D1376991

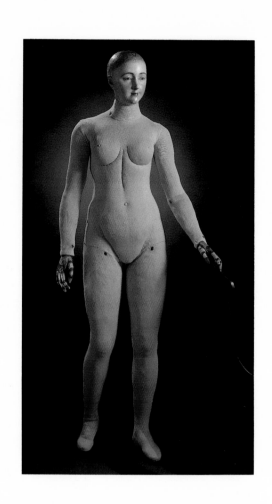

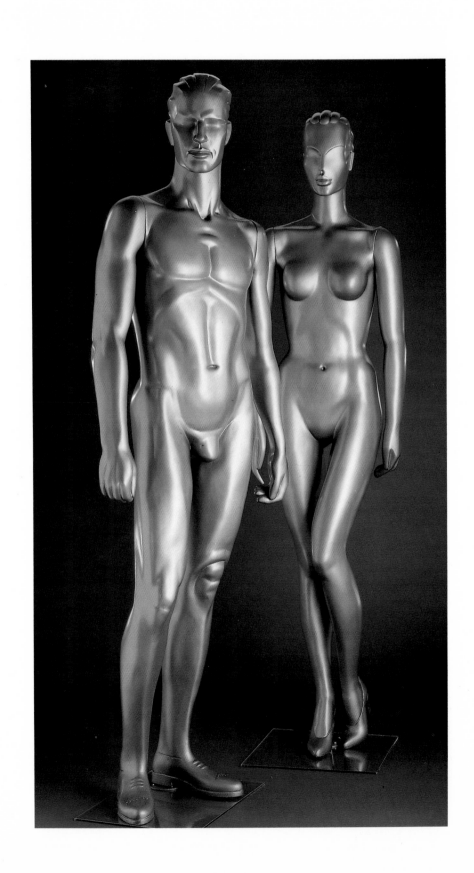

MEN and Women

Dressing the Part

*Edited by Claudia Brush Kidwell
and Valerie Steele*

Smithsonian Institution Press
Washington

Men and Women: Dressing the Part and the related exhibition at the National Museum of American History were made possible in part by grants from the Smithsonian Institution Special Exhibition Fund and from the National Cosmetology Association.

Color printed by South China Printing Company, Hong Kong
Text and all other illustrations printed in the United States of America
Manufactured in the United States of America

10 9 8 7 6 5 4 3 2 1

Library of Congress Cataloging-in-Publication Data:

Men and women : dressing the part / edited by Claudia Brush Kidwell and Valerie Steele.
   p.   cm.
   Bibliography: p.
   Includes index.
   1. Costume—United States—Sex differences. I. Kidwell, Claudia Brush.
II. Steele, Valerie.
GT605.M45   1989 391'.k001'9—dc19   88-18259
ISBN 0-87474-550-0 ISBN 0-87474-559-4 (pbk.)
British Library Cataloging-in-Publication data is available.

∞ The paper used in this publication meets the minimum requirements of the American National Standard for Permanence of Paper for Printed Library Materials Z39.48-1984.

Designer. Janice Wheeler
Editor. Antonia Gardner

Front cover. A woman's well-turned ankle framed in lace contrasts with the man's somber color trouser leg.
Back cover. The fashionable silhouette for a 1913 couple.
Half-title page. Artist's lay figure used by the American artist Thomas Sully, about 1840. The torso of this adjustable figure is formed to replicate the shape of the ideal woman's body, as molded by the fashionable corset of this period. Sully's customers were spared the necessity of spending hours of sitting for their portraits, since Sully could work by using their clothes on the posed lay figure.
Title page. Store mannequins, 1988, designed by Andrée Putman for Pucci International, New York City.

CONTENTS

During the 1950s, the differences in men's and women's appearances were extreme. In this 1955 *Mademoiselle* photograph, the male's dark business suit contrasts sharply with the colorful, curvaceous female silhouette. Thirty years later, talk about traditional family values frequently brings to mind stereotyped images of 1950s rounded, "nurturing" women and rectangular, "breadwinning" men. Fashions of the 1950s are made synonymous with then-desirable masculine and feminine behavior. This simplification obscures the complex processes of gender socialization, making it difficult for us to understand past and present changes. Exploring the historical relationship between appearance and our definitions of masculinity and femininity reveals some of these processes. George Barkentin.

PLATE 1.

In all times and places men and women have worn distinctively different clothing or adornment. But there is nothing intrinsically feminine or masculine about any particular fashion, fabric, or color. The meanings given to clothes are influenced by the history of a garment, and they can be changed by new situations. In cultures where trousers have become symbols of masculinity, women wearing trousers cause questions about women looking and acting like men. This photograph illustrated a 1985 article on the meaning of "the new androgyny." If appearance is a sign of identity, what does it mean when women lift weights and wear trousers, while men largely reject the sartorial symbols of femininity? Robert J. Steinberg.

PLATE 2.

You don't need a collar to need Wisk.®

© 1985 Lever Brothers Co.

WISK® GETS
RING AROUND
THE COLLAR
AND YOUR
WHOLE WASH
CLEAN.

Gender distinctions in modern children's clothing begin in infancy. The "traditional" symbols used in this 1985 advertisement—pink or blue, flowers or trucks—are actually recent innovations dating back only a generation or two. Is clothing for small children more gender specific today because their gender identities are now seen as malleable? Does the more public life for children require a more obvious system of gender identification?

PLATE 3.

Although men's clothing has often been at least as modish and body-revealing as women's clothing, it has seldom been perceived primarily in sexual terms. Our society has tended to place far more emphasis on the erotic aspects of women's fashions and under-fashions. In recent years, however, sexy young male models have been increasingly used in advertising and art, although cheesecake continues to be more common than beefcake.

This 1980s ensemble uses shimmering silk and delicate, see-through lace to enhance feminine beauty. A hundred years ago, a glimpse of a woman in her chemise, a long white cotton undergarment, might have been titillating. Thus definitions of sexy clothing vary according to the viewer and changes over time.

PLATE 4.

The essence of classic clothing.

Concepts of appropriate work clothing rest on a structure of ideas about which jobs are appropriate for women and for men. In nineteenth-century offices, business dress meant men's suits, since both the bosses and the clerks were men. As women sought to be accepted in the man's world of business, they often adopted elements of men's clothing. They were not necessarily adopting more practical clothes; rather, they were appropriating the conventional symbols of male status and professional colleagueship. Despite the ubiquity of the business suit, the totally mannish look for women is still taboo. As this 1985 advertisement of Jos. A. Bank Clothiers shows, there are still significant differences between the way men and women dress for work: professional women usually wear a softer suit with a skirt, not trousers, and a cravat or bow, not a necktie.

PLATE 5.

In the first half of the nineteenth-century, female athletes were viewed with suspicion. Initially it was easier for them to engage in vigorous exercise in the privacy of a girls' school gymnasium. As their numbers increased, there was a growing acceptance of women on the playing field. By 1927, when this athletic young couple appeared on a magazine cover, robust good health and trim bodies had become the ideal; strength and muscular development were stressed for men, while beauty with grace was the goal for women. At a time when youth was glorified, sports such as tennis played a critical role in shaping and maintaining the new physical ideal. For both sexes, the active player became the attractive partner.

PLATE 6.

It is not always obvious, when looking at the past, to determine which features of masculine and feminine fashions are potent signs of gender and which are simply fashionable design elements (and these may not always be mutually exclusive).

Conditioned as we are today to think of rounded women and rectangular men, we are likely to identify small waists and rounded hips as feminine and broad shoulders and narrow hips as masculine. Yet, in the 1840s, when middle-class men

PLATE 7.

and women wore very different clothing and did very different things, an hourglass figure simply denoted a fashionable *person*.

In the 1940s, as World War II was ending, square shoulders became identified with masculine styling, particularly with military uniforms, yet military men were not the first to sport broad shoulders. A decade earlier, the latest feminine fashions featured exaggerated shoulders that emphasized the new ideal for a small waist and small hips.

PLATE 8.

THE BLOOMER WALTZ.

When a new fashion involves a feature that has symbolized the opposite sex, the innovation can meet with strident opposition. In the early 1850s, the proposed Bloomer Costume drew national atten-tion, and the proponents of bloomers eventually abandoned the innovation. It was only many decades later that trousers became acceptable attire for women. When the Beatles appeared on American television in 1964, they shocked many Americans with their long hair. A num-ber of young men, supported by other youths, male and female, experimented with new lengths of hair. In spite of op-

PLATE 9.

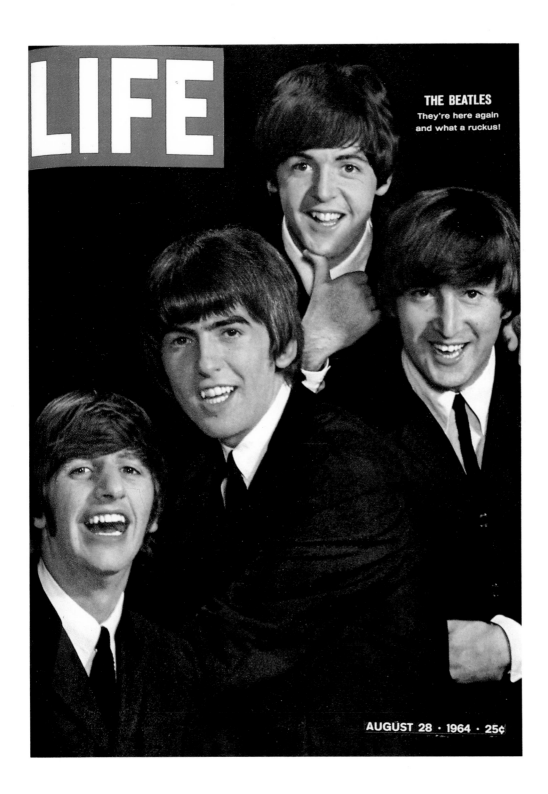

LIFE

THE BEATLES
They're here again
and what a ruckus!

AUGUST 28 · 1964 · 25¢

position from the older generation, longer hair on young men became acceptable, eventually influencing the hair styles of older men.

Long hair for men was accepted, while the Bloomer Costume was rejected—although both blurred a visual distinction between the sexes. The differing responses may be related to the different times when the proposed changes occurred and the different types of people who proposed and opposed the new look.

PLATE 10.

In 1970 the avant-garde designer Rudi Gernreich predicted that men and women would be wearing unisex clothes by 1980: older people would wear boldly patterned caftans to "abstract" bodies that "can no longer be accentuated," while young men and women would wear skirts and trousers interchangeably.

During the youth-dominated 1960s, new fashions included increased body exposure and pants for women. Gernreich felt that, after the changes of the 1960s, pants and skirts would lose their significance as gender symbols. But this has not happened. It took more than a century for women to wear pants in public; and few modern men have made skirts part of their wardrobe.

It seems that clothing distinctions will continue to be made between the sexes, but inveterate optimists hold out the hope that society will transform the meanings of masculinity and femininity to construct a more equitable system.

PLATE 11.

BARBARA A. SCHREIER

INTRODUCTION

The freedom to choose and to create an image of self, whether in the tangible forms of appearance or the abstract qualities of self-concept, has been a celebrated source of self-expression and a chronic source of conflict. Throughout our history, men and women have struggled to forge an alliance between their own ideas of personal image and the collective social vision of their gender. The struggle is complicated because it does not occur in a vacuum. It is rooted in our biological histories, shaped by our structures of power and interdependence, and informed by our cumulative experiences. And it changes as we try to balance home, work, leisure, and personal ties.

Untangling this web of complications as it is expressed in forms of dressing has been the central concern of the authors of this book. We did not set out to write a comprehensive history of gender roles or a chronological survey of costume styles. Instead, we wanted to explore the historical relationship between our outward appearance and our definitions of masculinity and femininity. In the process we discovered a dialogue anchored in polarities—between males and females, public life and private life, ideals and reality. It is a dialogue encompassing voices that resonate with cultural differences, class variations, and ethnic diversity. It is a dialogue that adjusts its vocabulary to accommodate the values and images endorsed by tradition as well as the promise of new gender arrangements. Finally, it is a dialogue in which we, as men and women, cannot help engaging.

Central to this discussion of the interaction between clothing and gender identity is the understanding that the term *gender* implies more than an identification with a biological sex. As Ann Oakley defines in *Sex, Gender and Society,* "'sex' is a word that refers to the biological differences between male and female: the visible differences in genitalia, the related differences in procreative function. 'Gender,' however, is a matter of culture: it refers to the social classification into 'masculine' and 'feminine'."[1] In analyzing gender identities, we use the term *gender conventions* to refer to the social and cultural expectations of behavior, clothing, and images that have divided men and women into separate spheres.

The essays that follow make it clear that there has been variety in expressing these conventions and that many styles of gendered clothing have their own history of resistance and conformity. Yet the existence of these behavioral standards has always been an integral part of our social structure. Therefore, although the early-nineteenth-century Dandy, a symbol of aristocratic elegance, appears to be the antithesis of the 1950s beatnik rebel, both men represented one version of the masculine ideal of their day. Similarly, the 1920s flapper and her Edwardian mother articulated very different views of femininity, but they are united within their adherence to timely gender conventions.

Because of its varied usage and its gender implications *fashion* is a problematical term in our discussions. In fashion, out of fashion, fashionable, and fashion-conscious are concepts commonly linked to women; men must be content with the description of old-fashioned. (Indeed, males who admit to an active interest in fashion are often viewed with suspicion.) How women look has been the principal validation of their femininity, whereas men have proved themselves through actions. At least this is the standard explanation. But do men ignore their appearance when taking a personal inventory of strengths and weaknesses? Are they free from the pressures to conform to a predefined image? Historical costume evidence answers these questions with a resounding NO! Therefore, we use *fashion* to describe a formal arrangement of male and female clothing that expresses the aesthetics and customs of a cultural period. *Fashion* includes widespread social norms that may be modified by individual self-expression. It is part of what Roland Barthes refers to as the "syntax of clothing."[2]

Because we are concerned with the interplay of fashion and identity, particularly gender identity, we use the term *appearance* in its broadest possible sense. If dress or costume implies merely the covering or decoration of the body, we encourage readers to incorporate other, more subtle cues in their definition of appearance. Postures, manners, and body gestures all play important roles in coalescing our private responses to socially legislated conventions. To examine garments outside of the realm of physical experience is to look at a lifeless prop. Consider, for example, the self-effacing, demure pose of a mid-nineteenth-century woman who glided, never walked, across a room, or the imposing stance of a male industrialist in 1900 who commanded attention by his aggressive posturing. These all-important mannerisms underscore the message of the fashions and reinforce the ideology of gender distinctions.

Likewise, costume historians must always be mindful of the schism between fashionable ideals and reality. To examine the ideal image alone is to look at historical evidence through a distorted window. As an image is

transformed into an ideal through an interconnected system of mass communication, social organizations, and personal choice, we become attached to it and committed to emulate it. It has the potential to create desire, motivate change, and invigorate the fashion system. It may be incorporated into our identity kit as a standard by which we judge ourselves and others. The Gibson girl, the sentimental heroine, the sex goddess, all are mythical inventions imbued with powerful messages that help us establish and recognize desirable modes of behavior and appearance. And as they shift over time, we continually structure and restructure ourselves and our interactions to conform to the changing image. The cowboy is replaced by the playboy who, in turn, must yield to the sensitive male. The question Who am I? is often asking, Who should I be?

We cannot forget, however, that these ideals are illusionary. Although it is important to examine the prototypical ideal in fashion plates, advertisements, or literary passages, these sources must be checked against the physical evidence of the objective reality. For us, the most significant records are the costumes themselves. In the following pages, we try to uncover the meaning of these objects. This involves asking questions: Who wore this? When, and for what occasion? How does it relate to the predominant ideal(s)? What importance was attached to it? Decisions about appearance occur on both a conscious and unconscious level and are guided by more factors than just the social norms (including gender issues). Yet even when the answers are clouded, contradictory, or incomplete, raising the questions is always instructive. The actual costumes must be reckoned with in order to understand how abstract ideals and real life solutions coexist and interconnect.

Our appearance and our models of gender identification are interrelated and overlapping constructs that strengthen, modify, test, qualify, and confirm each other. Therefore, when we examine how clothes define an individual, we must also set the man or woman within the context of their place and time.

This approach raises several problems: it demands new ways of seeing connections between gender and appearance without ignoring that each has its own internal development and structure; it involves focusing on the collective experience without diminishing the importance of individual choice—isolating the norms while insisting that the richness of variation not be lost. The problems are further complicated by the elusive nature of historical evidence. Even when information is available, abstract systems of fashionable ideals, gender conventions, sexuality, and societal roles often are not articulated. In our early discussions about this project, it became clear that some parameters had to be established if we ever hoped to present a consistent analysis. As a result, this study focuses on white, middle-class Americans who, we believe, have established the patterns for many of our dominant clothing and gender traditions. This limitation, however, must be noted, and we hope that it sparks a more comprehensive, comparative analysis of the interactive relationships between class and race, and gender and appearance.

Additionally, although our interpretations of gendered appearance draw heavily upon mass media images of men and women, it is beyond the scope of this book to examine how these gender images are produced or how they receive cultural legitimation. It is our intent as costume historians to use the images, and their messages, to detect, describe, and identify historical models of gender roles and to draw inferences about their social consequences. Ideally, our work will strengthen future research on the role of fashion-related mass media as a social mechanism and the relationships among producers, communicators, and consumers.

Although it is an enlightening process to trace the changing meanings of masculinity or femininity, the full impact of these gender conventions on fashion is only revealed when the two sexes in fashion history are examined side by side. It then becomes obvious that historically clothing has served to separate men and women. We define ourselves as being male or female through a system of opposition. At times, this impulse has been carried to extremes. In the 1950s, the curvaceous, full-bosomed woman, in her voluminous skirt and tight bodice, juxtaposed next to her hard-edged male counterpart in a gray flannel suit, represented a caricature of this sex-based imagery. Yet even when men and women outwardly were similar, such as in the 1840s when tiny waistlines and shapely hips were admired in both sexes, the need to distinguish between them asserted itself.

But does different have to mean unequal? Those who would answer yes to this question posit the theory that only by establishing a clothing pattern that transcends gender differences can the sharp division between the sexes be eliminated. Typically, they propose an androgynous appearance, where men and women share identical clothing, as the pathway to change. For example, when Rudi Gernreich proposed his vision of the future of fashion in 1970, he predicted that the traditional apparel symbols of masculinity and femininity would become obsolete: ". . .women will wear pants and men will wear skirts interchangeably."[3] This approach, however, implies that appearance has the power to cure the male/female contest. The evidence gathered in this book argues directly against such logic.

Yet while appearance alone does not create or break down systems of sexual oppression, it has reinforced inequalities between the sexes. Just as the well-tailored suit has been a dominant emblem of male opportunity and privilege, expectations of a woman's passivity have been embedded in a psychologically restrictive and physically limiting wardrobe. Before an in-depth analysis can be done on why these differences exist (and thrive, in some instances), we must first understand how the differences manifest themselves. Therefore, it is our intent to illustrate the historical patterns of male and female self-presentation, to examine some ways the forms and symbols change over time, and to explore the ways in which a dichotomous structure of clothing and appearance contribute to the complex process of gender socialization.

Our study of this time-honored formula of separation also includes the restless feelings it engenders. What happens, for example, when one sex adopts the gender signs of the other? Does this disruption of opposition change the meaning of the symbol, does it spark rebellion, or does it prompt the other sex to find new ways to distinguish itself? All of these responses have occurred at various times in our history. Consider the image of a women dressed in pants. It is a clothing symbol laden with gender meaning and a recurring subject of this book. Proponents of the trousered female have linked their campaign to a variety of causes, including the political implications of the nineteenth-century dress reform movement, the athletic rationale for bifurcated sportswear, and the functional benefits of pants in the workplace. Acceptance of a woman in pants, however, has been determined by time and setting, as well as by the age and the intention of the wearer; responses to this alteration of fashion have ranged from mild amusement to impassioned anger.

In the following chapters, we investigate institutions, events, and practices primarily as they affected, and were affected by, gender behavior and appearance. Although they stem from common traditions, the spheres of gender influence can differ in emphasis, purpose, and structure. Chapter one presents a cross-cultural perspective of the need to distinguish between the sexes, while chapter two describes how we inculcate our children with the messages of appropriate gender behavior. In chapter three, the focus is on how we expose, conceal, and display our bodies to attract sexual partners. Chapters four and five concentrate on the impact of gender conventions on the sectors of our daily life—work and play—and the concomitant influence on our professional image and sporting attire. Chapter six examines the gender metaphors and symbols that are expressed through the American fashion system. Chapter seven investigates the success and failure of two historical attempts to blur the visual lines between the sexes.

In the pages that follow, we explore the dimensions and the significance of our need to differentiate between masculine and feminine appearance. This knowledge is essential if we hope to transform the differences between gender roles toward a more positive valuation system.

VALERIE STEELE

APPEARANCE AND IDENTITY

In the beginning . . . each had a single, all-purpose wardrobe. He wore a king-sized fig leaf, and she wore a queen-sized. Adam's was manly, rugged, with an outdoor Hemingway look. Eve's was dainty, feminine, definitely slimming, accenting the fun in functional and the you in youthful. . . . Yet already the serpentine thought was insinuating: Why not two fig leaves in every wardrobe? A charming little blue denim number for Eve to garden in, and a more sophisticated version for her to wear into the city to see her analyst. . . .

Eve Merriam,
Figleaf: The Business of Being in Fashion (1960)

An article of clothing has no inherent meaning. Trousers do not have the idea of masculinity built into them, nor does a skirt automatically signify that the wearer is either female or feminine. The meaning of clothing is culturally defined. This becomes manifest in a cross-cultural perspective: "Turkish trousers" were designed to be worn by Middle Eastern women; a wrapped skirt is standard male apparel in much of Southeast Asia; and in China trousers were predominantly worn by members of the working class—male and female. Similarly, if we study the history of Western dress, we find that in Europe trousers only gradually became associated with masculinity. To take another example, is pink naturally a feminine color? In the eighteenth century, a pink silk suit was regarded as appropriate attire for a gentleman. Only over time was the color pink redefined as "feminine." And there were always exceptions to such laws of dress. It is the history of clothes and the context in which they are worn that determine the meanings that *we* ascribe to them.

In sorting out the messages of clothing, the idea of a "language of clothes," though currently a popular notion, may ultimately be too confining. Some types of clothes (such as, perhaps, the business suit) communicate a fairly direct message. But many clothing messages are more like music: they are expressive in an indirect and allusive way. There is rarely a single meaning attached to each article of clothing. Instead, its meanings depend on the context—Who wears it? When? Along with what other clothes? What was the history of the garment? Although we speak of a language of clothes, there are no true equivalents of nouns, verbs, and sentences. Nevertheless, clothing elements do have to fit together coherently, rather like words in a sentence. Bearing in mind these difficulties, it is still important to ask: What do our clothes mean? What is the relationship be-

In Western culture, trousers were associated with the military—and, thus, masculinity—since the Middle Ages, when knights wore trousers and short body armor when going into battle. This late-fifteenth-century Swabian School painting, *The Bridal Pair,* depicts the fashionable trouser-like hose and short doublet that had evolved from the military style by the fourteenth century.

tween our different—but changing—clothing and our identities as men and women? To penetrate beyond simplistic gender stereotypes, we must recognize that our clothed appearance—the persona we present to the world—is as complex as our selves.

As we stand on the verge of the 1990s, we are well positioned to analyze how clothing meanings are created. We have seen the pendulum swing from the distinctively different clothes worn by men and women in the 1950s to the supposedly unisex or androgynous styles of the mid-1970s and early 1980s, and now back to the so-called return of femininity in women's apparel. If dress says something about our personal identities, surely it also expresses aspects of our identities as men and women.

The sociologist Fred Davis suggests that at various times in history certain social ambivalences become prominent and may be expressed sartorially. Thus, people may want to express something about what Davis calls the ambiguities of masculinity versus femininity or androgyny versus singularity (or, for that matter, youth versus age, domesticity versus worldliness, or conformity versus rebellion).[1]

Nothing would seem more unisex than a fig leaf. Yet in the lines quoted at the beginning of this chapter, our mythical original clothes are explicitly associated with stereotypes of masculinity and femininity.[2] Not only are men portrayed as "rugged," but so are their clothes. By contrast, both women and their clothes are described as "dainty" and "charming." Thus Merriam simultaneously implies that men and women have significantly different characteristics and that differences in their clothes derive from these supposed biological differences. Moreover, she also suggests that women naturally have a greater interest in fashion than men do, since only Eve contemplates acquiring a multiplicity of fig leaves.

Truly unisex clothing does not exist. Even in the mid-1970s and early 1980s, despite all the talk about "unisex" or "androgyny," most men and women still wore different clothes. In nearly all times and places, men and women have worn distinctively different clothing or adornment. Although cultural outsiders may not perceive the differences between, say, a man's kimono and a woman's kimono, a Japanese person would not confuse the two styles. These clothing differences are related to the widespread belief that there are more or less dramatic contrasts between male nature and female nature. The concept of sexual dualism is seldom absolute or antagonistic, but rather relativistic and complementary. As the philosopher Jean Jacques Rousseau wrote, "A perfect man and a perfect woman ought no more to resemble each other in mind than in features. . . . In the union of the sexes each contributes equally toward the common end, but not in the same way."[3]

Differences in clothing have reinforced physical and social differences between men and women. The male author of *Ladies Toilette, or Treatise on Beauty* (1822) stated bluntly that men and women should wear completely different clothing and hair styles. Even their choice of materials should be different.

> A woman dressed in broadcloth is less feminine than when she appears
> to us, enveloped in a transparent veil, a light muslin, a rich gown of silk.

A woman, by taking on the clothing of a man, loses all the graces of her sex without acquiring any of the advantages of ours.[4]

He went on, with some disgruntlement, to complain that many women were nonetheless making themselves ridiculous by adopting styles inappropriate to their sex.

During the 1970s and 1980s, men and women seemed to adopt unisex uniforms—whether dress-for-success suits for work or jeans and T-shirts for leisure. Women's very bodies seem to be changing, becoming thinner, more muscular and (some would say) more masculine. But if this was the new androgyny, it was both one-sided and ambivalent. Women might have been imitating men's clothing and the male physique, but men were definitely not reciprocating. As Anne Hollander wrote in 1985,

Although the new ideal feminine torso has strong square shoulders, flat hips, and no belly at all, the corresponding ideal male body is certainly not displaying the beauties of a soft round stomach, flaring hips, full thighs, and delicately sloping shoulders. On the new woman's ideally athletic shape, breasts may be large or small—a flat chest is not required; and below the belt in back, the buttocks may sharply protrude. But no space remains in front to house a safely cushioned uterus.[5]

It was widely believed that these changes heralded women's growing social equality with men: men's clothing was more comfortable and practical; men's bodies were healthier. But is there really something better about men's bodies and men's clothes that women want to have, or have we been drawn to *symbols* of personal freedom and power?

If you are a woman, you may be wearing trousers, but it is unlikely that your entire ensemble, accessories, and hairstyle are masculine. Indeed, if you are pursuing a professional career, you might find that a distinctly mannish appearance is a liability. Men and women have worn different clothes even during periods when women appeared to be copying men's clothing. It would be difficult for a woman to achieve a totally male look. A few years ago, a female journalist deliberately tried to pass as a man. She had to bind her breasts, cut her hair, wear a false mustache, lower her voice, and change her body language, as well as put on a complete male clothing ensemble.

If you are a man, you are highly unlikely to be wearing a dress. A few years ago, some avant-garde fashion designers showed skirts and dresses for men, but this seems to have been a passing fad. The only possible exception, the kilt, is acceptable because we recognize that it is a nationalist symbol, *not* a female skirt. Most American men would face social disapproval if they appeared in public in woman's clothes—almost as much disapproval as if they appeared without any clothes at all.

Why do we wear any clothes at all? The ancestors of humans were covered with fur, like other animals. The "naked ape" evolved perhaps a million years ago, when *Homo erectus* developed a dramatic increase in brain size. Scientists have tried to come up with functional reasons for this hairless body. Was it better for running through the grasslands? Was it sexually attractive? Since relative hairlessness is characteristic of infantile mammals, scientists have more recently suggested that the absence of body hair might

These 1980s photographs from Angela Fischer's *Africa Adorned* show the Dinka people of East Africa: the man wears a corset-like garment that identifies him as a young warrior, the women wear a combination blouse and necklace that proclaims their wealth and fertility. Anthropologists believe that clothing is used essentially for symbolic identity (including gender identity) more than for practicality or modesty.

simply have been a side effect of the human's large brain and the related slow-down of human development (called neoteny).[6]

Lack of fur did not automatically lead to the invention of clothes, however. We know little about the origin of clothes some 20,000 to 50,000 years ago. Prehistoric evidence is scanty, and ethnographic comparisons with so-called primitive tribes can only be used with caution. We may assume that as *Homo erectus* and *Homo sapiens* moved from tropical to colder climates, they wrapped themselves in furs or skins for warmth, just as other peoples developed artificial protection from the blazing sun or torrential rains.[7]

Yet people apparently did not invent clothes because they needed them for warmth or protection. Practical body coverings have been ignored in many parts of the world, even in cold, wet climates. In Tierra del Fuego, for example, Charles Darwin observed the icy sleet freezing and melting on the skin of the Indians, who appeared oblivious to the cold, clad only in paint and jewelry. The Picts, ancient inhabitants of Britain, are also known to have been naked except for blue body paint—a situation that surprised the clothed Roman invaders of Julius Caesar's time.

Although there have been many cultures without clothes, everyone seems to have decorated their bodies. The Xicrin Indians of Brazil, for example, still wear no clothes, only dark blue body paint. Without this paint, they feel naked and embarrassed. The line between clothing and adornment can actually be difficult to determine, so nonfunctional are many items of dress. The Dinka people of East Africa, for example, traditionally went naked, and the men regarded it as unmanly to use a covering, even on cold nights. Even today many of the young men wear as their sole article of clothing a tight, beaded corset-like apparatus, whose color is a sign of the age group to which the wearer belongs. Young Dinka women also wear almost no clothing, although they may wear something halfway between a blouse and a necklace of beads and cowrie shells, symbolizing wealth and fertility.

The fig leave theory has been demolished: anthropologists no longer believe that shame or modesty led to the development of clothes. When people wear clothing, the genitals are often the first part of the body to be covered, but this seems to be done at least as much to call attention to them as to hide them. The enormous penis sheaths of New Guinea, for example, are an obvious exaggeration of the genitals. The cache-sex jewelry of many African men and women also serves to draw the eye to the genitals, while magically warding off evil influences. Symbolic ornament apparently preceded—and takes precedence over—considerations of warmth, protection, and sexual modesty. It is possible that there are biological roots for human self-decoration: captive primates will adorn themselves with flowers and ribbons. Yet among primates, only humans regularly use adornment, and they seem to have done so from an early date. There is evidence that humans used body paint (red ochre) as much as 50,000 years ago.

In many traditional cultures, women and girls tend to wear more clothing than men—at least on an everyday basis—since social standards of modesty have often been stricter for women. But on special occasions (rites of passage, religious ceremonies, warfare), men tend to wear more clothing and more elaborate body decoration. On such occasions, when splendor symbolizes power and status, men monopolize the "best" clothes. Men's ceremonial clothing displays the social and political power of chiefs, warriors, and priests. In West Africa, for example, the clothing of a hereditary ruler "is so highly symbolic that he can indicate an opinion or a change of plan simply by changing his costume and ornaments and reappearing newly clothed to the awaiting assembly."[8]

In American society today, many people assume that women pay more attention to dress and adornment than men do, and that this is natural. But in a number of cultures (such as the Tchambuli of Melanesia), the men are the leisured and decorative sex, while the women are hard working and plainly dressed. This has been the case often enough in world history that we cannot regard it as unnatural. Only when we stop believing that biology determines clothing behavior can we begin to understand how men and women have created the clothes they wear.

Biological differences between men and women do not cause different social roles or lead to different forms of clothing. Obviously, nature differentiates between male and female, as it does between young and old, but we attach a variety of different meanings to the biological facts. Among the Eskimos, an old person was often regarded as a burden to the family. Among the Chinese, an old person was a respected elder. Different cultural meanings are also attached to maleness and femaleness.

The so-called Peacock Revolution of the 1960s and early 1970s aroused tremendous controversy, in part because it attempted to revive elaborate male fashions. Contemporary observers speculated about the possible sexual implications of sixties male fashions. Even now some people ask: Is splendid male costume analogous to the peacock's tail? Since, among many species of animals and birds, the male is more colorful and decorative than the female, it initially seems plausible that there might be some natural relationship between the male animal's anatomical ornament and the man's sartorial ornament. In fact, this analogy is not valid.

The peacock's tail offers no biomechanical advantages for the bird. (Indeed, it makes flying more difficult.) But it does promote success in reproduction. Thus we say that sexual selection is a form of natural selection. The peacock's tail, the elk's antlers, the lion's mane, the robin's red breast, all say to females, Look at what a sexy, powerful male you have here! and to other males, Why don't you bow out of the competition—and the neighborhood—now, before you get hurt! A bright red female robin, on the other hand, would attract not only male robins, but also predators who might kill the mother or worse, her progeny.

But when human males adopt artificial ornament, they do so for cultural, not biological reasons. Unlike the peacock's tail or the tiger's sharp teeth, a man's top hat, for example, did not develop naturally either to enhance reproductive success or to help in the struggle for survival. Men in-

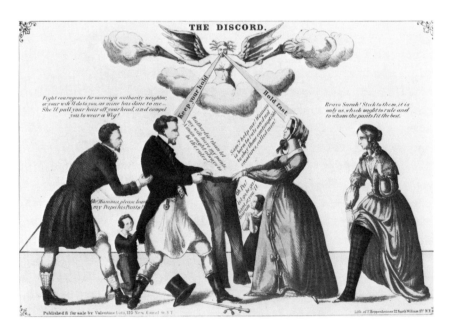

An American print from 1855 dramatizes the question, Who wears the pants? The central male figure exclaims, "Rather die! than let my wife have *my* pants. A man ought always to be the ruler!" But his female counterpart replies, "Woman is born to rule and not to obey those contemptible creatures called men!" Courtesy of The New-York Historical Society.

vented the hat. The process of clothing evolution proceeds at different rates and for different reasons than biological evolution. In some cases, men might be trying to attract women; more often, they seem to be sending public (or political) messages to other men. Human beings do not inherit their clothes genetically; they design them within the confines of a clothing tradition, and the forms their clothing take can be bewilderingly nonadaptive. Not only is cultural evolution very rapid, it can also be copied by other groups of people.

Both bodies and clothes have been interpreted in terms of gender stereotypes. "Big shoulders project power," declared the *New York Times* in 1985, but "strong shoulders are receding in favor of a rounder look" for women's clothes.[9] Perhaps the fashion change was occurring because women have achieved more power; but the article also implied that "women are thinking more about marriage and family." Some sociologists interviewed suggested that the later 1980s might repeat the history of the 1940s and 1950s, when the mannish Joan Crawford look yielded to the curvaceous Elizabeth Taylor look—together with all that implied of gender roles. Certainly padded jackets broaden the shoulder line, creating the silhouette of a man's big shoulders. But is a "softer," more rounded suit really the sign of a creeping feminine mystique? This would seem to be a serious oversimplification.

What do we really mean when we say, That pink silk blouse with ruffles looks *ultra-feminine*. Last year's fashions were *androgynous:* Women wore dark, *masculine-tailored* clothes. But this season, men look like men and women look like women. There is no rational reason why trousers signify masculinity and skirts femininity, why the fabric silk, the color pink, and the use of ruffles all say "femininity" to us, while wool, dark colors, the absence of trimming, and a tailored look are considered "masculine."

The most obvious division in clothing today is between trousers and skirts. Yet it is by no means true that men have always worn bifurcated garments and women not. Alexander the Great, Julius Caesar, Charlemagne—none of these men wore trousers, although they were aware that Persian men did. Men of Classical Greece and Rome, medieval European lords, and Chinese mandarins all wore flowing robes (i.e., skirts). By contrast, Turkish women in the harem, Eskimo women on the frozen tundra, and Chinese peasant women all wore trousers.

How did modern Western men come to wear trousers and women skirts? As the history of dress evolved, two basic types of clothing developed. In warm countries, where weaving was invented more than 10,000 years ago, a draped or wrapped and tied style predominated (like the Roman toga, the Indonesian sarong, and the Indian sari). In cold countries, by contrast, nomadic people favored clothing made of animal skins cut and sewn together to follow the lines of the body (like the trousers and jackets of central Asian and northern European people. An intermediate type of clothing was the binary style, made of pieces of fabric sewn together and loosely following the lines of the body (like the Japanese kimono and the North African caftan). Binary clothes and wrapped garments could be folded flat, unlike the tailored clothes of the north, which fitted together

In both medieval Europe and imperial China men and women of the elite tended to wear long, formal robes. In Europe the long robe eventually became identified as feminine, while in China it remained, until 1949, a mark of status rather than gender. These two townsmen are shown exchanging New Year's greetings in a photograph of Peking in the 1920s.

with darts and were three-dimensional. All three types entered the European clothing tradition as a result of cultural contact, population movement, and invasion. The same thing happened in China.

But whereas in Europe, over the centuries, flowing robes became associated with femininity and tailored trousers with masculinity, this was not the case in China, where robes and trousers indicated not different gender, but different social status.[10]

Trousers seem to have been invented in Persia in the late prehistoric period. They were then adopted by many northern European and central Asian "barbarians" (as they were referred to by "civilized" members of the Roman and Chinese empires), such as the Saxons. In many cases, barbarian women also wore trousers, especially when horseback riding was part of the nomadic way of life. In the cities of the two empires, however, both men and women of the elite wore long flowing robes (whether draped or binary). Even after the Roman Empire collapsed into a fragmented feudal Europe, noble men and women continued to wear long, quasi-Roman robes. Peasants wore short robes, and occasionally male peasants wore loose "barbarian" trousers.

Thus, the indigenous trouser tradition essentially died out in Europe—except in the clothing of soldiers. An aristocrat might wear a long robe at court, but he wore hose-like trousers on the field of battle, often under his armor. European men did not admire trousers, per se, but they did admire soldiers: the raison d'être of the ruling aristocracy was its status as a warrior caste. Women in Europe did not wear trousers because the garment had acquired such strong masculine connotations: what could be more masculine than a soldier?

In China, also, soldiers wore trousers (sometimes incorporated into suits of armor), but Chinese soldiers had no such exalted status, since the Chinese masculine ideal was the scholar-bureaucrat, who wore a robe. In China, peasants of both sexes wore trousers, so there was a basic division between rulers in robes, on the one hand, and peasants and soldiers in trousers, on the other. Women could and did wear trousers. Even upper-class Chinese ladies (and gentlemen) wore trousers for horseback riding or on less formal occasions.

Back in medieval Europe, aristocratic men gradually developed a new, high-fashion type of trousers. First, however, they shortened their robes. Not that they adopted the coarse short robes of peasants, rather they developed elaborate and very short robes worn over tight stockings. Eventually, this new robe turned into a doublet, and the top of the stockings turned into short, puffy bloomers, which turned into knee breeches. At the end of the eighteenth century, knee breeches merged with plebian long trousers to become modern men's pants. Women continued to wear long skirts—very long skirts for high-born women and their middle-class followers, and shorter skirts for peasant and working-class women.

The Victorians opposed female trousers and short skirts, not so much because they were prudish about female legs, but because they vehemently rejected clothing with mixed gender and class messages. Women could wear bifurcated garments only under special conditions: at fancy dress parties (Turkish trousers were popular), sometimes for hunting, as part of bathing dress, and eventually as underpants. A few peasant and pioneer women wore trousers, as did some women who worked in mines.

Trousers were only very gradually accepted after World War I. But in the 1920s, "Conspicuous Outrage" began to become as much a part of fashion as "Conspicuous Consumption." Even so, we forget how restricted most trouser-wearing really was during the Jazz Age. Trousers were acceptable in the form of beach pajamas, lounge wear, riding jodphurs, and eventually blue jeans. But it was only in the 1940s and 1950s that casual trouser-wearing became common among teenagers, college coeds, and suburban housewives ("a little blue denim number for Eve to garden in . . ."). Trousers were still unacceptable as urban street wear or for work. As late as 1960, *Harper's Bazaar* ran an advertisement showing a woman, first in a black shirtwaist dress and again in a white (bifurcated) jumpsuit, with the caption: "First we stole his shirt . . . now we steal his overalls"—indicating that both the button-down shirt and trousers were still regarded as masculine articles of clothing, no matter how long women had worn them.

Yet other clothing elements that were once worn by men (or by both sexes) have now become essentially feminine. We think of hats—especially fancy hats with feathers and ribbons—as a feminine accessory. But in the Middle Ages it was a daring innovation for women to abandon veils and adopt men's elaborate hats. Jewelry, of course, used to be worn by both sexes—not just necklaces, bracelets, pins, rings, and crowns, but even earrings. As late as the seventeenth and eighteenth centuries, men often wore silk stockings, cosmetics, long curled and perfumed hair, virtually everything except perhaps luxurious underwear—although they did wear "petticoat breeches."

We think that blue is for boys and pink is for girls, but the opposite used to be true. Until about the 1920s most Americans tended to regard red and its pastel derivative pink as more masculine, and blue as more feminine. The idea of blue boys and pink girls was apparently a nineteenth-century French innovation that was only gradually adopted here, but we do not yet know why it changed in France. In small amounts, of course, pink continues to be acceptably masculine, for example, in men's shirts. Indeed, periodically and under certain circumstances men can still wear ruffled shirts and silk garments. Thus, the language of clothes changes over time, as changing styles of appearance are constantly reinterpreted in terms of changing gender (and class and national) ideals, and biological males and females are transformed into particular types of men and women.

It is undeniable, however, that color, luxurious fabrics, and decorative ornament have largely disappeared from men's clothing in the past 250 years. Having given up fancy clothes, stockings, and jewelry, men find it difficult to adopt them again without running the risk of looking effeminate. Most men do not want to steal back their lost finery, but we are entitled to ask, Why not?

Men's clothing is more functional than women's clothing, many argue. Is this really the case? About trousers, one must ask, Functional for what? For riding to work on horseback? A century ago, men's clothing was relatively looser and sturdier than women's clothing, but as women's clothing has become shorter, lighter, looser, and more varied, it seems that women have a better and wider choice of clothing than men do. This is an extraordinary situation, quite at odds with centuries of dress, when men's clothing was usually at least as elaborate and luxurious as women's clothing.

Why did men abandon their splendid costumes in favor of a plain dark uniform? Until recently, costume historians believed that the change was caused by the rise of the middle class or the triumph of democracy and capitalism. These were certainly contributing factors, but historians now recognize that the shift to darker, plainer attire began in the mid-eighteenth century, *before* the French and American Revolutions, and *before* the era of high capitalism. Moreover, the use of darker colors and wool rather than silk was associated, not only with middle-class capitalists and democrats, but also with country and sporting clothing of the English aristocracy.[11]

The emerging idea that fancy clothing was effeminate was inextricably intertwined with eighteenth-century English political attacks on cosmopolitan and ultra-aristocratic courtiers. A fashionably-dressed man on the streets of London was liable to be attacked as a "French dog" or an "effete, degenerate Macaroni," hence the satiric song "Yankee Doodle Dandy" (about a man who "stuck a feather in his hat and called it Macaroni"), which was originally written by an Englishman to make fun of the poorly dressed American troops. But the inhabitants of the American colonies defiantly adopted the song, while also embracing the growing English sentiment against foppish French attire. Elaborate male clothing became associated with foreign culture—and specifically with the corruption of the French court. The new masculine ideal was the English country gentleman. The concept of this gentleman may seem elitist today, but in the eighteenth century it was a liberating idea. In place of the old belief that gentle birth alone made one noble was the new idea that by acquiring gentle manners any man might potentially achieve distinction. To be a gentleman identified an individual with a group of desirable fellow citizens, and apart from both corrupt courtiers and the mob. In the course of the French Revolution, Frenchmen also began to disassociate themselves from the old courtly style of dress.

With the development of the modern state, European monarchs gradually began putting officials into uniforms. Thus men's closer integration into government set them on the path to uniformity in clothing. Men's clothing emphasized their public position, women's clothing their private (and sexual) status. By the nineteenth century, the bureaucratic and military uniforms were followed by the business uniform—first for men, and then gradually for women as well, as they increasingly entered the public sphere.

As women sought to be accepted in the man's world of business, they often adopted elements of men's clothing. Nothing could be less functional than a man's necktie (and many men find them more or less uncomfortable), but neckties are an integral part of business and formal men's wear, so in the 1890s and again in recent years many women have worn blouses with floppy bow ties—a feminized version of the male necktie. In such cases, women are not adopting more practical clothes, but they are appropriating the conventional symbols of male status and professional colleagueship.

The *look* of functionalism is at least as important to us today as a real functional superiority. The men's business suit was not deliberately designed (like certain kinds of modern active sportswear) to be functional. It contains vestiges both from riding costume and from the formal dress of authority: jacket vents, white shirts, ties. The specialized clothing of modern firefighters or scuba divers was specifically designed to be functional under particular circumstances (and even the firefighter's uniform may include some traditional, nonfunctional elements). But for true comfort, perhaps a bathrobe or pajamas would be best for work, with foot covering appropriate to the climate and topography. Indeed, under most circumstances, we actually need no clothes at all, or only a rain poncho and sandals, which could be discarded at the workplace.

Of course, if we follow these ideas, we may well be arrested or fired, but that would be the result of artificial social standards: requirements of modesty (no nudity at the office) or requirements of appropriate dress (no bikinis either). True, some dress-for-success consulting firms purport to have proved that conservative attire actually contributes to increased productivity, but even if their methods and statistics were a great deal more reliable than they appear to be, the obvious conclusion is rather that when people feel they look professional, they may do a more professional job, and others will probably regard them as more professional. It has little to do with the clothes, as such, and everything to do with the way people interpret their clothes and the clothing of others.

As fashions in clothes change, so do fashions in bodies. At any given time there are a wide range of physical types that are more or less fat, thin, or muscular, youthful or aged, of varying skin colors, features, and proportions. Because people have come from all over the world to live in the United States, our population is unusually heterogeneous in appearance. But only certain of these physiognomies are regarded as beautiful at any given time—and the ideal has changed dramatically over the centuries.

For the ancient Greeks, a certain type of young male body was regarded as ideally beautiful. Greek statues of rather heavy-set goddesses were also intended to be beautiful, but the overwhelming emphasis was on male beauty (an estimation that was related to the practice of homosexuality and a generalized cultural homophilia). The Victorians, however, spoke of "Man's Strength, Woman's Beauty," and argued that, to the extent that male beauty existed *at all,* it was defined as being the opposite of feminine beauty: broader shoulders, for example, and perhaps a full beard. Although they frequently claimed to admire the Classical ideal, a work like Hiram Powers's *The Greek Slave* (1847) shows a remarkably Victorian-looking female nude, with a long waist, sloping shoulders, and rounded arms, an ideal body that was reflected in the forms of contemporary Victorian dress.

The changing clothing of men and women appears related to changing physical ideals, which are themselves connected to wider social and cul-

Fashions in clothes change and so do fashions in bodies. *Adam and Eve* by Roger Van der Weyden shows the late Gothic physical ideal: slender and ethereal, with small breasts for women and small muscles for men. The Renaissance painting of *Neptune and Amphitrite* by Jan Gossaert depicts a far more massive physical type.

tural ideals. In the Middle Ages, for example, the ideal body type for both men and women was slender and ethereal, as Gothic paintings of Adam and Eve indicate. The design of medieval clothes subtly stylized the human body into the artists' perception. Men were usually portrayed in art, looking to modern eyes like pathetic weaklings, with narrow shoulders, scrawny legs, and big feet. Their bodies were designed to wear hose and doublets. Evil and plebian characters (like Christ's executioners) were portrayed as muscular. Beautiful women (whether virgins, saints, or temptresses) were shown with small, high breasts, a fashionably long torso, and an equally stylish swollen belly (which was not an indication of pregnancy). This idealization of slenderness was intended to reflect, in part, a religious purity of spirit.

With the rise of Renaissance humanism, the body was reinvigorated. Female sexual beauty and male physical strength were admired. In art, the fine bones of earlier Gothic nudes were now covered with layers of flesh—indeed, to modern eyes, rather a lot of flesh. Although based on Classical prototypes, the Renaissance physical ideal was more massive. In fashion, too, barrel-shaped clothing was modish, and the female bosom was de-emphasized in dress and in art.

By the eighteenth century, however, the substantial, fleshy, powerful body was increasingly regarded as plebian, and a more delicate and refined ideal arose among the upper classes, for both men and women. To ask, in twentieth-century America, why eighteenth-century men dressed in such a feminine way is to misunderstand what the style meant at the time.

American history begins with the massive, heroic type of the seventeenth century gradually evolving into a more slender and cosmopolitan ideal characteristic of the eighteenth century. Like earlier types, it represented the self-image of the Anglo-American elite, but it influenced middling and even humble people as well—both men and women. In the course of the nineteenth century, however, the cultural ideal of a delicate physique became increasingly associated with women in general, rather than with men and women of the upper class. In the popular imagination, women were both the new aristocrats (every woman potentially a lady) and the spiritual sex. Hence, their supposedly more ethereal appearance.

In the second half of the nineteenth century, a heavier body type was increasingly regarded as desirable and healthy for both sexes. For men and women, it appears to have been associated with the possession of a "substantial" position in society. At the most basic level, it was regarded as healthy because it meant that the individual had more than enough to eat. In many parts of the world, fat still carries positive associations: in West Africa, for example, brides are deliberately fattened to make them more beautiful.

The feminine ideal did not suddenly shift from one of delicacy to one of voluptuousness. Women were always supposed to be both simultaneously. But in the later nineteenth century the balance tilted toward opulence of figure—except, of course, for the slender waist and extremities. Men, too, sought to give the impression that they were larger and more massive. With the development of a capitalist economy and the shift from agriculture to industry, muscles were less important for men than the appearance of having power, which was increasingly an attribute of wealth rather than brute force or hereditary status. A solid, middle-aged captain of industry was thus more powerful than a muscular young farmer or a refined but poor aristocrat.

The development of the modern physical ideal—younger, taller, thinner, and more muscular—began around the turn of the century, again for both sexes. New historical circumstances meant that these physical characteristics were given new interpretations. Now, a thin, strong body was associated, not with hard physical labor, but rather with prestigious sporting activities. Leisure was no longer perceived in terms of a precapitalist lifestyle (aristocratic, ladylike), but with a late-capitalist consumer society. Increasingly, the basic unit of society was the individual, instead of the family, which meant that women and young people had greater autonomy. The bearded, older *paterfamilias* gave way to the clean-shaven sporting youth, playing golf with the Gibson Girl who was herself, in a sense, the harbinger of today's women weight-lifters. The spread of birth control also helped loosen the connection between female sexuality and constant maternity. In terms of appearance, this meant that the new ideal woman was no longer the voluptuous mother, but the young woman with the girlish figure.

But the triumph of thinness was slow in coming, and seemed to many people antithetical to female sexual beauty. The Gibson Girl looked willowy and athletic compared with her smaller, more rounded Victorian mother—but she looked heavy and matronly compared with the twenties flapper. Yet, although the twenties are notorious for thin, flat figures, in fact, by today's standards, both ordinary women and famous twenties beauties were usually rather plump. One of the most famous movie stars of the twenties, the "It Girl," Clara Bow, was short and round with masses of flaming red hair and an hourglass figure. The trend partially reversed itself from the 1930s through the 1950s, when high fashion, movie fashion, and everyday fashion all emphasized a womanly figure—strategically shaped by figure-controlling garments. It was really only in the 1960s that significant numbers of women threw away their foundation garments and internalized the process of figure control through diet and exercise.

A recent study indicates that many American women still think they are too fat; they think that men would find them more attractive if they lost weight. But the men, clinging to an older ideal, think many women are too thin (a *Playboy* model versus a *Vogue* model). Meanwhile, the men are satisfied with the way they look, happily unaware that women tend to think that American men are also too fat. Thus, as physical ideals change, people try with varying degrees of energy and success to alter their appearance—both from the outside by means of dress and adornment, and from the inside by means of diet, exercise, body language, and facial expression.

Today's more muscular, slightly androgynous body ideal is not really any more natural (or even necessarily significantly healthier) than the plump or slender bodies favored in other times and places. Certainly nutri-

In 1913 the fashionable silhouette for both men and women was straight and narrow. This fashion plate appeared in *Journal des Dames et des Modes,* which was among the first fashion magazines to declare that fat was out and thinness was desirable.

tion has improved and (some) people are less sedentary than they were in the recent past, but it is false to interpret changes in physique in terms of progress. Both luck and effort are needed to approximate the cultural ideal, which is an aesthetic ideal as well as a product of nutrition and exercise.

And no matter how athletic and well nourished a young woman may be, she is unlikely to be as tall, muscular, and thin as her male counterparts. If women in the mid-1980s were, to some extent, copying male styles of dress and appearance, does this mean that they were finally accepted as equals? To the extent that the male image is still the norm to be copied by women, the answer must be no. But it is also yes, to the extent that more of us now believe that men and women are primarily people, and only secondarily people of a particular sex.

Do men and women have to wear unisex clothing to prove that they are equal? The idea that women's rights and dress reform went hand-in-hand is not borne out by the facts. In the nineteenth century, the women's movement advanced without being accompanied by the widespread adoption of rational clothing. Rational, natural clothing has never been successful—not after World War I, not in the 1960s, and not today.[12] Instead, women have adopted new forms of sexually attractive clothing—brassieres (and exercise) instead of corsets, miniskirts in place of longer dresses—as the ideal of feminine sexual beauty has changed. In China, the great revolutionary experiment of one uniform for everyone was rapidly dismantled after Mao's death, as men and women both claimed the right to beautiful and individual dress.[13] Perhaps we will also decide that differences between men's and women's clothing are valuable to us as a way of affirming our individual identities (including our gender identities). In 1985, when fashion historian Anne Hollander explored "The New Androgeny," she implied that while both men and women dressed more or less like men for work, they both dressed rather like little boys for leisure. But by the end of the 1980s, there was a noticeable revival of traditionally feminine styles.

It is possible that in our culture clothing that differentiates sharply between men and women will increasingly be restricted to social settings, where sexual display retains greater significance. In the meantime, this book will explore—in the various contexts of sexual behavior, work, sports, and simply growing up—the relationship between appearance and identity.

JO B. PAOLETTI and CAROL L. KREGLOH

THE CHILDREN'S DEPARTMENT

There has been a great diversity of opinion on the subject, but the generally accepted rule is pink for the boy and blue for the girl. The reason is that pink being a more decided and stronger color is more suitable for the boy; while blue, which is more delicate and dainty, is prettier for the girl.

The Infant's Department (June 1918)

Although we may think the gender differences we see in today's children's clothing are traditional, few of them date back further than the turn of the century. In fact, each generation of children has been raised according to a different set of rules and practices, depending on the prevalent fashions in child psychology and child rearing. Liberated parents of the 1970s, embracing the principles of non-sexist child rearing, ardently believed that dressing their daughters in frilly pink dresses and their sons in three-piece suits would teach them undesirable gender stereotypes. A decade later, many parents believe equally strongly that unisex clothing will confuse their children and undermine the process of learning gender conventions.

For all their differences, both sets of parents are acting on the assumption that clothing is a potent force in the way children learn to be masculine or feminine according to society's rules. There is no question that it is an important way in which children learn the symbols of gender. By the age of three or four, most preschoolers have learned what kinds of garments are appropriate to each sex. But pink and blue color coding was a novelty at the turn of the century and only became widely practiced after the Second World War. For most of our history, there has been little differentiation between the clothing of male and female children under the age of five. A hundred years ago, both boys and girls wore dresses until about that age, yet there is no evidence that these conventions had any effect on the gender identities these children assumed in adulthood.

Does that mean that gender differences in children's clothing bear no relation to adult gender conventions or imagery? Functional differences in boys' and girls' clothing do exist. Today many girls' dresses, blouses, and nightgowns button down the back, while boys' clothes pull on over the

A boy's first pair of trousers, like his first haircut, represented a significant rite of passage until early in the twentieth century. A bittersweet moment in a mother's life is portrayed in this 1860 illustration from *Peterson's Magazine*.

head or open in front, permitting boys to dress themselves independently more easily. Boys' clothing is more likely to have pockets than girls' clothing. However, boys do not reap all the functional advantages; girls' lightweight dresses are more comfortable in hot weather than are the close-fitting tops and shorts usually worn by boys. In addition, while the presence or absence of strong gender distinctions in children's clothing may have little effect on their eventual conformity to prevailing gender conventions, they may have a great deal to do with their parents' beliefs about how gender identity is acquired. Modern child psychology teaches us that children acquire their gender identities in a series of overlapping stages of development that begin at birth. Accordingly, parents today perceive—and dress—infants as sexual beings, while a century ago babies were asexual cherubs. The dress of modern preschoolers reflects their parents' attitudes toward the teaching of gender conventions: traditional, non-sexist, or laissez-faire ("I let them pick their own clothes because it won't make any difference anyway").

While the changing styles of children's clothing may be fascinating on the surface, the truly important changes in gender imagery are less obvious: functional changes in dress, much more than color and trim, have affected children's learning of gender conventions, and even more fundamental, changes in gender imagery used in children's clothing reveals a great deal about their parents' beliefs about children and gender.

You don't need a collar to need Wisk.

WISK GETS RING AROUND THE COLLAR AND YOUR WHOLE WASH CLEAN.

Wisk

It is easy to tell the girl from the boy in this 1985 advertisement. Light colors, gathers, puffed sleeves, and bows are familiar symbols of femininity, just as dark colors, pockets, and bold stripes are "masculine." Both children can get dirty, play soccer, and run for president when they grow up, but their clothing emphasizes their differences more than ever before in history. Do clothes make the man (or woman), or do we overestimate their importance?

INFANTS

It's a boy!

Even a quick review of birth announcements will tell you: the most important thing to announce to friends and relatives about a new baby is its sex. Around the world and throughout history, a child's sex has been a deciding factor in its upbringing, its education, and even its survival. The importance of a child's sex—specifically, the historical preference for male children—is deeply ingrained in every cultural group that has come to our shores and, through them, in American culture as a whole.

Given this, the development of infants' clothing in America seems to be a complete paradox. If gender were so fundamental to an infant's identity, why did parents prior to this century dress all their babies alike? If modern gender conventions are becoming less distinct, why are infants' fashions today more sex-typed than those of previous generations? The key to this paradox may lie not only in understanding beliefs about gender, but also in the overlapping beliefs about infancy, which have changed considerably since the eighteenth century.

Prior to the end of the seventeenth century, European and American parents perceived children as being vessels of evil, tainted with original sin. Practices that we would consider physical or emotional abuse were commonly used to wrest even infants from the hands of Satan.[1] But John Locke, in his 1692 work *Some Thoughts Concerning Education,* suggested a revolutionary vision of the child as a "tabula rasa"—an unmarked slate—

upon which parents and teachers could inscribe beliefs, behaviors, and knowledge. Instead of a predetermined evil character, the child was perceived to have a benign, potential character that could be molded into a more desirable form through gentle example and firm discipline.

Throughout the eighteenth century, Locke's philosophy influenced child-rearing practices, particularly in England and America. More mothers nursed their own infants, after centuries of turning them over to wet nurses. Infants' clothing changed as well. Prior to the 1700s, babies had been swaddled, immobilized in strips of fabric wound around the body, to hold the child's limbs in place so that they would grow straight. Swaddling also had the advantage for the nurse or mother of converting a wriggling, squirming baby into a neat manageable bundle that could be hung on a peg on the wall out of harm's way.

By the early eighteenth century, swaddling was falling into disfavor. Instead, small infants wore diapers (then called clouts) and long dresses, which often extended well beyond the child's feet, to protect the baby from drafts. When they began to learn to walk toward the end of their first year, they graduated to shorter ankle-length dresses with no diapers underneath. Bowel training started early, often before six months, so that a certain predictability (if not real control) was achieved by one year. Undiapered toddlers were allowed to urinate outside on the ground until bladder control permitted the use of a chamber pot or privy. These loose dresses were worn until the child was between two and four years old, when infancy abruptly ended and training for adult life began. One characteristic of baby clothing did not change during this wave of reform, however: neither swaddling clothes nor infant dresses distinguished between boys and girls. The usual color of these garments was white, and embroidery and other ornamentation was added with no regard to the child's sex.

All of this suggests that, in the eighteenth century, infants were not perceived as individuals to the extent that they are today. The eighteenth-century child was not generally thought of as having a personality, much less a gender, until it reached the age of two or three (or later). What personality it was acknowledged to have was more that of a darling pet than of an adult in embryo. Because infant mortality was so high, perhaps the parents were protecting themselves from becoming too attached to the child, but beyond that, the truth is that at one time babies were not the sentimentalized cherubs they were to become in the nineteenth century. While a child's gender may have been of interest and importance to its parents, its status outside of the family was that of a *potential* individual, a status that seems to have been the overwhelming determinant of infants' costume.

In the nineteenth century, popular writers and transcendentalist philosophers provided a new model of the nature of the child. No longer either sinful beings or empty vessels, babies were perceived as innately good, even saintly creatures. A careful balancing act began, as parents sought to prepare their children for the responsibilities of adult life while still preserving for as long as possible the innocence by then synonymous with the word *infant.* This resulted not only in the continued use of genderless dresses for infants through the entire nineteenth century, but also contributed to the extension of unisex styles several years beyond infancy. There was, throughout the nineteenth century, still no differentiation between boy and girl infants. Both wore embroidered or lace-trimmed garments. Both wore bonnets. White was the universal color of infancy, perhaps because of its connotation of purity, but also as a visible sign of the conscientiousness of the mother in keeping her child clean. Equally important was the practical matter of fading or bleeding colors, making white a better choice for frequently laundered garments.

By the end of the nineteenth century, important changes had occurred in the popular view of infants as psychologists began to discover the extent to which young children and babies were aware of and affected by their surroundings. This led to an increasing emphasis on the role of the mother as her baby's teacher, not simply its caretaker. Mothers had long been responsible for the moral education of children as well as for their early lessons in reading and other skills. But, where the eighteenth-century parent believed that a baby boy would become a man by instinct, directed by his masculine nature, the late-nineteenth-century parent was being told that masculinity could, and *should,* be taught. Psychologist G. Stanley Hall (the father of modern child psychology) wrote repeatedly and forcefully in popular magazines that early sexual distinction was essential to correct adult development.[2]

From the turn of the century until the 1950s, infants' clothing gradually lost its genderless styling and became progressively more sex-typed. The first change in baby clothes appeared in the early twentieth century, with the introduction of rompers or creepers—one-piece garments with gathered leg openings and buttons or snaps closing the crotch. Originally introduced in the 1890s for older children's playclothes, within a short time these clothes were available for babies as well. They were a significant departure from traditional infants' clothing on two counts. First, they were bifurcated. Second, creepers were usually made of colored fabrics—solid blues and reds, gingham checks in pink, red, and blue, and blue or gray ticking stripes—in vibrant contrast to the white traditionally used for dresses. Both of these characteristics signaled the acceptance of the concept of infants' individuality and allowed parents to dress their babies in costumes regarded as appropriate to each child's personality and activities.

Like most Americans born in 1916, Joseph Barraclough of Port Norris, New Jersey, wore long white dresses at least until his first birthday.

Rompers and creepers began to be popular daytime play outfits for infants and toddlers after the turn of the century; they replaced white dresses, except for dressy occasions, by the 1940s for both boys and girls. Unlike clothing for today's young children, these typical examples from 1917–18 were unisex.

One of the results of these parental choices was the creation of a system of gender symbolism where none had previously existed.

This is not to say that the introduction of creepers resulted in an immediate end to centuries of genderless costumes for babies. Until the rules of gender coding for infants evolved completely, most rompers were essentially unisex, since not all parents or manufacturers agreed on the appropriate styles, colors, and decoration for boys and girls. Even bifurcation was not uniformly perceived as masculine styling. On the one hand, creepers were worn by little boys whose parents thought that dresses were too unmanly for their sons, but creepers also offered progressive parents of daughters a practical alternative to dresses for playclothes. Until clearly distinctive styles were available for each sex, a baby boy and a baby girl could wear the same style romper, although they might be wearing them for different reasons.

To see how long the introduction of this gender symbolism actually took, consider the conventions of modern baby clothes. Pink is for girls; blue is for boys. Only girls may wear dresses. Even trim materials and pictorial motifs (trains, flowers, baseballs, butterflies) are selected according to the sex of the intended wearer. (This may seem to ignore the unisex styles sold in gift boxes and intended as shower gifts, but these are notable for their conscious *avoidance* of any gender symbolism.) None of these conventions was true of most infants' clothing prior to World War I, and some of them did not become traditional until the postwar baby boom.

Take, for example, the fairly common practice of dressing girls in pink and boys in blue. Many exceptions to this rule can be found as late as the 1940s. In the beginning of the century the rule was the opposite—pink for boys and blue for girls. Between 1900 and 1940 both colors were often used interchangeably, even while the modern pattern was gradually emerging. A set of twin paper dolls (boy and girl) published in the late 1930s shows identical blue buntings as well as matching pink bathrobes, although the boy holds a blue rattle and the girl's rattle is pink.[3] Since prepackaged layette sets are intended to be purchased before the baby's arrival, it is interesting to note that Sears, Roebuck and Co. did not offer its layettes in a neutral color (yellow) until the 1950s. Before that time, layettes were offered only with a choice of pink or blue trim. It would appear that it took forty or fifty years of colored baby clothes for our present pink and blue symbolism to evolve completely.

Nor did boys suddenly stop wearing baby dresses with the introduction of rompers. Dresses remained a staple item in infant wardrobes well into the twentieth century, still trimmed with delicate embroidery and other handwork. As late as the early 1950s, infant boys still wore white dresses, even though rompers, overalls, and footed sleepers were far more common by then. Christening gowns remain the one remnant of the practice of dressing both boy and girl babies in trailing white dresses, although today's infant male need not suffer the indignity of wearing girls' clothes at all. Christening suits, with vests, short trousers, and satin bow ties, have made it possible for parents to eliminate every hint of femininity from their sons' wardrobes.

It is interesting to note that most of the gender symbolism added to infants' clothing in the twentieth century seems to have affected boys' clothing more than girls'. Boys' clothing borrowed style and details worn by older boys and men and was gradually purged of anything symbolic of femininity, according to current definition. Comparatively few changes occurred in girls' clothing. Since the 1940s, most of the changes in both boys' and girls' clothing have served to eliminate ambiguity, as the new gender symbolism became familiar. Today's infants' wear is easy for even a non-parent to read, impressive testimony to the power of the system of symbols developed in so short a time.

Why is it so important to modern parents that the sex of their child be evident? Not that long ago the Mellin's Baby Food company used to amuse

How many parents today would find a sex-guessing contest amusing? Readers of this 1905 Mellin's Baby Food advertisement apparently found gender ambiguity less threatening than we do.

MELLIN'S FOOD BABIES
Result of the Guessing Contest

The above portraits were shown in our exhibit at the St. Louis Exposition. We offered $250.00 in gold to the person who could correctly guess the boys and girls in the 20 numbered pictures.

No one guessed 20 correctly.

Mr. George Harrison, Enfield, N. C., was awarded the $250.00, the only person guessing 18 correctly, this being the largest number of correct guesses.

Mellin's Food received the GRAND PRIZE, higher than the Gold Medal, the Highest Award of the St. Louis Exposition 1904.

No other infants' food received so high an award.

MELLIN'S FOOD CO., BOSTON, MASS.

the readers of *The Ladies Home Journal* with contests to guess the sex of babies shown in their ads.[4] It is hard to imagine today's parents enjoying such a contest, especially if their man-child was consistently guessed to be a girl. Part of the answer lies in our present-day view of babies as impressionable beings, learning from birth. Like G. Stanley Hall, many twentieth-century parents believe that such an important lesson as gender can not be taught too early. The truth is that most children are unaware of sexual distinctions or their meaning until the second or even third year of life, so gender distinctions in the clothing of a month-old infant can have little effect on the child's training. However, it is highly effective in molding the expectations and behavior of the parents and others who hold, speak to, and play with the baby.

This has been repeatedly shown by psychologists who have observed adult behavior when confronted with babies dressed in a variety of outfits. These test subjects reacted differently when they thought the child was a girl than when they were led to believe the baby was a boy. The most interesting reaction, however, was when they were confronted with a baby of unknown sex. Some responded by choosing neutral toys to offer the baby or by guessing the child's sex, usually erroneously, based on the baby's size, appearance, or behavior. A few, clearly frustrated by an ambiguous social situation, persistently asked to be told the baby's sex.[5] These studies show that the primary function of gender-specific infants' clothing is to enable others (especially strangers) to make appropriate social responses to the baby. This reflects the more public life of modern infants, in contrast to the turn-of-the-century baby, who spent its first months at home surrounded by family and friends who already knew his or her sex. Today's parents often admit to dressing their babies for outings conscious of the need to provide strangers with cues to the baby's gender. Even non-sexist mothers may put pink bootees on their otherwise ambiguously dressed daughters.

The sex of a baby is probably as important today as it was two hundred years ago, but the immediate symbolic communication of a child's sex is expected, even demanded, in America today. The key to this transition lies in the combination of two factors: changing beliefs about early personality development and the increasingly public lives of babies.

EARLY CHILDHOOD (ONE TO FIVE YEARS)

Most children do not begin to learn the rules of gender imagery until their second year of life; by age five the lessons are thoroughly absorbed. It follows that the way in which children are dressed during this stage could have a considerable impact on the development of gender identity. Historically, gender distinctions in clothing for small children have ranged from obviously sex-typed to virtually identical styles. Nor has this been a progressive evolution. Prior to the middle of the eighteenth century, all children went from infants' dresses to adaptations of women's clothing at the age of two, and then donned miniature versions of gender-specific adult fashions by the age of four. During the late eighteenth century, children no longer in baby clothes wore gender-specific styles intended especially for children. Most nineteenth-century clothing for young children was once again based on that of adult women, making little distinction between boys and girls. Then, at the beginning of the twentieth century clothing for toddlers and preschoolers started to become gradually more sex-typed, a pattern that has continued to the present day, despite a brief vogue for unisex styles for children in the 1970s.

Like the changes that occurred in infants' dress, the evolution of clothing for early childhood has been influenced by changing child-rearing practices based on beliefs about the nature of childhood. Unlike infants' clothing, however, clothing for children during these important learning years might be expected to affect patterns of gender identity in their later childhood and adult lives. Apparently they have had little effect. Certainly boys, who have worn an amazing range of styles in the last three centuries, show no evidence of growing up into dramatically different styles of manhood from generation to generation; boys in skeleton suits, boys in kilts, boys in velvet cavalier suits, and boys in denim overalls grew up to be typical American men in all the usual varieties. Girls' clothing has changed far less, and mainly in the twentieth century, so it may be premature to assert that wearing trousers instead of skirts has had no impact on girls' gender identities. More likely is that clothing changes have only had an effect on children's development when they were accompanied by changes in education, activities, and expectations. Otherwise, what appear to be significant shifts in children's clothing patterns may be nothing more than new fashions in window dressing, with the same old merchandise for sale inside.

Before 1760, children's clothing, like their education, was not suited to their needs. At two or three, boys and girls exchanged their infants' clothes for stiff formal gowns that were much like a grown woman's. Boned, back-lacing bodices molded youngsters' torsos into a fashionable cone shape. These bodices were worn with full, ankle-length skirts. Only the long fabric leading strings that hung down the dress back and the padded crash helmet, or pudding, distinguished their clothing from that of their mothers. When they were four years old, children changed into clothes that proclaimed them to be young men or women. A girl's hair style, gown, and high-heeled shoes echoed her mother's, while a boy put on exact replicas of his father's shirt and stock, knee-length breeches, waistcoat, and coat. Lessons in formal self-presentation, including posture, movement, and courtesies began at the same time that a little boy or girl donned adult clothing. The unyielding garments and learned mannerisms imposed the illusion of physical and mental maturity upon very young children.

In the second half of the century, education reform acquired a new champion, French philosopher Jean Jacques Rousseau, who based his work on the earlier writings of John Locke. In *Emile* (1762), Rousseau suggested a more relaxed approach to child rearing, with formal lessons postponed until the age of six or later. He believed that little boys and girls should be encouraged to engage in outdoor play and physical activity before schooling began. Like Locke, Rousseau believed that children should be carefully

The Grymes children (c. 1750) are dressed in clothing typical of well-to-do eighteenth-century American colonists. The youngest, two-year-old Charles, wears a loose white dress, a style recently adopted for infants. Brother John (second from left) has, at three or four years of age, graduated from baby clothes to a costume more like adult clothing. In a few more years he will give up his skirts for his first pair of breeches and, like older brother Thomas (age twelve), be dressed in adult clothing. Seven-year-old Lucy is already old enough to wear the same styles as a grown woman. Collections of The Virginia Historical Society.

taught expected behavior at an early age; both disapproved of any coddling, spoiling, or encouragement of inappropriate childish activity. It was during the 1760s, coinciding with the publication of *Emile,* that children's clothing began to suit children. At that time the formal, boned toddler's dresses were replaced by ankle-length, loose-fitting muslin dresses simply adorned with wide sashes at the waist. These gowns, in fact a version of the infants' dresses already in use, were at first worn by children aged two to four. Later, gradually, they were adopted for girls until their early teens. In the 1770s, a new style for boys was introduced—the skeleton suit, a soft shirt buttoned onto a pair of long, but loosely fitted, trousers. The skeleton suit and the muslin dress were the first true children's fashions, reflecting the growing conviction that children had needs distinct from those of adults. In terms of gender, they introduced one significant new pattern. With the skeleton suit, boys were given a style that was not men's clothing, but still different from the clothing worn by girls their own age. Not only did the new styles acknowledge that childhood was distinct from adulthood, they also reflected the special status given to boyhood. Girlhood, on the other hand, had merely changed from being perceived as early womanhood to prolonged infancy, at least as far as clothing was concerned.

In the nineteenth century, children changed from blank slates to little angels—perfect beings who were not only without sin, but who offered adults a model of unworldly goodness. To nineteenth-century parents, their children's maturation, beside being a positive process of growth and mastery, also entailed an inevitable loss of innocence. Years of infancy and toddlerhood were a period of "bliss . . . before consciousness begins . . . ,"[6] the prelude to "that blank well of foregone conclusions which shuts out

The Smith children, shown here with their mother in 1796, wear clothing that is markedly different from that worn by the Grymes family half a century earlier. The baby wears a soft white dress, but so does the older sister. The oldest son wears a man's suit, but the two younger boys wear skeleton suits, a newly introduced intermediate stage between skirts and adult clothing for small boys.

fairyland."[7] Sexual awareness, it seemed, would come soon enough; there was no need to hurry it.

Paralleling this sentimental view of children as innocents, children's clothing throughout most of the nineteenth century worked to obscure gender differences for as long as possible, as well as postpone adult clothing until the early teens. As in the eighteenth century, infants of both sexes wore long white dresses until they began to walk. Toddler boys and girls then wore short, loose-fitting dresses (usually white or pastel colors) until they were two or three years of age. From then until the age of five or six, children wore dresses or suits with short skirts. (In effect, a boy's graduation to trousers took place slightly later than had their skeleton-suited

Is the smaller boy on the left in this detail of a *Godey's Lady's Book* print dressed like a girl? Perhaps in our eyes, but in 1843, skirts also signified infancy or immaturity. His cap identifies him as a boy, just as the bonnets and trim on their dresses proclaim the figures on the right to be girls.

Left. Van Loo (Charpentier)'s painting *The Cup of Chocolate* (c. 1755) shows how a colorful and highly ornamental style of dress was regarded as appropriate for both men and women. *Right*. By the nineteenth century, indeed, by the late eighteenth century, men's clothing had become dark in color and plain in style. Ford Madox Brown's painting *The Bromley Family* (1844) shows a variety of colors available for the women's dresses but a more limited range for men.

PLATE 12.

The shapes of store mannequins change in accordance with contemporary fashions in bodies and clothes. The c. 1974 figure by Adel Rootstein, c. 1938 Kayser underwear display accessory, and the c. 1890 dress model (missing wax head and jointed hands) illustrate different ideal postures. They also document different opinions about the desirable proportion of fat to muscle as well as how body tissue should be distributed, rearranged, or, if necessary, augmented.

PLATE 13.

Children's clothing communicates age as well as gender, and the two are often intertwined. In the eighteenth and nineteenth centuries, more age-distinct styles existed for boys than for girls, who moved more gradually from infancy to womanhood. John Grymes, second from the left in the upper portrait (c. 1750) is wearing skirts because he is only three or four years old and not old enough to wear breeches. In the lower portrait, dated 1796, the little girl wears a dress similar to the baby's, while her two brothers on her left wear skeleton suits, specifically intended for boys too old for baby dresses but not old enough for men's clothes.

PLATE 14.

Store bought or homemade, dress-up costumes encouraged children to try on adult roles. Traditionally, soldier, cowboy, and fantasy hero outfits have been aimed more at boys, while girls' options included nurses, brides, and ballerinas. Since the 1970s, superhero outfits for girls have grown in popularity, reflecting the acceptance of aggressive play for females.

PLATE 15.

Historically, men's fashions have been at least as flamboyant, modish, and body revealing as women's fashions. The portrait of Henry VIII (1536) by Hans Holbein from the Walker Art Gallery, Liverpool, England, shows the notorious codpiece, which emphasized the man's genitals. His clothing also exposed his legs and exag- gerated the breadth of his shoulders. But was this costume intended to express sexuality or power and status?

PLATE 16.

The play of eroticism in fashion is not usually explicitly sexual. A person may dress to look attractive, but this should not be confused with the use of clothing as a direct sexual lure. Evening dress, for example, creates an image of subtle sexual beauty for both men and women. The Arrow Shirt Man was a famous sex symbol, but the woman in this Arrow Shirt advertisement of 1914 exposes much more of her body than the man.

PLATE 17.

Clothing originally intended solely for the bedroom and the boudoir has sometimes gradually moved into the semi-public realm. The woman's dressing gown (or peignoir) evolved into the tea gown, which played a significant role in the development of freer modern fashion. As men's clothing became darker and more uniform, the man's dressing gown permitted a degree of fantasy and fluidity that was unacceptable elsewhere. The two illustrations here, both from French fashion magazines of the 1830s, show examples of "undress" that evaded the standard rules of dress.

PLATE 18.

When long skirts were worn, a fleeting glimpse of delicate feet and well-turned ankles, even in plain hose, could be tantalizing. The fancy-patterned stockings that became popular in the mid-nineteenth century contributed to the effect. The fashion for lavishly trimmed petticoats, in the early twentieth century, gave a woman the opportunity—through the skillful handling of her skirt—to flirtatiously make her audience even more aware of her shapely legs.

PLATE 19.

counterparts of the late eighteenth century.) Both boys' and girls' skirted styles bore a strong resemblance to women's dress of the period, usually reflecting current fashions in sleeve, neckline, and so on. This pattern of dress for children under six persisted from about the 1830s until the turn of the century. However, that is not to say that the boys were dressed *exactly* like girls. Descriptions of toddlers' clothing in fashion magazines make it clear that there were subtle differences between male and female styles:

> For boys of a year or a year and a half the blouse dress is worn, for morning wear confined at the waist with a belt. But little difference is noticed in the general style of their dress except the hat and less elaborate trimming on their dresses.[8]

> . . . little boys' dresses button up the front, those of their sisters fasten in back . . .[9]

Boy or girl? The silhouette, sleeve style, and dark green trim of this white wool dress do not offer a clue, nor do this three-year-old Brooklyn boy's long curly locks. In 1873 George Musgrave's mother and father did not think it necessary for his clothing to announce his gender. Nor were small children a century ago believed to need gender-specific clothing in order to learn appropriate gender identities.

Dressing boys in skirts for so long may have helped parents, especially mothers, delay the symbolic loss of their son's innocence. First haircuts and breeches were often described in the popular literature as traumatic for a mother, first steps toward the inevitable day when she would lose her son forever to the world outside the home. When long trousers briefly became fashionable for small boys in the 1890s, the *New York Times* fashion columnist wrote, "The little suits look so cute that no mother will be able to resist them, however unwilling she may be to lose her baby in her boy."[10]

Many of these anecdotes implied that breeches and short haircuts were the catalysts for boys beginning to behave "more like boys," though there also was often a suggestion that more masculine behavior was inevitable and could not be held off forever. One author compared mothers of small boys to a hen who mothered ducklings: "The point comes when they grow into something unfamiliar."[11]

Ostensibly, it was the mother who decided when her son was old enough to wear short trousers or knickerbockers instead of dresses. But this decision was not necessarily an easy one, or even one made without pressure from the father, relatives and friends, or the boy himself. The actual age at which this happened was extremely flexible; the most guidance that fashion advisors would offer was that the decision be based on the boy's size and appearance, not his age. A small, delicate six-year-old might still be wearing skirts, while his bigger, sturdier neighbor could already have graduated to knickerbockers at five. Whatever the effect of this practice on individuals, the overall result was that acquiring masculine clothing was not merely a matter of being old enough, but also of looking and behaving in a masculine manner.

> Her disposition, with her natural feminine tastes and tenderness, is always inclining her to deck her child with the gewgaws of finery and coddle him with the delicate appliances of luxury. The timely check from the manly boy may therefore prevent her from persisting in an effeminating process which would be sure, if continued, to deprive him of his best characteristics.[12]

Throughout the nineteenth century, the transition to adult clothing for boys was mainly one of the defeminization of his clothing between the ages of one and six. For girls, it was a simpler process. In contrast to the distinct stages found in boys' costume—infant dress, toddler dress, preschooler's skirted suit, schoolboy's knickerbockers, and finally, long trousers—girls' clothing changed less dramatically between infancy and adolescence. The most visible change was a gradual lengthening of the skirt. At puberty, girls began to wear their hair arranged in adult fashion and wore dresses identical in style to those of adult women, except for formal clothing. The "correct" ages for these transitions were seldom discussed in magazine articles or advice columns and were apparently not particularly controversial.

By the 1880s the care of children, like many other endeavors, was becoming more influenced by scientific theory and experimentation. Increasingly sophisticated physical and psychological research probed every stage of childhood. By the turn of the century, this child study movement had made it possible to compare individual children with their age-mates, giving new significance to the word *normal*. Freudian-influenced psychoanalytic theory placed great emphasis on a child's early experiences and the process of identification with the same-sex parent. Parents, especially mothers, were inundated with information and advice on the care and training of children, from prenatal care to the problems of adolescence.

At the same time, clothing styles for children underwent several important changes. Increasingly casual American lifestyles and a new emphasis on active play and organized sports for children encouraged the adoption of more practical and comfortable children's clothing. For girls this often meant the acquisition of masculine styling—shirts, knickers for sports dress and play clothes, and simpler styling for everyday clothing. By 1910 some women's magazines were advocating that girls as old as ten or twelve wear bloomers or knickers for play, although other evidence suggests that outside the gymnasium the practice was more likely limited to younger children. Girls' rompers were shown in Sears catalogues during that time period but were sized only to seven years.[13]

As girls' clothing acquired features once exclusively masculine, boys' clothing lost much of its resemblance to female dress. This was particularly true of styles for boys aged two to seven years, who were put directly into trousers, rather than the skirted styles. Elaborate, Little Lord Fauntleroy costumes for boys, based on earlier men's fashions, also fell out of favor:

> I saw a boy with a predestinate idiot of a mother, wearing a silk hat, ruffled shirt, silver-buckled shoes, kid gloves, cane, and a velvet suit with one two-inch pocket which is an insult to his sex.[14]

By the end of the 1890s, though boys wore dresses only until the age of two or three years rather than five or six, these changes were not intended to hurry the boy toward adulthood. For adolescent boys, the age of transition from short pants to long trousers had not changed, continuing to take place between the ages of twelve and fourteen. The transformation in little boys' clothing was meant to differentiate boys from girls at an earlier age than before, in accordance with the new beliefs about gender identification. Turn-of-the-century books or magazine articles for parents rarely even discuss the issue. Charlotte Perkins Gilman was the lone voice in favor of the older practice of delaying gender differences in dress:

> The most conspicuous evil here is in the premature and unnatural differentiation in sex in the dress of little children. . . . a little child should never be forced to think of this distinction. It does not exist in the child's consciousness. It is in no way called for in natural activities, but is forced into a vivid prominence by our attitude.[15]

Since the turn of the century, researchers have further explored the learning and socialization process. We are still not entirely certain how many of our gender behaviors and abilities are the result of our cultural environment and how much is inborn or instinctive. This nature versus nurture controversy lies at the heart of any discussion of gender differences in children. Yet the way in which we dress our children displays much less ambivalence. Clothing for small children, like that of infants, continued to become progressively more gender-specific. Just as in baby clothes, pink was still occasionally used for toddler boys' clothing as late as the early 1940s, but by the end of World War II was exclusively used for girls' clothing. At about the same time, very small boys began to wear adult-style suits and ties for dressy occasions, usually including long trousers. Although shorts and trousers remained popular for girls and even became acceptable for school in the early 1970s, stylistic differences (color and trim) and functional differences, such as zipper placement and number of pockets, usually distinguished girls' from boys' pants.

During the 1970s, there was a brief fashion for unisex clothing for children, echoing the gender-ambiguous styles worn by adults. With the use of brighter colors and long hair for boys, plain overalls and T-shirts for girls, it seemed that non-sexist clothing, if not completely non-sexist child rearing, was to be the wave of the future. But the fashion passed, and children's clothing in the 1980s, like adult clothing, has reverted to more sex-typed patterns.

Before we leave the subject of clothing for very young children, it is worth mentioning one very important component of children's experimentation with role imagery—dress-up games. Borrowing articles of adult clothing in order to heighten the realism of imaginative play would seem to be a very natural impulse for a child. In 1772, Virginia tutor Philip Vickers Fithian observed two of his young pupils (aged seven and eleven years) playing this venerable game:

> Among the many womanish Fribbles which our little Misses daily practise, I discovered one to Day no less merry than natural; Fanny & Harriot by stuffing rages & other Lumber under their gowns just below their Apron-strings, were prodigiously charmed at their resemblenc to Pregnant Women![16]

Likewise, in the nineteenth century, it is possible to catch occasional glimpses of children using costume in informal play or amateur theatricals, such as the March sisters enjoyed in *Little Women*. The old chest of clothes, hats, and boots has helped fill many a rainy afternoon, right up to modern times. Beginning around the turn of the century, ready-made costume playsuits—cowboy suits, Indian outfits, and many others—became popular.

How do costumes such as these function in children's play? The urge to play make-believe is at its height in most children from eighteen months to seven or eight years, with dress-up activity a frequent part of this play.[17] Wearing mommy or daddy's clothing is a favorite of preschool children, and by the age of four or five, wearing other kinds of clothing becomes equally fascinating. The form of play in which such outfits are used varies as the child matures. An eighteen-month-old, for example, may enjoy trying on different hats for the sheer fun of looking different or wearing something associated with another person. From age two to five, the child is more likely to use clothing to try on different roles or pretend to be a specific character. A pull-on skirt and Mommy's old patent leather pumps may be the costume for a tap dancer one day and Minnie Mouse the next. In dress-up play, the involvement or reaction of parents or teachers can provide the child with very important information about approved behavior—most parents would react differently if Minnie Mouse were their son rather than their daughter.

Between the ages of three and five, when gender identification occupies so much of a child's interest, it is not surprising that boys and girls already play different forms of dress-up games. Although both may enjoy what psychologists call "chase play"—good guy/bad guy games involving cowboys, soldiers, or superheroes—it is more common among boys. Girls are much more likely to engage in grooming and beauty-oriented play.[18] Again, parental attitudes influence the choice of game and costume, and these attitudes are subject to change with child-rearing philosophies. Prior to the turn of the century, "tomboys" who wanted to join their brothers in chase play were looked at askance, and it is a recent fashion to encourage boys to don aprons to play "house husband" instead of "Daddy coming home from work."

As a way of learning appropriate gender conventions and imagery, grooming play for girls stands alone in its importance and durability. American girls have always been raised to think about their appearance.

Although good grooming is supposedly desirable for boys and girls, girls are expected to show more interest in appearance and clothing. Girls' dress-up and grooming toys enjoy perennial popularity, from fashion dolls to ponies with manes for combing. An extreme example is this doll with long hair for styling—and nothing else—shown in a 1979 J.C. Penney Christmas catalogue. © J.C. Penney Company, Inc., 1979. Reproduced by permission.

The message that personal attractiveness is a feminine responsibility has permeated the toys and lessons directed toward little girls for centuries. This beauty is duty concept transcends lessons of personal neatness, which have been directed at both sexes. Beauty and grooming toys comprise a huge complex of toys for girls, from Barbie to ponies with manes for combing, and from cosmetics for preschoolers to dress-up kits featuring satin skirts and feather boas. There is no parallel for boys, and beauty play for girls has enjoyed continuing popularity even during those times when non-sexist child rearing was at its height.

RITES OF PASSAGE: ADOLESCENT DRESS

In many cultures throughout history, a child's entry into adulthood has been marked by a formal ceremony, or rite of passage. Very often a change in costume also marks this transition—the Roman youth donning his *toga virillis,* for example. In the United States, adult roles and adult clothing have not always been acquired at the same time, nor has either necessarily coincided with puberty. Yet Americans have, since the end of the eighteenth century, made varying distinctions between the clothing of adults, adolescents, and children. How has adolescent dress functioned in rites of passage in our culture? Have these functions differed for young men and women?

The stage of life we call adolescence was not popularly known by that name until the early twentieth century, nor has it always been perceived as an extension of childhood. As late as the middle of the nineteenth century, what we might call "boys and girls" of fourteen or so were considered young men and ladies, not old children. In the eighteenth century, adolescence was clearly treated as an early part of adult life. Many thirteen- and fourteen-year-olds left their homes and participated in adult life. (This is not to say that they were expected to be as competent as their elders; even two hundred years ago, youth was recognized to be a potentially difficult time of life, due to the young person's inexperience and lack of judgment.) Boys left home for work, travel, or, more rarely, college; girls remained at home until they married but were permitted a larger social life than their younger sisters.[19] There was no distinct change in clothing to mark these changes in status. Young adults had been dressed like mature men and women since childhood.

By the end of the eighteenth century, however, the changes that had occurred in children's clothing had effectively postponed the acquisition of adult clothing until the age of ten or twelve. There was still no hard and fast rule governing the age at which the transition should be made. No doubt class played a part in it, since lower-class children left home, married, and went to work earlier than upper-class children. Sex, too, was a determining factor—young women frequently married at an earlier age than did men, while unmarried teenaged girls enjoyed less freedom than their male counterparts. Since these practices were not standardized, the matter was left up to the child's parents, a situation that persisted until the middle of the nineteenth century.

By the mid-nineteenth century, more formal guidelines were emerging, perhaps through the influence of ladies' magazines, mothers' manuals, and etiquette books. For girls, puberty marked the final transition to long skirts, after nearly a lifetime of wearing progressively longer dresses. This was also the age at which corseting was introduced, or became more restrictive in the case of girls who had been wearing children's stays. Girls in their teens abandoned the simple flowing or braided hair styles reserved for little girls and instead wore their hair arranged up in the latest adult styles. Boys, too, marked their entry into sexual maturity with a change in costume. By the late 1860s and early 1870s, the transition from short trousers or knickerbockers to long trousers, usually between the ages of twelve and fourteen, was one of the most important occasions in a young man's life. The main difference between adolescent dress for boys and girls was that a girl's clothing changed in style when her figure became more womanly, whereas the corresponding shift for a boy had no such obvious stimulus.

During the late nineteenth century, the tendency was to soften the transition to adulthood for girls by creating special styles for them in their teens. These were generally simpler and younger-looking than those intended for women aged eighteen or above, favoring lighter colors and more delicate trimmings. Their appearance marks the beginning of a separate clothing market for teenaged girls. By the end of the first decade of the twentieth century, a separate, standardized size range for this age group—junior miss or junior—was being used. This resulted in the creation of even more styles, especially for junior high and high school girls, styles that reflected their interests in active sports, informal parties, and dancing, as well as meeting their needs for school. Equivalent styles did not appear for boys until slightly later in the century. As the buying power of teenagers increased, so did the importance of this market and the number of styles designed specifically for the twelve-to-twenty-year age group.

By this time, the popular image of adolescence had changed dramatically from what it had been a century before. Psychologists had begun to focus on the negative aspects of the age group—rebellion, ambivalence about adult roles, vulnerability to peer pressure. Often, they noted, these problems expressed themselves through the teenager's dress. Some troublesome tendencies were found in both boys' and girls' behavior; for example, teens were observed to dress in ways that were at complete odds with their parents' taste of standards of modesty. From the scantily-clad, be-rouged "Flapper Janes" of the late 1910s and 1920s to the 1980s punks with their brightly-colored hair, each generation has invented its own means to outrage its parents.

Many young adolescents (twelve- to fourteen-year-olds) go through a careless asexual phase, seemingly attempting to evade or reject adult gender conventions. For boys, this expresses itself as slovenly grooming and a strong resistance to any form of dressing up, especially in order to attend coed events such as dances or parties. In girls, the equivalent period became known as the tomboy phase, since the adolescent's rejection of femininity often included wearing masculine or androgynous clothing and engaging in male activities. This phenomenon undoubtedly existed earlier in history, as Jo March and other famous tomboys illustrate, although the availability of trousers and shorts for older girls after the turn of the century certainly made an androgynous appearance much easier to attain. At the same time, educators and psychologists began to stress that tomboy behavior was not a cause for alarm. Parents were reassured that this was a very necessary stage in their daughters' development, and some writers even believed it was desirable. Joseph Lee, founder of the Playground Association of America, asserted, "A girl should be a tomboy during the tomboy age, and the more of a tomboy she is the better."[20] Cross dressing or equivalent gender-bending behavior among young males won no similar endorsements.

Another component of teenage clothing behavior is the strong drive to dress like their peers. As the teenage fashion market became more defined and the distinctions between adult and teen dress more pronounced, local fads or informal dress codes became more evident. Peer pressure began to play an increasingly important role in a teenager's struggle to be granted adult dress or grooming privileges. Decisions about when a boy might wear long trousers or when a girl could put up her hair were once left up to the parents' discretion, though parents were no doubt aware of how their children's age mates were dressing. Adolescent psychologists, by emphasizing the teenager's need to conform, lent additional weight to the argument that "everyone else is doing it," especially when the dispute was over a relatively unimportant aspect of dress or grooming.

These arguments were apparently more common for girls than boys, since girls are traditionally encouraged to be more concerned with their appearance. The "beauty and duty" lessons of childhood backfired when the girl reached her early teens and began pressuring her parents—usually the mother—for permission to choose her own clothing, use makeup, and wear more grown-up clothing. Judging from the advice columns in teen magazines, which began appearing in the 1940s, many girls want to assume these adult privileges at twelve or thirteen, while mothers have tried to hold out until high school age, usually between fourteen and sixteen.[21] In contrast, the once significant male transition from knickers to long trousers was completely abandoned by the early 1940s, and parents usually permitted their sons to start shaving—the principal masculine grooming rite—whenever it became necessary.[22] The resulting pattern is of greater acceptance for a boy's sexual maturation than for a girl's even though girls usually enter puberty earlier than boys.

In modern teenage culture, we have no clear rite of passage for either girls or boys. Perhaps the closest possibility is the high school prom, particularly the boy or girl's *first* prom, which is the first occasion for which most adolescents wear formal attire. The preparations, the photographing of the young couple in their adult finery, and the parental emotions that accompany this event have all the signs of a ritual marking the child's entry into adulthood—except, like Cinderella's, the transformation only lasts one night. Modern maturation is a process, not an event, and the granting

The grown-up dress and rented tuxedo are this 1953 couple's ticket to one night of fantasy adulthood at their Senior Prom in Berkeley, California. In reality, adulthood comes much later to modern teens than to their counterparts in earlier times. A sixteen-year-old's clothing in 1787 was gender-specific and adult; in 1987 a sixteen-year-old looks masculine or feminine, but not grown-up.

of adult privileges has passed from being a parental prerogative to a long process of conflict and negotiation. Childhood in America today, if defined in terms of a period of learning adult roles and being economically dependent on the parents, extends through the high school years and even into college. Accordingly, the acquisition of adult gender symbolism, particularly by girls, now extends over a period of nearly a decade.

In American culture of the 1980s, children's clothing transmits a confusing message to us and to our children. On the one hand, infants' clothing proclaims that gender identity is important from the moment of birth. Young children are encouraged to express that identity, usually according to fairly restrictive definitions of masculinity and femininity. Yet at the same time, children may be learning that gender does not matter in some situations, that men can be nurses, that women can be police officers. Children are, in short, dressed in a more sex-typed manner than we may actually expect them to behave. This is in dramatic contrast to the pattern for children prior to the end of the nineteenth century, when the symbols of gender imagery were not introduced until well into toddlerhood and their acquisition was rationed out according to fairly distinct levels of maturity. The modern child's clothing is sex typed from the beginning, and adult gender imagery is introduced gradually as the child grows, with few rites of passage to mark the stages of maturation, even among adolescents.

These differences reflect the changes that have occurred in adults' perception of childhood and gender over the last century. Today's infants are acknowledged to have gender, even if they are unaware of it. Children are believed to acquire gender identity in a continuous process of development. Given this model, the notion of distinct stages of dress makes little sense and has therefore been discarded. At the root of the mixed messages found in children's clothing is our own ambivalence about modern gender conventions. What is appropriate male or female behavior? Must a businesswoman wear a gray flannel suit in order to look competent? Is it all right for a man to have a face lift? If we are not sure of the patterns we should be following now, we are even less sure of what we ought to be teaching our children. As a result, we are teaching them a complex lesson, one that reflects our own times: that clothes may express one facet of a person's personality, but they no longer reveal every nuance of his or her social identity.

VALERIE STEELE

CLOTHING AND SEXUALITY

It goes without saying that the Erotic Principle has, for almost the whole of human history, been the dominant factor in female dress. . . . The function of fashion is to increase the erotic appeal of the female body by constantly shifting the emphasis from one part of it to another. Hence we find that at one period the bosom is the center of attraction; at another, the legs.

James Laver,
The Concise History of Costume and Fashion (1969)

*M*any costume historians have assumed that the role of clothing in sexual attraction differs significantly for men and women. The most influential of the Sex Appeal theorists, the late James Laver, argued that, "Women's clothes . . . are governed by the Erotic or Seduction Principle." By contrast, *men's* clothes are said to be governed by the Hierarchical Principle (dressing to indicate one's position in society).[1]

Do women dress to attract men? Certainly, women's clothing has frequently emphasized female sexual beauty, through selective concealment, exposure, exaggeration, and occasional titillating cross-dressing. But is it true that sex appeal is the *primary* purpose of women's dress? Is Laver's famous theory of the Shifting Erogenous Zone correct in maintaining that fashion change occurs because male sexual interest fluctuates from one erotic zone of the female anatomy to another? Contemporary journalists and sociologists have often agreed with Laver. "Fashion and Passion," reads one 1984 headline. "Designers are Shifting the Erogenous Zones Again."[2]

But fashion does more than say, Look at my breasts! Oh, are you bored with breasts now? Then look at my legs! No one has ever offered any convincing evidence that heterosexual men become bored with breasts, not even during the 1920s when fashion flattened the breasts and exposed the legs. Laver's idea that the female back became eroticized in the 1930s because men were tired of legs is surely mistaken. Instead, the bare back style seems to have been influenced by swimsuit designs, which were cut low in back to maximize the area of skin being tanned. Moreover, Hollywood may also have contributed to the new style. Beginning in 1934, there was much stricter film censorship. Prevented from showing dresses cut very low in front, filmmakers sought to evade censorship by exposing the flesh in back.[3]

The low-backed evening dress
was a popular style in the 1930s.
But does this type of body exposure support the theory of the
Shifting Erogenous Zone? The
illustration is from *Vogue* (1934).
Reprinted with the permission
of Joanna T. Steichen.

And no one has ever suggested that changing male fashions reflected women's shifting sexual interests. Laver's idea that male sexuality is centered exclusively on the genitals, while women's sexuality includes many different erogenous zones (which may be exploited by fashion), is absurd in both psychological and historical terms. Fashion history reveals numerous examples of male clothing that has accentuated the shoulders, chest, legs, buttocks, and even the penis.

But although men's clothing has often been at least as modish and body-revealing as women's clothing, it has seldom been *perceived* primarily in sexual terms. Men seem to be reluctant sex objects. Conversely, no matter how modest women's clothing has been, it has consistently been *interpreted* as a mode of sexual attraction. That Laver interprets women's clothing in general as being primarily seductive says more about his image of women's role in society than it does about the clothes themselves.

Nor is Laver the exception; many other costume historians also betray a serious misunderstanding of what sexy dressing means, to the wearer as an individual and to the society as a whole. Consider the following quotations from two recent books on fashion:

> . . . everything can be boiled down to sexy dressing . . . selected to provoke the crucial clash of two parties to produce a third.
> Prudence Glynn, *Skin to Skin: Eroticism in Dress* (1982)

> As well as telling us whether people are male or female, clothes can tell us whether or not they are interested in sex, and if so what sort of sex they are interested in.
> Alison Lurie, *The Language of Clothes* (1981)

The history of sexuality is as much a recognized discipline as the history of work or sports, but the subject of *clothing* and sexuality is rather more difficult to define and analyze, as these quotations indicate all too well. Work clothes are worn by workers at work, sports clothes by athletes during the game. But when, and by whom, are sexy clothes worn? Clearly, we are not speaking primarily of the clothes worn by lovers during the act of making love. Instead, we seem to be facing the question of what constitutes sartorial sexual attraction: what makes clothes sexy?

Glynn assumes that the purpose of fashion is to promote heterosexual intercourse (and, ultimately, procreation). But human sexuality is more than a simple biological drive. It is also a complex social construct that is organized differently in different times and places—and differently for men and women. The conventions of sexual expression in dress are clearly dependent upon the ways in which sexuality is organized in the culture as a whole. Lurie recognizes this, but focuses primarily on the codified use of clothing as a deliberate sexual lure.

SEXUAL ATTRACTION

According to recent studies, sexual arousal in human beings is not "an automatic and instinctive response to the sight or touch of another person's body [that] . . . leads to sexual contact."[4] Nor is the human male necessar-

ily "the agressive, easily aroused partner." Human sexual attraction is
learned behavior, and it varies according to personal experience and the
customs of society. "What a man finds attractive in a woman is not biolog-
ically determined, but depends on his age, his social class, his personality,"
and what he looks for from the woman. One study, for example, showed
that "porters and soldiers preferred photos of large-breasted nudes in 'bed
room poses' . . . whereas the psychologists liked young, *predominantly
dressed* girls who were 'unconventional' or 'provocative,' and who were
'displaying arms and legs'. . . ." Both groups thought that prospective
wives should dress relatively modestly. Similarly, working-class women
tended to prefer photographs of mostly undressed "muscle men," while
professional women "found the 'Charles Atlas' types not merely unattractive but positively repulsive. Like their male colleagues, they preferred unconventional, *mostly dressed* men."

Not only is the distinction between dressed and undressed significant,
but the value placed on different body types is also directly relevant to sartorial preferences, since clothing can so easily alter the apparent shape of
the body. If men distinguish between clothing appropriate for wives and
clothing that is attractive on casual sexual partners, this also throws a mon-
key wrench into Glynn's overly simplistic picture of sexually enticing female dress.

Lurie implies that clothing functions simultaneously as a sexual lure and
as a code, indicating the wearer's preferred type of sexual partner. Prostitutes certainly use clothing as a direct sexual lure. In New York City in the
1980s, for example, a woman wearing hot pants, high heels, and a halter
top may well be a prostitute. It is also true that some homosexuals have
used a sartorial code (involving keys, earrings, or handkerchiefs—to say
nothing of the ubiquitous mustache) to inform other gay males of their
sexual preferences. But in most cases, the play of eroticism in fashion is
not explicitly sexual, and clothing only sometimes functions as a direct
sexual code.

A woman may dress to look beautiful, sometimes to attract sexual admiration, but only rarely with the aim of actually seducing the viewer(s).
Physical beauty is ultimately derived from sexual attraction, but they are
not synonymous. Fashion serves both to make the individual look more
beautiful and also, to some degree, directly to emphasize his (or her) sexual
charm. We may say that a particular dress makes a woman look beautiful
and a good suit makes a man look handsome, but that a low-cut or see-
through blouse makes her look sexy, just as tight jeans or an unbuttoned
shirt make him look sexy.

Even clothes that are intended to be sexy (to attract someone else) may
be subtle or obvious. Thus, a successful lingerie manufacturer insisted,
"Our image is elegant, romantic, and sexy. We believe in subtlety. We are
not selling items for women who stand in doorways with a come-and-get-
me pose."[5] By contrast, at least until recently, a *Frederick's of Hollywood* catalogue featured overtly sexual underwear, such as "crotchless panties." As
these examples indicate, women's lingerie is one of the major categories of
clothing that many Americans regard as being sexually stimulating. There

is much less general consensus about the eroticism of men's underwear, to say nothing of other types of clothing, where individually determined preferences abound.

The issue of sexual symbolism in clothing is also problematical. At various points in *The Language of Clothes,* Alison Lurie indicates that 1) "it might be proposed that the narrow woven cord or leather thong ties often favored by elderly American men suggest a withering or drying-up of the passions"; 2) "According to a journalist of my acquaintance, a casually burgeoning paisley scarf, especially if red, announces 'I can get it up'"; and 3) "A shabby, small, or—worst of all—ill-functioning umbrella is a source of shame that often seems excessive unless some erotic meaning is presumed." Similarly, in her section on "Sexual Signals: The Old Handbag," Lurie describes how the use of "the term 'purse' for the female pudenda . . . may be subliminally responsible for the female readiness to discard even a slightly worn purse."[6] But does an old handbag really reveal its owner to be an "old bag"? Comparisons such as those between umbrellas or ties and the state of a man's genitals, while amusing, seem overly simplistic.

In the real language of clothes, a garment seldom conveys such direct and specific information. If it did, there would be no chance of misinterpretation—whereas, in fact, the motive of the wearer in choosing a particular style of clothing may conflict dramatically with the viewer's perception of what that clothing projects. Sexiness (however it may be defined) is not an intrinsic attribute of clothing; it is a meaning ascribed to particular clothes by particular people.

Perhaps not surprisingly, recent research indicates that men and women often disagree on which clothes are most sexually attractive. In one study, men reported that they were most attracted by women's clothing that reveals the bust (such as see-through blouses or the absence of a brassiere). Yet women told another researcher that they thought men perceived bust-revealing styles as only "moderately attractive." The women believed men were most attracted to clothes such as midriff tops, short skirts, and revealing slits (although men reported otherwise). Furthermore, the women interviewed said that they only "infrequently" wore the clothes that they thought men liked, which would appear to cast doubt on the popular belief that women dress primarily to please the opposite sex.[7]

In the many cases of rape and sexual harassment in which the defendants maintain that the victims were "asking for it" by dressing "too provocatively," men's and women's differing perceptions of women's clothing can have tragic results. Despite the fact that rape is clearly a crime of violence rather than of passion, studies still indicate that many American men who are not rapists *also* tend to blame female rape victims. Moreover, they frequently cite sexy clothing as a contributing factor in the assault, although (as clothing psychologist Susan Kaiser pointedly observes) women in "unsexy clothes such as baggy sweatshirts and jeans" have also been raped.[8]

This type of social science research is only beginning to answer some of our questions concerning the role of clothing in sexual attraction—for both men and women. But subjective accounts still dominate the field, as

What features of women's clothes do men find most attractive? Apparently, men and women do not agree. Are low-cut, see-through, bust-revealing clothes sexiest? Is a prostitute's obviously sexual clothing necessarily more attractive than a more subtly sexy dress? What about leg-revealing short skirts, as seen in this 1987 fashion illustration? Andrea Blanch.

books like *The Sensual Dresser* offer advice on how to use clothing to increase sexual appeal:

> When speaking about the right clothes, the first rule is to put on less not more. I'm not talking about nudity.[9]

However helpful (or merely entertaining) such literature may be, it is long on intuition and short on evidence that other people may share the author's particular interpretations of dress.

Are men more easily aroused by visual stimuli, and women by the sense of touch, as the Kinsey reports have implied? According to more recent research, "the idea that men and women differ substantially in what turns them on is almost certainly a myth," although it can be self-fulfilling, if enough people believe it to be true.[10] Sexual behavior, including arousal and attraction, is culturally conditioned, and men may have been encouraged to respond more to certain kinds of sartorial eroticism. Today's highly sexual advertising appears to assume that many women are also favorably impressed by, for example, the sight of a good-looking man in tight jeans, an open shirt, and even a partially opened zipper.

EROTIC IMAGES

A woman stands in her bedroom or boudoir, dressed in her underwear. She wears a short, lacy white petticoat and a blue satin corset over a white chemise. Embroidered silk stockings rise to just above the knee. She also wears high-heeled shoes, earrings, a gold bracelet, and a finger ring.

Manet's *Nana* (1877) is an archetypal image of the seductive woman, not naked, but dressed only in underwear, jewelry, and high heels—and observed by a man who is fully clothed from his top hat to his polished shoes.

In 1975 photographer Helmut
Newton reversed the conventions of erotic art by showing a
clothed woman observing a
half-naked man. But a closer
look at this photograph from
Vogue reveals that although the
woman is dressed, her bodice is
open, her skirt is short, and her
legs are spread apart. Moreover,
although his torso is bare, the
man does wear trousers.

Nearby, a man sits, fully clothed from his top hat to his suede gloves and his black shoes. He watches her. Until a moment ago, she was looking at her reflection in the mirror, and applying powder and lip rouge. Now she pauses and looks out at us.

A century later, another young woman sits on a sun-drenched couch. Her legs are spread, her skirt just above the knee. Her legs are bare; there are sandals on her feet. The top of her dress is open over her throat and upper chest. She is staring hungrily at a young man who passes in front of her, wearing only a pair of white trousers. His torso is naked, tanned, and muscular. The shadow of his head appears on the wall behind her, but the photograph has been framed or cropped in such a way that his body is cut off at the shoulderline. All visual attention is focused on his body, half-clothed and half-naked, and on the intensity of the stare that the woman directs toward him.

Manet's painting of the courtesan Nana was exhibited in 1877. In 1975, *Vogue* reversed the conventions of erotic art and printed a photograph in which the sexual subject is a clothed woman and the sexual object is a half-naked man. At first glance, the fashion photograph appears to be the opposite of Manet's painting, but if we look longer we notice significant similarities. The woman in *Vogue* is not so clothed and self-possessed as she first appeared to be. Of course she is dressed, but her bodice is open, her skirt is short, and her legs are spread. Nor is the man so unclothed: he wears considerably more than his underwear. We are not surprised to learn that the photographer is Helmut Newton, who is known for his highly sexual (some say pornographic) fashion photography. Newton is no artistic feminist, but he has done more than introduce the tradition of erotic art (directed toward a male audience) into the realm of the women's fashion magazine.

Before the twentieth-century sexual revolution, a picture like Newton's would have been virtually inconceivable. Only when women began to assert that they, too, could be sexual aggressors were men presented as objects of desire *for women*. It is only in this context that we can understand how radical it is to portray a (mostly) clothed woman watching a half-naked man. Today, sexy young male models are increasingly used in advertising and art. Nevertheless, images of beautiful women still seem to have a far greater appeal (for both men and women). Cheesecake is more common than beefcake, and male objectification remains very different from the representation of women as sex objects. The most successful images of men as sex objects have caused controversy because a number of viewers have interpreted them as homosexual erotica. Nevertheless, Bruce Weber's photographs and Calvin Klein's advertisements have achieved something of a breakthrough in the depiction of the sexually attractive male.

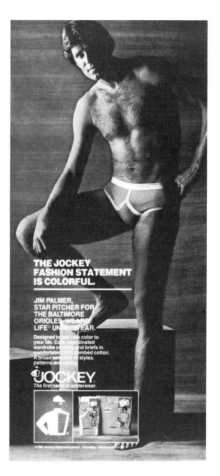

Are men reluctant sex objects? Until recently only men who were regarded as ultra-masculine (like baseball star Jim Palmer) were willing to pose nude or dressed only in their underwear. But this advertisement for Jockey underwear, which appeared in *Time* magazine in 1981, was soon followed by even sexier advertisements presumably intended to appeal, in part, to the many women who purchase their men's underwear.

FASHION AND EROTICISM: THE VICTORIAN EXAMPLE

Today's short skirts and tight trousers seem to us much sexier than the clothing worn a hundred years ago. The long skirts of Victorian women

Historians have greatly exaggerated the prudishness of Victorian dress. At fancy dress parties women often wore fairly short skirts and even Turkish trousers. Yet the Bloomer Costume, which was intended to be worn *in public,* was vehemently rejected. By comparing a fashion plate from the American *Le Bon Ton, Journal de Modes* (1860) and an American illustration of the Bloomer Costume (c. 1850), we can see the distinctions involved in the private-public controversy.

seem an outward sign of their repressed sexuality and their social oppression. In fact, the Victorians were well aware that women had legs. Their ideals of femininity and class status led them to insist that most women wear long skirts for most occasions. For centuries, long skirts had been the feminine norm—in the "permissive" eighteenth century as much as in the "repressive" nineteenth. Working-class women (and little girls) wore shorter skirts, but middle-class adults seldom copied them. The rules governing physical exposure depended heavily on context, as, indeed, they still do: a bikini is fine on the beach, but not in the boardroom or the ballroom. Short skirts *were* acceptable, however, for certain sporting activities and, significantly, for fancy dress parties held in *private.* The private/public distinction meant that, just as women wore low-cut dresses at evening parties that could not be worn on the street, so also might they display their lower legs at indoor costume parties that were restricted to a circle of friends. Fancy dresses with short skirts had been worn for private court theatricals since the Renaissance, when ladies played fairies and milkmaids. Under these circumstances, there was absolutely no danger that someone might think a lady was really a milkmaid! Turkish trousers were acceptable for nineteenth-century costume parties, but bloomers were thoroughly rejected as street clothing. Yet even the clothing worn on the street could be sexually attractive: from the swinging of the crinoline, which revealed legs clad in colorful embroidered stockings, to the tightly formfitting dresses of the 1870s and 1880s, which emphasized every line of the waist, hips, and thighs, Victorian dress was hardly as body-concealing as we might suppose.

The Victorians were also aware of the appeal of seductive and luxurious undergarments, although for many years pretty lingerie was primarily associated with ladies of easy virtue. Underpants were also slow to be accepted, because they were regarded as a semi-masculine garment. Nevertheless, Anglo-Americans were less prudish than they seemed. As early as 1858, the American magazine *Home Journal* printed a piece called

"The Red Petticoat Connubially Whip-Up-Alive," which suggested that Queen Victoria wore red petticoats in order "to reawaken the dormant conjugal susceptibility of Prince Albert."[11]

As more luxurious lingerie became fashionable around the turn of the century, earlier concerns about its doubtful morality gave way to lectures on good taste. A typical beauty writer favored pure white taffeta ribbons for the corset cover and chemise, but she was willing to accept the more risqué colored ribbons, so long as they did not "show through" the woman's "peek-a-boo" blouse. Excessively decorated lingerie was the mark of the vulgar, not necessarily the depraved.[12]

Because the history of Victorian sexuality has long been misunderstood, the clothing of the period has been misinterpreted accordingly. Today historians such as Peter Gay argue that we have greatly exaggerated the prudishness of Victorian women (and men) and have neglected their celebration of sexuality. (The term "Victorian" is now frequently applied to America and Western Europe as well as to Great Britain.) My own research in nineteenth-century fashion history also indicates that, despite their long skirts, high collars, and corsets, Victorian women were neither prudish nor masochistic. Nor did women's long dresses turn men into foot or corset fetishists.[13]

While there are obviously significant differences between the nineteenth and twentieth centuries in the degree of generally accepted sexual explicitness, the historical pattern of increased explicitness in lingerie, for example, began in the late nineteenth century. Early underwear advertisements showed plain white underlinen neatly folded, with perhaps a little embroidery work visible at the top of the chemise. And as women's underwear became more luxurious and erotically expressive in the 1880s and 1890s, so also did advertisements become more explicit. Silk, lace, ribbon insertions, and even color became fashionable. Fine linens and cottons were augmented by more diaphanous and luxurious silks and chiffons. This development occurred simultaneously with the increased popularity of "healthy" underwear made of supposedly hygienic fabrics like wool, and sometimes also designed to permit greater mobility for sports.

Women were thus moving away from a single Victorian standard of pretty but proper white cotton underwear toward both athletic underwear and seductive lingerie. Not only were women more active, but there was an increasing emphasis on the importance of companionable marriage and a happy sex life—and it was believed that erotic lingerie could help a wife attract her husband. This shift began in the 1890s and had become a dominant cultural theme by the 1920s. The increasing use of birth control may have played a role in this development.

The period from about 1890 to 1910 was the great epoch of underwear and dishabille. Month after month fashion writers elaborated on the theme: "lingerie is an enthralling subject."[14] They rhapsodized about the "exquisite, subtle, adorable art of filmy, beautiful underclothing." The English fashion writer Mrs. Pritchard dedicated a whole book to the fashionable enthusiasm for lingerie, in which she argued that, "The Cult of Chiffon has this in common with the Christian religion—it insists that the invisible is more important than the visible." She assured her readers that, "Dainty undergarments . . . are not necessarily a sign of depravity . . . The most virtuous among us are now allowed to possess pretty undergarments without being looked upon as suspicious characters." She linked "exquisite lingerie" with sexual satisfaction and blamed failed marriages on the wife's unwillingness to wear more seductive lingerie: "Can one wonder that marriage is so often a failure, and that the English husband . . . goes where he can admire the petticoat of aspirations?" She advised unhappily married readers to "try the expedient of a much-befrilled petticoat or some illusions in nightgowns." In her view, a woman might be "the most virtuous and careful of wives," but if she were "without mystery and without coquetry," she would be far from attractive to the ordinary man.

THE MYTH OF THE SIXTEEN-INCH WAIST

The image of the Victorian woman has long been that of a person strait-laced and dressed to kill. Most historians have perceived the corset in particular as an instrument of women's oppression and a frequent cause of debility and disease.

But just how tight were these corsets? Did Scarlett O'Hara's real-life counterparts faint, sicken, and even die because they were laced into sixteen-inch corsets? Visitors to costume exhibitions exclaim with horror at the sight of nineteenth-century corsets. Yet the measurement of existing nineteenth-century corsets and dresses are not excessively small: twenty-one- or twenty-two-inch waists were not uncommon, but eighteen- or nineteen-inch waists seem to have been rare, and sixteen-inch apparently nonexistent. Moreover, the size alone (usually advertised as eighteen to thirty inches) does not indicate how tightly the corsets might have been laced. According to a booklet on *The Dress Reform Problem* (1886),

> A distinction should be made between *actual* and *corset* measurements, because stays, as ordinarily worn, do not meet at the back. . . . Young girls, especially, derive intense satisfaction from proclaiming the diminutive size of their corset. Many purchase eighteen and nineteen inch stays, who must leave them open two, three, and four inches. . . .[15]

A great deal of misunderstanding has arisen because historians have accepted some bizarre accounts of tight-lacing as not only authentic but actually *typical* of the period. The notorious "corset correspondence" in *The Englishwoman's Domestic Magazine*, for example, is widely quoted as evidence of torturous practices. Many correspondents described tight-lacing to fifteen or sixteen inches, or even less. Some of the anonymous writers dwelled salaciously on the painful aspects of tight-lacing; others described experiencing mingled sensations of pain and pleasure. For correspondents such as "Alfred," the appeal of the tightly-corseted waist may have derived from sadistic fantasies associated with tight-lacing:

> There is something to me extraordinarily fascinating in the thought that a young girl has for many years been subjected to the strictest discipline of the corset. If she has suffered, as I have no doubt she has, great pain . . . from

Both the libido for looking and the erotic appeal of corsetry are expressed in this American trade card (c. 1882) for the Adjustable Duplex Corset: "The Secret Out At Last—Why Mrs. Brown Has Such a Perfect Figure."

their extreme pressure, it must be quite made up to her by the admiration her figure excites.[16]

After the *EDM* correspondence came to an end, other periodicals such as *The Family Doctor* were sporadically taken over by the self-proclaimed "votaries of tight-lacing." Yet the more of these letters one reads, the more their scenarios seem part of an ongoing pornographic novel, and any indignation on the reader's part gives way to a suspicion that these letters should be analyzed as sexual fantasies. As another correspondent wrote, "I don't believe a word of these stories."[17]

Many, perhaps most, of these letters could actually have been written by male fetishists. Perhaps an unknown number of individuals did tight-lace, but not under the circumstances that they described—at the foreign boarding school, in the bosom of the fetishist family, at the hands of the sexy and sadistic governess—and not to the degree claimed. The subject of fetishism as a whole is too large to explore here, but fetishism was and remains distinctly a minority sexual practice. It should not dominate our picture of normal Victorian corsetry.

Today, when corsets conjure up images of painful, almost orthopedic instruments, we should look at Horst's famous 1939 corset photograph for *Vogue* magazine. In its stylized tracing of the female torso and in the sym-

The corset never disappeared; it changed into other types of foundation garments. Horst's famous 1939 photograph for *Vogue* shows the sexual appeal of the twentieth-century corset, its very shape an icon for the sexually dimorphic curves of the female body.

bolism of the back lacing, it gives a sense of the corset's longstanding appeal. The very shape of the corset is an icon for the sexually dimorphic curves of the female body, just as the brassiere reproduces the form of the female breasts.

Many normal men and women also thought that corsets could be sexy. The act of unlacing the corset, for example, was the prelude to sexual intercourse and appears in a number of erotic stories, such as this one from *La Vie Parisienne:*

> Trembling, happy, your husband unlaces you with an uncertain and clumsy hand, and you laugh, mischievously, joyously ascertaining that his confusion is caused by the sight of your beauty. You are happy to feel your omnipotence; you take care not to help him untie the knots or find his way among the lace-holes; on the contrary, you take pleasure in prolonging his tentative gropings, which tickle you deliciously.[18]

The corset was designed not only to slim the waist, but also to support and emphasize the breasts, since the brassiere had not yet been invented. The evidence indicates that most nineteenth-century women regarded the corset much as their daughters regarded bras and girdles—as a practical necessity that could also be an attractive item of lingerie. It could be argued that the corset never really disappeared: it just changed into new types of foundation garments, such as brassieres and pantyhose or lycra "control top" panties. Although most contemporary feminists decry this type of elegant bondage, a minority opinion holds that "high heels and corsets . . . are not just visual stimuli for men; they are also tactile stimuli for women."[19]

Corsets for men also existed in the nineteenth century. European accounts mention military men wearing stays, while advertisements suggested that stays helped support the male body during athletic activities such as horseback riding. Even today one occasionally sees advertisements for male girdles, designed to support the back and suppress the paunch. Balzac's fictional character Baron Hulot adopted a corset when he began to gain weight because he wanted to remain attractive to his youthful mistress.

Men, as well as women, have tried to restructure their bodies to conform to the current physical ideal. However, this social imperative has seemed to weigh more lightly on men, perhaps because definitions of the attractive male have not been as explicit. To the extent that men seek to approximate a bodily ideal, it has more often been through physical exercise or the sartorial concealment of physical flaws, rather than the use of foundation garments. Even if women's foundation garments are not physically unhealthy or psychologically oppressive, they do indicate a greater social preoccupation with the improvement and support of female bodies. Perhaps today the corset has been internalized, as women (more than men) try to diet and exercise their way to an ideal figure. If they reject corsetry, it is partly because they rebel against male standards of beauty, but partly also because they think that both girdles and "flab" are ugly.

INTIMATE BODY FASHIONS

From Casanova to Freud, the attraction of concealment has played a recognized part in the eroticism of clothing. Concealment is sexually attractive, because it stimulates sexual curiosity—what Freud calls the "libido for looking"—which is a basic part of the human sex drive. Like the original fig leaf, clothing simultaneously hides the body and calls attention to it. Anthropologists have shown that a cache-sex or penis sheath actually draws attention to the hidden genitals. Today, peek-a-boo materials like patterned lace only pretend to hide the body. Cartoonists and pornographers, of course, are alert to the erotic possibilities of concealment. Magazines like *Playboy* seldom show models who are *entirely* naked; instead, the women usually wear a few titillating items such as garter belts and high heels.

Why is the partly clothed figure often perceived as being sexier than the nude? Underwear provides an important clue. In the apparel industry, underclothes are known as "intimate body fashions," a highly revealing expression. All clothes are body fashions, but the more intimate the connection between body and clothes, the sexier the clothes will be. Clothes may seem to us intrinsically sexy, because they touch the body. In a sense, the sexual power and charm of the body "rub off" onto the clothes. But the clothes are then perceived as providing an additional erotic stimulus of their own.

Clothes are especially sexy when they call attention to the naked body underneath, and when the situational context implies sexual contact. Lingerie is high on everyone's list of sexy clothes, because it is most intimately associated with the naked, sexy body. It actually touches the body, hugs the torso, slides over the skin. Furthermore, underclothes are secret garments, hidden under the outer clothing just as the body itself is hidden, to be revealed only in the privacy of the bedroom in the presence of intimate friends. A person wearing underwear is simultaneously dressed and undressed. We have reviewed its importance to Victorian fashion.

Sexual display is inextricably connected with this strategic concealment. The exposure of part of the body draws attention there, as does decoration and exaggeration, from epaulets and padded shoulders to ribbons and padded bras. The very presence of a zipper or buttons implies the possibility of opening them. Tight clothes outline the shape of the body, while loose clothes can give the sense that the hidden body is moving within. Fabrics from silk to velvet and leather recall the sensation of touching the skin. Clothes are sexy in many ways, all of them potentially characteristic of both men's and women's clothing.

Many people think women's underwear is sexy, but apparently not many people think men's underwear is sexy, even when it is short, tight, silky, and colored. In the early 1980s, however, when women started buying man-styled underwear, many people thought that was sexy. *Women's Wear Daily* called it "the hottest look in women's lingerie since the bikini brief," and the vice president of Bloomingdale's said that "It will bring women's underwear into the '90s." *Time* magazine reported nervously on Calvin Klein's "Gender Benders," complaining that the string bikini looked like an athletic supporter, while the boxer shorts still had a "controversial" fly opening. Klein replied: "It's sexier with the fly. These things are seriously thought out." In other respects the garments were not exact copies of men's underwear: the bikinis were cut higher on the thigh, and they came in twenty-four colors as well as plain white.[20]

Androgynous underwear was frequently worn as exercise clothing, perhaps hinting that sex itself was a contact sport. Certainly the style reflected a new ideal feminine body—strong and sexy, slim and muscular. As the androgynous look in fashion faded in the mid-1980s, underwear manufacturers shifted toward more classically feminine styles. Definitions of sexiness continued to evolve.

But *men's* underwear has seldom carried the same erotic connotations—of undress as a prelude to sexual intimacy, the attraction of concealment, and the libido for looking (and touching). Silky and colorful men's underpants have been in existence at least since the 1930s, but according to *Es-*

Advertisements for women's underwear range from the frankly sexual (Frederick's of Hollywood style) to the more romantic and elegant approach seen in this example from the Victoria's Secret catalogue (Winter 1985). Intimate body fashions—women's lingerie—are widely regarded as being highly erotic because they are intimately associated with the naked, sexual body, and because they are "secret" garments.

Men's underwear has seldom carried the same erotic connotations as women's underwear—of undress as a prelude to sexual intimacy, of the attraction of concealment (and the arousal of sexual curiosity), and of the libido for looking and touching. But recent Calvin Klein advertisements have stressed the potential sexual appeal of masculine-style underwear for both men and women. Indeed, the women's version of men's underwear has been described as "the hottest look in women's lingerie since the bikini brief."

quire magazine, white boxers remain the "true underpinning of the Ivy League style, the top drawers."[21] The owner of an upscale men's store in Harvard Square said that he stocked no other kind—no Jockeys, and none of the snug, "Italian-stallion" variety. "All the rest are tacky. . . . They're like bikinis. They're effeminate." Definitions of sexiness vary according to individual taste, as conditioned by ethnic group, age, social class, and geographical residence. But as the comments in *Esquire* indicate, the history of male underwear is also related to status anxiety and fear of effeminacy. According to historian Jo Paoletti, "such sex-role related criticisms are . . . powerful motivators of male behavior."[22] There are innumerable printed images, magazines, even calendars, devoted to female lingerie, but only a handful of comparable male images.

As men's clothing in the nineteenth century became darker and more uniform, indoor clothing like the dressing gown and smoking jacket permitted a degree of color and fantasy unacceptable elsewhere. Meanwhile, women's clothing that was originally intended solely for the bedroom and the boudoir moved gradually into the realm of semi-private occasions, such as tea parties, and eventually into the wider world. The woman's dressing gown became especially significant, as it evolved into the more erotic peignoir and tea gown.

Due to its unique position halfway between dress and undress, the tea gown played a significant role in the development of modern, post-Victorian fashion. Since it was designed for intimate, at home parties, it evaded the otherwise almost universal requirement of corsetry. Its image as an artistic garment of poetry and fantasy permitted it to become more diaphanous and overtly seductive and allowed designers a greater degree of artistic experimentation, thus paving the way for the radically new twentieth-century look in fashion and beauty.

It was via the tea gown that many of the loose and flowing, high-waisted

Perhaps the ultimate contemporary example of erotic dress is underwear-as-outerwear, whether in Jean-Paul Gaultier's *haute couture* version, a 1988 spring suit with sheath skirt and jacket opened on underwear, or in the use of bras, slips, and petticoats as evening wear.

and no-waisted design ideas associated with the Aesthetic Movement entered the mainstream of fashion. None of this would have been possible had there not existed a semi-private, interior realm within which such sartorial experiments could be conducted. Furthermore, the tea gown was not perceived as an anti-fashion statement (a type of dress reform), but rather as an individual expression of the wearer's taste and beauty.

Women's lounging pajamas also became acceptable among the avant-garde for at-home parties even before the First World War. By the 1920s they were widely adopted for parties and at the beach. *If* American men ever do adopt skirts, the style may well appear first as loungewear, as with the unisex caftan, which appeared briefly in the 1960s and 1970s. Trousers for women and flowing robes for men have historically been more acceptable within a semi-private setting, especially one characterized by an element of playful fantasy.

One of the most erotic styles of recent years has involved the use of underwear as outerwear. Because it violates one of the most powerful clothing taboos, the unexpected exposure of secret, sexual garments potentially carries a strong erotic charge. Already in the 1960s, there was a fad for wearing turn-of-the-century petticoats as skirts. By the 1980s, colorful silk slips passed as evening dresses, while camisoles were used as party tops. Avant-garde French fashion designer Jean Paul Gaultier showed 1950s-style brassieres and corsetry as outerwear; one of his "girdle" dresses was prominently featured on the cover of several important fashion magazines. The emergence of the T-shirt may be the most significant and pervasive example of underwear-as-outerwear. Not only does it flaunt rules about hidden clothing, but it also violates taboos against cross-dressing (since the T-shirt has become virtually unisex) and against male sexual display. Hollywood's portrayal of Marlon Brando in his undershirt helped set the fashion.

Fashion is rather like the legal profession: once a precedent has been set, a host of later decisions can be based on that first case. The development of sartorial symbolism derives in large part from the associations that particular clothes acquire. A 1984 article in *The Wall Street Journal* exemplifies the way in which women's clothes, even shoes, tend to be viewed in sexual terms: "Low-Cut Trend in Women's Shoes is Exposing Toes to New Scrutiny."[23] Apparently, "The classic, closed toe pump has developed a low-cut look in the so-called throat line, which means the shoe shows more of the cracks between the toes." The industry calls this "cleavage" and many observers find it "a sexy kind of look." But others think the style looks unprofessional. Susan Bixler, who wrote *The Professional Image,* is quoted in the article: "You have a nice suit, you're all put together, and then you look down and all of a sudden the feet are just screaming sex!"

If the cracks between women's toes are seen as "cleavage," then it seems people are ready to interpret women's bodies and clothes as being essentially erotic. Women habitually go topless in many cultures because the breasts are seen as primarily maternal, not erotic. For centuries (even in the Judeo-Christian and Islamic worlds), the sight of a woman nursing was accepted as normal. This factor contributed to the fairly rapid acceptance of dresses with low necklines, which were introduced in the fifteenth century. Initially perceived as a direct incitement to lust, it gradually became accepted as a form of aesthetically-tamed eroticism.

Since the nineteenth century, low decolletage has been more characteristic of evening wear than day dress. Those who regard it as sexually hypocritical or immodest to wear body-exposing fashions at night miss the point entirely. Low decolletage for formal evening wear was the *conventional* mode of dress, one that applied for aged matrons as much—or more—than for marriageable young ladies. Sexual display in dress does not invariably have a sexual purpose such as catching a husband or winning sexual admiration.

A tight sweater, a low neckline, or a black lace brassiere creates a very different effect than total toplessness. In a modern topless bar, the hostesses are, in effect, selling the sight of their breasts to a male clientele. At a topless beach, the message is that the breasts have become partly de-sexualized again. But when clothing merely hints at the sight of the bosom, the message can be playfully erotic. A woman in a low-necked evening dress may be saying, "I have beautiful breasts. Some lucky person may get to see them—not just anyone and not in public. You are free to fantasize." Then, again, she may simply be indicating that she is at a formal evening party.

At the turn of the century, Charles Dana Gibson drew an amusing cartoon in which he suggested that men, too, might adopt a low neckline for evening wear. This never caught on. A brief experiment during the Renais-

The display of a man's fine white shirt corresponds visually to the woman's exposure of skin in a décolleté evening dress, as can be seen in this 1889 illustration from *Collier's*. Charles Dana Gibson spoofed these conventions in an 1889 cartoon, when he portrayed men in low-cut evening wear.

sance in male decolletage was jettisoned in favor of the exposure of a fine white (under) shirt—a status symbol rather than a symbol that combined status with sex. Male body exposure usually occurred, instead, under non-sexual circumstances, especially for manual labor and sports. But only recently has female body exposure *in public* been accepted as non-sexual. Today even the shortest of running shorts is accepted on U.S. streets, but joggers who travel to foreign countries quickly learn that the sphere of nonsexual female body exposure is far more restricted elsewhere.

THE MALE SEX OBJECT

The issue of clothing and morality has almost always been associated with questions of female modesty and chastity. Costume historians have frequently asked, Do women dress to attract men?—while ignoring the ample evidence that women dress as much for reasons of status as for sex appeal. Even when it is clear that women are dressing for an audience of other women, it is suggested that they are all rivals for male attention. But what is the reaction when the question is turned around: Do men dress to attract women? Presumably, heterosexual men want to look sexually attractive to women, but their primary goal, they say, is to look active, powerful, and rich. Furthermore, they are strongly inhibited by anxiety about appearing effeminate—or, indeed, as a sex object at all. The male sex object is regarded with ambivalence and even disapproval. Only men regarded as ultra-masculine (such as baseball or football stars) can pose with impunity as centerfold models.

Men and women both report that there is a stigma attached to the man who looks too beautiful or ultra-fashionable. Heterosexuals openly suggest that beautiful, fashionable men look effeminate (which is, in part, a code word for homosexual). In a broader sense, however, effeminacy implies the quality of being like a woman, which is somehow less than a man.[24] Evidence of strength and success attracts many women, and the men's experience of their own sexuality has made it undesirable to seek acceptance or approval of their sexual charms. Men's *bodies* have never stood simply for sex; consequently, their *clothes* never have either. Pity the poor man who wants to look attractive and well dressed, but who fears that by doing so he runs the risk of looking unmanly.

Does men's clothing indirectly attract women by making them look rich and powerful? Both young women and their families have traditionally taken into account a man's ability to be a good provider. Unlike many men, women claim to be attracted most by indications of intelligence, strength, and virility rather than a good body or perfect facial features. In short, male beauty has traditionally been perceived in terms of inner qualities and personal accomplishments more than physical characteristics.

American advertisers do observe, though, that there has recently been a shift away from the father/husband image and toward the young, pretty gigolo image, which may indicate that women's priorities are changing. The advertising strategy for Corbin men's suits wavers between the usual dress-for-success imagery and the unconventional appeal articulated by a sultry young woman: "He's wearing my favorite Corbin again." In one ad, the male model is somewhat older, and good looking in the familiar manner of Cary Grant; in another version he is younger and more dramatically handsome. Are these men sex objects? Is the Corbin business suit intended to be perceived as sexy?

"HE'S WEARING MY FAVORITE CORBIN® AGAIN."

For three generations, Corbin quality men's suits, jackets, and trousers have been tailored in the United States

CORBIN,
Call for the store nearest you... 1-800-4CORBIN
See Reader Service Card after page 220

Is this man a sex object? Although the man's suit is not body-revealing and overtly sexy in the way many women's clothes are, researchers have found that "males appear more 'potent' when they are dressed in high-status clothing." The 1980s advertising for Corbin suits has emphasized the traditional dress-for-success strategy, together with a new focus on the sexual appeal of the well-tailored business suit.

Researchers believe that "qualities like competence (appearing qualified and expert) and potency (boldness, aggressiveness, and powerfulness) are attributed to individuals on the basis of their dress." A study done in 1979 "found that males appear more 'potent' when they are dressed in high-status clothing (in this case, a suit, dress shirt, tie, and dress shoes, as opposed to blue-collar work jeans, shirt, and boots)." This "potency effect" did not apply to women in high-status clothing.[25]

The Corbin suit is certainly not sexy in the way many women's clothes are. It is not body revealing or body exposing. But it may be perceived as sexy by women for whom (as Henry Kissinger once said) "power is an aphrodisiac." In an equation where earning power and status equal masculinity, the business suit represents a very potent source of sexual appeal.

Yet there is no consensus today about sexiness in modern men's clothing. A man's "power suit" may seem attractive to one woman, yet seem bourgeois and repressed to another. Still another woman might distinguish between various men's suits, concluding that a suit by Armani is sexy but that most other suits are not. It is not accidental that the main character in the film *American Gigolo* was dressed entirely in Armani clothes, and whole scenes were devoted to his shopping trips and the contents of his closet. More recently, there have been a number of articles suggesting that the television program *Miami Vice* has launched a new sexy look in men's clothes, one featuring white or pastel sports coats over T-shirts. It seems long ago that John Travolta's shiny polyester shirts, open down the front, were widely regarded as erotic. If we look further back in time, we find that the Arrow Shirt Man was perceived as a sex symbol. (When the shirt company first launched advertisements featuring a square-jawed and muscular young man, a number of women apparently wrote, proposing marriage.) More recently, Christian Dior has advertised men's shirts with the slogan "The prime need of fashion is to please and attract."

Whereas women's sexy clothing frequently plays on the themes of body exposure and disrobing, men's sexy clothing more often relies on indirect associations with particular men, such as movie stars or rock stars, or male archetypes, such as cowboys or secret agents, who are themselves regarded as being sexually attractive. Their personal charisma then becomes associated with the types of clothes they wear. Personal qualities such as daring, unlimited courage, and power—or men's involvement with some prestigious or adventurous *activity*—become associated with their clothes. Through sartorial extension, a western hat, boots, and jeans may conjure up images of rugged individualism.

Many women insist that men's clothing does not have clear sexual connotations—that men's bodies or personalities are more significant than their clothes. Men, too, frequently say that women's bodies, not their clothes, are sexy. Yet it is undeniable that certain female garments (such as garter belts and high-heeled shoes) are also widely perceived as sexy *objects*. The sight of Marlon Brando or James Dean in a black leather jacket is often regarded as sexy—but why? Leather has a certain intrinsic tactile appeal, as does silk or cashmere. But in the twentieth century leather has also acquired tough, even sado-masochistic connotations that may appeal to a

Many people find black leather sexy for both men and women, as emphasized in this 1985 advertisement. Not only does leather have a certain tactile appeal as a "second skin," but it may also carry a variety of erotic connotations. From Marlon Brando's black leather jacket to Saint Laurent's black leather miniskirt, the message combines seduction and danger.

number of people, at least on the level of fantasy. Ultimately, sexual fantasies may lie behind the perceptions that certain styles (such as military uniforms) are sexy.

The South Carolina Legislative Assembly passed a rule in 1986 requiring men of their staff to wear jackets and ties—and women to wear skirts. Only a few legislators argued that women should be allowed to wear trousers. A few days later, the *New York Times* reported that America's "No. 1 model for bathing suit . . . is 36-23-35." Apparently the fashion for androgynous figures was over, and the full-figured woman was replacing the muscular female beauty.[26] Similarly, the fashion for androgynous (i.e., man-style) athletic underwear was also waning, while sales of luxurious feminine lingerie were increasing—or at least, as in the 1880s, the athletic and the seductive styles were coexisting. By the time you read this chapter, the pendulum may have swung back again, toward relative androgyny.

Nothing seems to be more characteristic of fashion than this constant shifting of emphasis, so that an advertisement in February of 1985 announces: "Surprise! Women will dress like women this spring," while by July, the message reads, "Come fall, you're through with froufrou."[27] This, of course, is the phenomenon that led James Laver to hypothesize the theory of the Shifting Erogenous Zone. But a more accurate analysis might stress, instead, the significance of novelty and the continual evolution of our ideas about personal identity. In the past two hundred years, men's clothing has changed more slowly than women's dress, but it also evolves and expresses the current ideal.

At one time, we idealize pretty femininity and an elegant gentlemanly style; in another year we are attracted by the "exotic erotic" and fantasy (often ethnic) looks, or by a classic, natural, all-American look. Clothing may emphasize the differences between men and women, or minimize them—usually by bringing women's clothes closer to the male model. Different styles of eroticism are variously perceived as being most attractive, in part because our personal identities are constantly being redefined. Recently, postmodernist styles of fashion have played with the ideas of artificiality, androgyny, and ugliness, calling into question the canons of good taste and sexual appeal. If the aesthetic of the ugly becomes dominant, how will eroticism and gender identity be expressed sartorially?[28] Whatever happens, the real erogenous zones are the skin and the eyes and, of course, the brain.

At the moment, American society seems most preoccupied with the issue of work, so that even questions of sexual display tend to be seen in the context of the workplace. For example, in 1986, one Bali bra advertisement showed a woman in a tailored business suit, the jacket opened to expose a luxurious brassiere. The caption read, "Underneath this grey flannel suit beats a heart of satin and lace." By late 1987, however, the advertisement may have been less appropriate as women's business clothing became more traditionally feminine.

VALERIE STEELE

DRESSING FOR WORK

The younger type of business girl . . . appreciates the fact that a part of doing her work well is to dress suitably for it. A man does this—why shouldn't a woman. A man doesn't wear a frock coat and a white ascot tie when he runs a steam engine; and a woman of sense doesn't go to her office desk in a peek-a-boo waist [i.e., transparent shirtwaist blouse] and a trailing velveteen skirt.

The Ladies' Home Journal (1907)

*D*ress for success is not a new idea. As early as 1907 *The Ladies' Home Journal* printed an article on the subject, "As Business Women Should and Should Not Dress."[1] For centuries many women have worked for pay, while others performed unpaid labor at home or on family farms. Nevertheless, the article on business dress was a sign that the nature and significance of women's work was changing. Today we often find similar articles advising women to model their clothing on that of men, and warning them against wearing provocative or overly feminine clothing to the office. The peek-a-boo blouse did not actually expose the bosom, but by showing the lingerie beneath it was perceived as being too sexual for the workplace. Similarly, the long trailing skirt was not merely impractical, it also carried inappropriate connotations of leisured femininity. The "girl with too much feminine finery" gave the unfortunate impression of being more interested in men "and ice cream" than in doing a day's work. Equally reprehensible, however, was "the misguided person who has gone severity-mad . . . and makes herself ridiculously masculine." Such a person, concluded the anonymous author, "is only a feeble imitation of a man."

How do our ideas about gender (and class) affect both the work we do and the clothes we wear to work? Although the literature on dressing for work has probably been useful for individuals seeking practical guidance, our purpose here is to analyze the symbolism of work clothing, focusing on gender issues.

Until recently, people assumed that there were natural reasons why jobs tended to be sex-linked: men are strong (so they make good construction workers), brave (good firefighters), aggressive (good lawyers), intelligent (good doctors), while women are kind (good nurses), love children (good

There are many jobs that have "changed sex"—as when the male clerk was replaced by the female secretary. Yet whenever such changes occurred, new sexual stereotypes developed. The "business girl" in this 1913 Ivory Snow advertisement wears the recommended tailored costume with some feminine touches; she is an efficient-looking, attractive subordinate. Her boss presents a more professional, authoritative image in his dark sack suit.

teachers), vain (good beauticians), neat (good servants), follow instructions meticulously (good assistants), and so on. People recognized that there were exceptions to every rule—from female soldiers to male prostitutes—but such ideas seemed anomalous.

Historically, there are many jobs that changed their gender connotations. During the nineteenth century, the male clerk was largely replaced by the female secretary, and the female midwife by the male physician. In the textile industry, hand looms operated by skilled male weavers were replaced by power looms run by unskilled women (and children). Yet, whenever this occurred (usually in response to changing labor market conditions and technology), people came up with reasons why the new situation was natural and sex-linked. Even feminists who wanted women to enter new jobs often argued that women were naturally better suited to particular jobs than men. Women supposedly had greater manual dexterity, for example, so they would be good typists. The *clothes* worn for various jobs have also been designed and perceived through the lens of sexual stereotypes.

But aren't work clothes designed to be practical for the job at hand? Certain types of work clearly require some sort of *protective clothing:* the firefighter wears a helmet; the welder needs a face mask; some metal workers wear goggles. Other workers need even more specialized forms of body covering: the deep sea diver, the astronaut on a space walk, the people who work with highly radioactive materials or dangerous chemicals. Many of these clothes, however, are *equipment* rather than apparel, and are thus outside the realm of this chapter. Most types of work can be performed in a wide variety of clothes, and have been. If a particular type of clothing has become conventional for a job, this may be due to its symbolic value rather than to purely practical considerations. Other work clothes combine the practical and the symbolic. The doctor's white coat, for example, was a relatively late development in the history of medicine and was related to the germ theory of disease. It was a sign of hygiene. But in a world of washing machines and disposable cover-ups, much of its practical value has disappeared. The personal symbolism of doctors' white clothing lingers on, but it depends for its prestige on an appropriate (hospital) setting. One doctor in Washington, D.C., recalled that he had proudly worn his white coat everywhere until, at the supermarket, someone mistook him for a clerk and asked him where the tomatoes were.[2]

The two main criteria for work clothing are suitability for the job and suitability for the worker. In both cases, definitions of suitability may be practical and/or ideological (or symbolic). Consider a maid's formal uniform, often a black dress with white apron, cuffs, and cap. If an employer is looking for someone to clean the house, answer the door, and serve guests, presumably either a man or a woman could do the job. Any sturdy, comfortable clothing would be adequate. But in twentieth-century America, the housecleaner is usually a "maid," whose employer may want her to wear some kind of uniform (although usually a plainer one than that used for formal service). If, however, the employer should elect to clean his own house and serve dinner to his guests, he would not do so in the maid's uniform. He would not want to be identified as a servant—as many housecleaners have also objected to wearing what they regarded as servile livery.

If we see a doctor wearing his white coat even in the supermarket and a maid who is reluctant to wear her apron even on the job, we begin to understand how a uniform can function either as a badge of professional status or as an emblem of service. Men do not always wear professional uniforms or the uniforms of skilled laborers, nor do women always wear uniforms for service jobs, but historically there is a tendency for the lines of division to fall in this way.

A 1974 article in *Psychology Today* suggests that if you want to be obeyed, you should put on a uniform. Does this apply more for men or women? Men have been more likely to wear the uniforms of hierarchical authority. This situation may be changing, however, as men and women in occupations of authority increasingly wear minimal uniforms, or eschew uniforms altogether. Many doctors, for example, have returned to wearing ordinary upper-middle-class clothing, at least when they have no need to reinforce their authority. Professional women—including women doctors—may still need such symbols of authority.[3] As with the language of clothing in general, the history of a job and its specific context in society help determine the meaning of the uniforms that men and women wear.

MEN (AND WOMEN) IN BLUE

"I found out that to most people, I was a uniform." In 1985 a young black woman, a New York City police officer, recalled her first days on the force, when she wondered how people would react to her. Most civilians perceived her simply as a police officer; and this was especially true of criminals who saw "the blue uniform" and fled.[4] As far as they were concerned, her individual identity was totally subsumed by her professional role.

The idea for police uniforms was borrowed from England and only gradually introduced in the United States on a city-by-city basis beginning in the 1840s. The mayor of New York City tried the experiment of uniforming two hundred policemen in 1844, but "the populace threaten[ed] to mob the Police, whom they designated as liveried lackeys." Uniforms were temporarily abandoned, and the police identified themselves only by wearing a star-shaped copper shield, hence the name "cops." The policemen themselves continued to oppose attempts to introduce uniforms on the grounds that the uniform "conflicted with their notions of independence and self-respect."[5] They demonstrated in front of the Police Chief's house. Ordered to wear the new official uniform, they refused, "because, they said, it would give them the appearance of footmen." According to a nineteenth-century history of the New York City Police Department, the police were gradually convinced that, far from being "a badge of servitude," the uniform would look more "reputable" than the motley clothes generally worn: "'Well, if that be what they call the uniform, it is a first-class thing. No one can object to that.'"

By 1856, both law and public opinion had changed. "All persons, legally endowed with authority, should be so uniformed, as to carry with them,

Historically, men have been more likely to wear the uniforms of hierarchical authority (such as police uniforms), while women have been more likely to wear the uniforms of service (such as maids' uniforms). Policemen initially objected to being dressed as "liveried lackeys," but their uniform soon gained quasi-military status. This engraving is from *Gleason's Pictorial Drawing-Room Companion,* January 7, 1854.

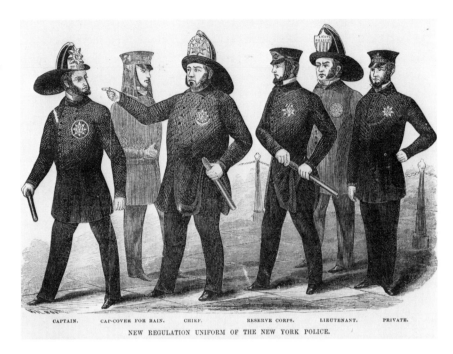

CAPTAIN.   CAP-COVER FOR RAIN.   CHIEF.   RESERVE CORPS.   LIEUTENANT.   PRIVATE.
NEW REGULATION UNIFORM OF THE NEW YORK POLICE.

even to the casual passerby, the *sign of their authority,* and then no one would pretend to dispute it." As the police historian wrote in 1885, the uniform gave a "trim and soldierly appearance . . . lent dignity to the men, and added to their official importance and self-respect."

The new regulation uniform in New York consisted of a "double-breasted frock coat of navy blue cloth" with a "black silk-velvet collar," two rows of buttons (this varied according to rank), a shield (the captain's silver star, the sargeant's copper star, etc.), and "a navy blue cloth cap, made in the style of the officers of the highest grade in the navy." For night patrol duty, the policeman would wear "a leather cap in the form of a helmet with a rim around it, resembling the cap worn by the New York Fireman."[6]

It took time before uniformity was enforced. A wide variety of hats were worn, from the high "Keystone Kops" helmet to the Confederate-style kepi; Panama hats were part of the uniform of the Second Precinct in the 1870s. But note the themes emphasized: authority, organization, hierarchy, and a trim and military look.

Meanwhile, as early as 1845 America's "first prison matrons were hired in New York City." By the 1890s in many cities there were police matrons in charge of female prisoners. In New York City, police matrons wore long, dark blue skirts and bodices decorated with a row of buttons and a badge. The first regular policewomen began to be appointed between 1905 and 1910 in a few cities, such as Portland and Los Angeles; in New York City they first joined during World War I.[7]

But not only were their uniforms different from the men's--to the extent they wore uniforms at all—but so was the character of their work. Although popular illustrations sometimes showed them in uniform collaring male criminals, in fact their jobs resembled social work, focusing specifically on the care of women and children. In 1912 when a law was passed in Maryland providing policewomen for Baltimore, horrified legislators had to be assured that "the women would not be uniformed," and would not have "beats," because the senators had terrible "visions of women in uniforms and brass buttons, parading the streets . . . arresting . . . drunken men." Similarly, Mrs. Alice Wells, the first woman to become a regular police officer in Los Angeles, wore no uniform, carried no weapon, and kept her star in her handbag. According to an article in *Good Housekeeping* (1911), Mrs. Wells did not want "a star with lace ruffles."[8]

In the 1920s, the duties of New York's first female Deputy Police Commissioner consisted "largely of preventive police work . . . and the supervision of conditions and people that might lead to debauch or pervert women and the young of both sexes. Her field of activity constitutes the most noble of police work, that of protecting the innocent and helpless. . . ." Policewomen were segregated in a division of their own. Mary Hamilton, the first director of the New York Bureau of Policewomen, wrote in her book, *The Policewoman: Her Service and Ideals* (1924), "It is

"Have you ever tried to get a gun or handcuffs out of a purse?" asked one policewoman in 1985, recalling the uniforms of the past. "It's just not practical, especially if you need to get them out quickly. Of course, a skirt is not practical. . . . I guess they just didn't know how women should dress when they first came in." This photograph from the *New York Daily News* shows a policewoman of 1951.

certainly a fact that no woman can really be a good policewoman, unless she works as a woman and carries into a police department a woman's ideals." She can cope better with women, girls, and children, "merely because of the fact that she is a woman."[9]

New York City policewomen did begin carrying revolvers in 1934, as ordered by Police Commissioner Valentine. The policewoman carried her gun in a purse, however, not in a holster. The purse was a leather over-the-shoulder bag, with one compartment for her 32 and another for her cosmetics.

An article in *Good Housekeeping* (1941) reported that policewomen in Washington, D.C., also carried revolvers, but seldom had to use them. Their duties still focused on women and children, from fingerprinting women prisoners to investigating complaints about cruelty to children. Washington, D.C., policewomen "dress[ed] in simple, tailored clothes" and either clipped the police badge "under a lapel" or carried it "in a purse."[10]

The policewoman's uniform evolved over time, but it retained the skirt. The hem rose from the ankle in the 1890s to a modest mini in the 1960s. A New York City police photograph from about 1965 shows policewomen in their newly updated everyday uniforms, complete with pocketbooks, lady-like white gloves, a little cap that needed to be pinned on, and moderately high heels. According to one recent historian, police departments introduced "a 'cute,' little stewardess-type hat" in a deliberate attempt to feminize the policewoman's uniform.[11]

In 1985, Helene M. Cassell, now a captain in the Fairfax County Police Department (Virginia), recalled how the uniform has changed:

> When I first came on they issued skirts. A patrol officer carries a four-inch revolver. At that time, they issued the women two-inch revolvers. They gave

It was only in 1972 that police departments across the country began to assign policewomen to do the same patrol work as policemen. In 1973 skirts were replaced by trousers. As this illustration of the New York City police shows, uniforms are now virtually identical.

women a purse to carry with a holster built into the purse versus wearing a gun and regular holster around your waist. It really wasn't practical. Have you ever tried to get a gun or handcuffs out of a purse?—it's just not practical, especially if you need to get them out quickly. Of course, a skirt is not practical as far as actually going out into a patrol area and enforcing the law. You can't climb a ladder very easily or anything else. I guess they just didn't know how women should dress when they first came in. Basically, our uniform has been transformed into almost the same thing the men are wearing, mainly because it's functional and the other really wasn't practical at all.[12]

Why did female police officers have to wear impractical uniforms? Was it just that the top brass "didn't know how women should dress," as Cassell suggests? Or was it, rather, symptomatic of the many limits on the use of women in the police force, limits that actually hindered the purpose of police work: fighting crime. Were women fully utilized searching women prisoners, guarding children, and doing clerical work? A few women were detectives and undercover police officers, but many promotional exams were arbitrarily closed to women. On the other hand, until the 1970s trousers for women were still widely regarded as informal and inappropriate for any sort of work, so perhaps police departments were merely reflecting social attitudes.

Only in 1972, when Congress amended Title VII of the 1964 Civil Rights Act (prohibiting state and local governments from discriminating on the basis of race, ethnicity, or gender) that police departments across the country seriously began to integrate policewomen into the force as a whole and to assign policewomen to do the same patrol work as policemen. In 1973 skirts were replaced by trousers. Again, it was only in the 1970s that trousers for working women became generally acceptable, but in police work the connection was clear: the same uniform went with the same duties for men and women.

Today, as they gain greater acceptance on the force, some female police officers say that they would like uniforms that are a little more tailored to the female body, more comfortable and attractive; others prefer absolutely unisex uniforms; still others (in some departments) have a choice of wearing skirts "inside" and trousers on patrol duty.

If we look at the symbolism of the police uniform—and, in particular, its recognizable resemblance to military uniforms—we begin to understand why *Psychology Today* chose to illustrate an article on "Uniforms and Social Power" with a picture of a policeman. This rather menacing illustration of a highway patrolman in jodphur pants and mirrored sunglasses is an easily comprehensible image of the uniform as a symbol of authority. Conversely, the earlier versions of the policewoman's uniform mixed symbols of authority (like the badge and gun) with those of femininity and gentility (like the pocketbook, high heels, and white gloves). It is reasonable to conclude that the feminized uniforms indicated a certain ambivalence about the woman's role as an authority figure, especially since the standard police uniform has always carried quasi-military associations.

The military uniform has also been the prototype for a host of other uniforms associated with traditionally masculine jobs. Indeed, this has sometimes caused problems, as when a New York City patrolman com-

Today uniforms remain a symbol of power and authority. When, in 1974, *Psychology Today* published an article on the meaning of uniforms, they chose this rather menacing drawing of a motorcycle policeman for the cover of the issue.

APRIL 1974 ONE DOLLAR

psychology today

MEDITATION:
Hard Facts on TM and
Who Can Benefit

Older Men Make
Better Fathers

Class War in
Beauty Shops

A Powerful Use for
MEGAVITAMINS

Conversation While Dying:
A Philosopher Holds Out the
Heroics of Everyday Life

Some People Like
to be Crowded

Father Monkeys

Sugar Pills
Can Kill Pain

OPEN
PRISONS

Uniforms and
Social Power:
Clothes
Do Make
The Man

plained that he was "getting pretty tired of being asked if he is a mailman or a member of the Air Force."[13] Part of the public's confusion is a result of the growing size and diversity of military and urban police forces, with the consequent variety of specialized uniforms. But some of the confusion is quasi-intentional.

Uniform manufacturers favor two basic styles: "the law enforcement knockoff . . . and the 'soft look' uniform—blazer and slacks—for the growing number of clients who prefer their security low-key." A recent attempt to have security guards wear "commando-style guard uniforms"— khaki-colored and worn with military berets—has not been successful, however. It conveys the wrong image, says Pinkerton's director of purchasing: "We would very much avoid a uniform that would convey combativeness."[14] Eastern Airlines has decided to retain its new uniforms for flight attendants, despite fears that the uniforms look "too military." The deciding factor was the argument that "in-flight assaults on attendants had dropped markedly after the uniforms were introduced, apparently because passengers took the military style as more than just appearance."[15]

Predominantly female, flight attendants benefitted from looking tough, while security guards, predominantly male, in commando uniforms attracted controversy. Clearly, sexual stereotypes do affect how well particular uniforms work. Meanwhile, an experiment designed to cut down on violence toward police officers and to promote a more positive public image by having the police wear "friendlier" blazers and slacks was abandoned as ineffective. Apparently, for police uniforms, the traditional, tougher look works: "Navy is good."[16] The uniform intimidates criminals and reassures the public. However, if the main purpose of police work is to *apprehend* criminals, then some police officers argue that this could be done most effectively if the majority of the force wore no uniforms at all, if they were plain clothes cops. Such an experiment is unlikely. What we do find is that Americans are increasingly accepting women on the police force—a woman, like a man, is seen as "a uniform."

MEN AND WOMEN IN WHITE

The doctor's white coat and the nurse's white uniform look superficially similar, but their origins and symbolism differ significantly, despite the fact that doctors and nurses perform complementary functions within the hosital. When we trace the history of the two uniforms and the two professions, we find that doctors' and nurses' uniforms have very different connotations, which are closely related to the phenomenon of sex segregation in the workplace.

Along with the stethoscope and the black bag, the doctor's white coat is one of the main symbols of the profession. But the white coat was a late-nineteenth-century development that originated in scientific laboratories, spreading first to operating rooms and then throughout the modern hospital. Until that time,

> The only correct garb of the surgeon was a frock coat (the oldest and shabbiest in his wardrobe), which was kept in the surgeon's room and never renewed or cleaned during his twenty years of operating work.

In 1867, the British doctor Joseph Lister reported that he had had good results with washing his hands *before* surgery instead of after. Furthermore,

> Instead of wearing a dirty old coat with dried blood and pus on it, to operate

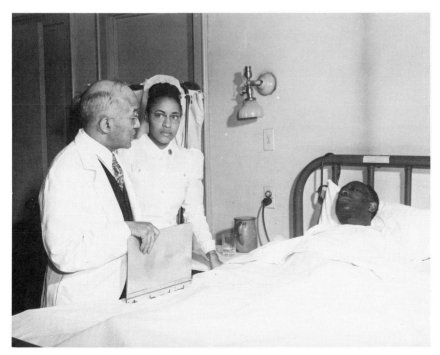

The doctor's white coat was derived from laboratory clothing, and symbolized the man of science, while the nurse's white cap and uniform originated *before* the development of the germ theory of disease and represented a badge of service. This 1942 photograph of Provident Hospital in Chicago also indicates the physician's dominant role vis-à-vis the nurse.

73

Lack of hygiene frequently killed the patient until Dr. Joseph Lister discovered the benefits of wearing a clean linen apron during operations. Thomas Eakins's painting *The Agnew Clinic* (1898) shows the surgeon wearing clean white surgical garb, although not yet a face mask or gloves.

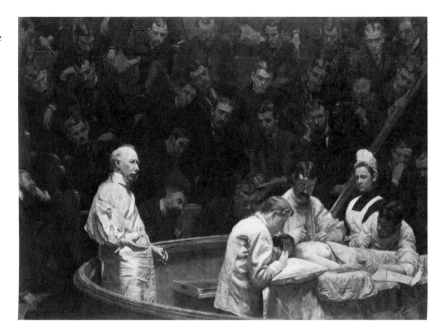

in, he wore a clean linen apron. Instead of having a needle and thread stuck in his lapel, he invented a way to sterilize ligatures.[17]

Other doctors ridiculed Lister, and for almost two decades they ignored his antiseptic principles. Thomas Eakins's painting *The Gross Clinic* (1875), for example, shows the famous American surgeon in the operating room wearing a black frock coat. It was only after about 1889 that American surgeons began to wear clean white gowns (or aprons), that they began washing their hands and boiling their instruments. Even then, surgeons still did not wear face masks or surgical gloves, as can be seen in Eakins's *The Agnew Clinic* (1898).

Photographs from 1889 in the Massachusetts General Hospital Archives "show the surgeons and nurses (but not the anaesthesiologist or observers in the balcony) wearing short-sleeved white coats over their street clothes."[18] According to Dan Blumhagen's historical study of "The Doctor's White Coat," this operating room garb was originally derived from the clothing worn in scientific laboratories—a connection that reinforced the contemporary image of the doctor as a scientist. The operating room gown served to protect "both the patient and the physician" from contamination. Blumhagen stresses, however, that such operating room "gowns" were not practical for other types of patient care, since they tended to have a back opening "for sterile technique." Furthermore, because "the term 'gown' in our culture usually refers to women's clothing," the garment was regarded as being "not suitable as a symbol for . . . 'active, scientific men.'" Thus, there was an early distinction between the operating room gown and the white coat.

The term "lab coat" is still popularly applied to the doctor's white coat. Yet,

> Originally, laboratory coats were tan and appear to have changed to white as they became associated with medicine. Why was not another, perhaps more functional, color adopted?

Apparently, the answer lies in the "cultured significance of 'whiteness.'"

In the Chinese and Indian cultures, for example, white symbolizes death. But in the West, whiteness carries desirable connotations of life, purity, and power, especially in contrast to black, which is the color of death and mourning. Doctors and the general public were "profoundly disturbed when Nobel Laureate Alexis Carrel wore *black* gowns in his laboratories and operating rooms at the fledgling Rockefeller Institute of Medicine." By contrast, the purity of white gave patients the sense that doctors intended them no harm. According to *Revelations,* Christ and the Saints are robed in white. Since the doctor also might be said to hold the power of life and death, it is better if he looks like one of the "good guys." Finally, whiteness is perceived as innocent, in the sense of being asexual. As patients must undress in front of a doctor, the white coat gives the patient "a sense of protection and lessens embarrassment."

Blumhagen concludes that the doctor's white coat symbolically emphasizes "the authority and supernatural powers of scientific physicians and the protection of patients." Introduced from the laboratory and the operating room, the white coat became even more significant as health care shifted decisively from the home to the hospital. Twentieth-century observers noted that, far from being practical, the white uniforms of physicians and interns were actually "difficult to launder." But symbolism was more important than economics, and Chicago's Michael Reese Hospital was only one of many where the rule was that "all people connected with the healing process (including patients and visitors) were to be dressed in white, whereas *nonmedical* employees were to be given colored uniforms." Thus, white became a symbol of medicine, even as surgeons themselves shifted to the use of light green or blue operating gowns "when high-intensity lighting made the glare from white . . . unbearable."[19]

The nurse's uniform evolved along very different lines. "Every woman is a nurse," wrote Florence Nightingale.[20] Nursing was part of a woman's work at home, justified by her feminine sympathy and sense of duty. Professional nurses, on the other hand, were usually lower-class women (sometimes even prisoners or paupers), who served both as nurses and maids. (Men have never made up more than five percent of American nurses.) As one English doctor said in 1854, "No respectable person would undertake so disagreeable an office. . . . The duties they have to perform are most unpleasant, and . . . it is little wonder that many of them drink."[21] Far preferable were the amateur nurses at home and the nursing sisters in Catholic hospitals. But all of them, whether kind or drunk, had little or no training in caring for the sick.

Nor did they wear a special uniform until the second half of the nineteenth century, with the development of nurse's training schools. The Bellevue School of Nursing opened in 1873 and adopted a uniform, but not immediately, since "the first suggestion of a uniform evoked an outcry against livery."[22]

> The members of the committee [responsible for the reforms at Bellevue] understood very well the moral effect of uniform, for they had said in their reports: "A uniform, however simple, is indispensable, and should be rigidly

enforced. *It is advantageous on the ground of economy as well as neatness, and its effect on a corps of nurses is the same as on a company of soldiers."* [23]

Each hospital had its own corps of nurses, whose uniforms identified them within the hierarchy of the particular schools and hospitals. The various insignia were thus important emblems of professionalism.

The principle was established that trained nurses should wear a uniform that was "simple, quiet in color, well made, and spotlessly clean." Late-nineteenth- and early-twentieth-century uniforms tended to be blue, blue and white striped, gray, or gingham dresses, worn with white aprons, cuffs, collars, and caps. (The small number of male nurses wore similarly colored trousers and jackets.) The short-sleeved, all-white, one-piece uniform (worn *without* a bib and apron) came in gradually in the 1930s: white "cannot fade with repeated launderings," reported hospital administrators, and the "simplified uniforms" were cheaper and more adaptable. [24]

The development of the nurse's uniform was not simply an issue of professional *esprit de corps* and functionalism for the job, however. Although later generations of nurses emphasized the hygienic virtues of washable white, in fact early nurses wore white aprons and caps several decades *before* the germ theory of disease was applied in American medicine. Nineteenth-century photographs make it clear that nurses' uniforms were stylistically almost identical to contemporary maids' uniforms. The apron was as suited to cleaning the house—or the hospital—as it was to tending the sick, appropriately enough when we remember that nurses were also expected to perform cleaning tasks.

"Why a Cap?" asked *The American Journal of Nursing* in 1940. [25] The first suggestion was that "Florence Nightingale wore a cap. No properly dressed lady of her day would forget her cap indoors, or her bonnet when she stepped out." But most nurses were not ladies like Miss Nightingale, and by the 1860s caps were becoming old-fashioned. Next it was suggested that the cap served a "very practical purpose"; i.e., "to cover the hair and keep the appearance modest and neat." The Board of Bellevue was probably typical of many employers of 1875 in insisting that, "it should be impressed upon our nurses that the caps were intended to *cover the hair* and not to be simply coquettish ornaments."

The early caps were small and round, with a puffed crown—identical to the typical maids' caps, except for the bands, which were symbolic of the nursing profession. Later hats tended to be folded with a turned-back cuff, a style that came in around 1925 and soon became emblematic of nursing. In between the servile cap and the professional cap there were occasional experiments with veils (similar to those worn by Catholic nursing sisters); some World War I Red Cross nurses, for example, wore this style.

Today, many nurses have abandoned their caps and uniforms:

> [Hospital dress codes have] "dramatically changed," said Christine Sheppard, a registered nurse and assistant director of clinical services at Lenox Hill Hospital. "In the past," she said, "nurses were viewed as subservient, so they were in uniform. A person in uniform has less autonomy." Today's nurses have more education and independence, she said, "so we no longer dress the same." [26]

As this illustration from *Scribner's Magazine* (1888) shows, the nurse's cap and aproned uniform were similar to contemporary servants' uniforms. The quasi-domestic cap of the nineteenth-century nurse evolved into the professional cap of the twentieth-century nurse.

Until the 1970s, women made up no more than six percent of American doctors, yet until the early nineteenth century, almost all midwives (and abortionists) were women. Only as medicine became more professionalized were they replaced by male obstetricians. By the end of the nineteenth century, although most doctors were men, there were also more than seven thousand female physicians practicing in America, including more than a hundred black women. Popular stereotypes about innate womanly dignity and sympathy sometimes even helped their acceptance, especially when they worked out of their homes, treating women and children. But it was a difficult fight: Elizabeth Blackwell, one of the first professionally-trained female doctors, feared in 1847 that she might have to "go to Paris and don masculine attire to gain the necessary knowledge."[27]

There is little evidence that women's clothing hindered their progress; only the rare eccentric like Dr. Mary Walker (of Civil War fame) adopted masculine dress. Other female doctors wore ordinary middle-class dress of the plainer tailored style. As the *Newport Daily News* put it in 1896, "One cannot imagine a woman physician coming to a case in a lace-trimmed muslin gown and a rose-trimmed round hat. There is for her the trim, taut tailor-made costume, in which she looks professional and dignified."[28] Meanwhile, male doctors tended to wear a "highly professional frock coat," together with the other sartorial attributes of gentility such as "polished boots, neat cuffs, [and] gloves."[29]

In the 1920s, when women's clothing was becoming physically lighter and less restrictive, the number of women doctors began to decrease. Changes in the structure of medicine—greater professionalization, higher medical school costs, quotas limiting the number of female medical students, the move from the home office to the hospital—contributed to the decline, as did social changes, such as the decline of feminism. Women patients increasingly no longer requested women physicians. The practice of medicine became more self-consciously scientific and specialized. Women were thus increasingly excluded from medicine, at a time when the profession was reaching new heights of prestige.

The last ten years have seen the number of women medical students increase dramatically—and the prestige of the profession has dropped somewhat. There has been a partial abandonment of the doctor's uniform, not the specialized garb for surgery, of course, and attending physicians at hospitals and medical schools still favor the white coat on the grounds of suitability. But private practitioners have begun going without it, and members of the house staff (at least in some California hospitals) profess to find it "subservient" and "not cool." Perhaps also, patients increasingly refuse to accept doctors as godlike authority figures.

Thus, the doctor's white coat may become increasingly less common, at the same time that the nurses' white uniform is also seen less. But just as the two uniforms emerged for different reasons, they may be disappearing for different reasons, as well. And although both men and women now practice medicine (just as they do police work), nursing is still overwhelmingly a feminine profession. Such sex segregation cannot help but affect how we perceive the clothes they wear.

BLUE COLLAR/PINK COLLAR

The terms *blue collar* and *white collar* graphically illustrate how American society is divided into working-class and middle-class people. The issue is one of class, and not simply one of money, since many blue collar jobs actually pay more than many white-collar jobs. The term *pink collar* is a later variant, referring to feminine jobs.

Although the ideology of egalitarianism downplayed class distinctions, in Colonial and Revolutionary America the clothing that men and women wore indicated their social status. During the Stamp Act violence of 1765, the gentlemen participants were "disguised with trowsers and jackets"—clothing more characteristic of the "meaner sort."[30] (Urban men of the elite were more inclined to wear knee breeches and long formal coats.) But over the course of the nineteenth century, men of all classes gradually came to wear *more or less* the same type of clothing (as did women), a phenomenon that has been called "the democratization of American clothing."

Some middle-class Americans objected to this increasing uniformity of dress, finding it inappropriate, impractical, "unpicturesque," and spend-thrift. More to the point, they correctly traced the popular aversion to distinctions of costume back to the ideology of political equality. Specifically, they believed that "our working-people" tried to "vindicat[e] their claims to social equality" by wearing fashionable middle-class clothing, such as the "stove-pipe hat and flimsy bonnet," "tight-fitting coats and flowing robes."

> It would be as well to put Hercules in a strait-jacket . . . as for our muscular sons of labor to clothe themselves in suits of fashionable cut, and so to strive at their mighty work.[31]

Despite the pseudo-heroic language, it was clear that the writer wanted working-class men to restrict themselves to specific working-class costumes. Why didn't the laborer adopt, for example, the blouse of the French workman? Such a smock would be "more graceful, convenient, and economical."

> The free American citizen has no reason to scorn it as a symbol of slavery. The French blouse has vindicated its title to the drapery of a freeman in many a bloody encounter with tyranny on the barricades and in the streets of Paris.

This was, unfortunately, a specious argument—coming, as it did (in a book of 1872), directly after the Paris Commune had been crushed by right-wing French forces, and when the American press had viewed the Communards as dangerous radicals.

Working-class women, too, were supposed to dress "appropriately—to their spheres we do not say, but to their occupations." Rather insultingly, the author insisted that "the rude freshness of natural beauty appears to the greatest advantage in a plain setting"—something such as a white cap, a plain jacket, and a "short skirt of simple stuff." No crinolines or trains for working women, no saving up for silk dresses in which to try to look like a "sham lady." Working-class women, like their male counterparts, tended to resist such attempts to reintroduce sumptuary rules.

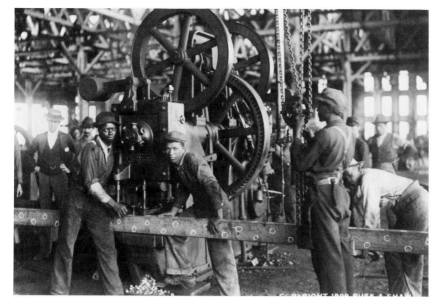

Long regarded as appropriate only for men, heavy factory work has often required considerable physical strength, as can be seen in this 1898 photograph of workers fabricating part of the steel structure for the battleship USS *Illinois*. Factory work was also frequently dirty. American workers led the world in the introduction of uniforms worn on the job. As one English observer noted in 1912, "A mechanic in the United States does not . . . go to and from his work in oil-stained dungarees. He changes his clothes at the works."

Skilled craftsmen, however, frequently have worn distinctive forms of dress. Craftsmanship, professionalism, and, frequently, unionism are characteristics of skilled workers, who have tended to be proud of their clothing, whether they wore uniforms, quasi-uniforms, or suits (and many *did* wear business suits at their work benches). A recent article in a craft journal, "Why Painters Wear Whites," elicited revealing answers from painters all around the country, which deserve to be quoted:

> As a policeman's uniform is a symbol of respect for law and order, a painter's uniform is a symbol of craftsmanship.

> Similar to feelings a person has for his lodge ring as a symbol of brotherhood, a painter's uniform boasts to the world, "I am in an elite membership." We are professional and we should look and act professional.

> A banker has his suit, so a decorator has his whites. It's sort of a badge of pride.[32]

Skilled jobs have tended to be men's jobs for a variety of complex historical reasons. In Colonial and Revolutionary America, for example, women's access to apprenticeships was severely restricted. If they did learn a marketable skill, like weaving, they were usually "taught with household subsistence, not income, in mind."[33] Women working at home, in isolation, clearly needed no distinctive uniform. Thus, although the subject of women's work at home is receiving increasing historical attention, it is less relevant to a study of work clothes in Early America.

Women entered the paid labor force in large numbers between 1770 and 1830, when there was a crucial shift from a mercantile to a laissez-faire economy, and the skilled artisan was increasingly replaced by the unskilled factory worker. The Lowell, Massachusetts, "mill girls" of the 1820s earned relatively high wages and wore relatively good clothes, although not uniforms. By the later nineteenth century, female workers in textile factories were poorly paid and wore dresses made of cheap fabrics such as gingham, serge, and coarse woolens.

Women entering the labor force tended to congregate in the light industries (or in light jobs in heavy industries). They often worked under male supervisors, as can be seen in this photograph of a silk mill in Paterson, New Jersey, in 1914. The female textile workers wear long skirts and sometimes aprons, hardly a specialized work uniform. Their male supervisor wears a (professional) business suit, and demonstrates his attitude of superiority toward the workers by taking off his coat.

Male and female factory workers in other industries, however, often wore a better grade of ordinary street clothes, sometimes protected by an apron; or they changed into uniforms at their place of work. Indeed, factory uniforms became an important subcategory of blue-collar clothing. Factory work was usually segregated by gender. Factory managers were usually men, and dressed differently than the workers—often in a formal suit—as can be seen in many early photographs. With increasing standardization of work procedures came a trend toward standardized clothing; uniform manufacturers produced a variety of inexpensive work clothes, from dungarees and boilersuits to aprons and coveralls.

American work clothes were praised in the English paper *The Spectator* because they allowed the worker greater self-respect:

> The [English] factory workers lack pride in personal dress, and the dirty, oily nature of their work, the fashion of semi-naked, slovenly, uncouth working clothes, are great deterrents against the popularizing of millwork. . . . The clogs and the shawl for head-covering frighten away the girl who takes a pride in her appearance. . . . Americans have already set us an example. A mechanic in the United States does not . . . go to and from his work in oil-stained dungaree[s]. He changes his clothes at the works. To change one's clothes is to change one's whole outlook. Nothing so symbolic as clothes! If the clothes are not changed, a grimy occupation means a normally grimy life. That is justly objectionable. . . . Why should not a Lancashire girl put on her working clothes in the mill . . . ?[34]

This practice of changing clothes at work helped make possible significant innovations during the First and Second World Wars, when women wearing boilersuits and trousers took on "men's jobs."

At the time of the First World War, it was easier for people to accept women wearing trousers at the factory than on the street. Moreover, it was seen as their patriotic duty temporarily to replace men who were off to war. "Skirts or Overalls for Women," asked an article in *American Machinist* in 1918.[35] Was it true that "the 'Womanalls' now worn in munition factories and on other war emergency work" were "ugly"? Did skirts necessarily hamper women's movements? The author concluded that, "it can hardly be expected that they will be comfortable in men's clothes." Rather, let them be careful with their dress, and especially their hair, and that alone would contribute sufficiently to "their safety in the shop." By contrast, an article on "Safety Equipment for the Protection of Women Operatives" in the automotive industries announced firmly that, "the hair and the skirt problems are being satisfactorily solved by the compulsory wearing of bloomers and caps."[36]

Many working-class women praised the new sartorial freedoms as well as the enhanced job opportunities. Said one ex-stenographer working in a World War I munitions factory, "I should hate to go back to work in the old long skirts."[37] It would be a serious mistake, however, to think that the war itself led to the "liberation" of women's clothing: the raising of women's skirts, for example, began *before* the war, as did the occasional use of trousers.

In 1924 Anne Rittenhouse wrote a book on *The Well-Dressed Woman,* with an important chapter on "The Wage Earner's Sartorial Struggle." It

During World War I women performed heavy industrial work, for which they often adopted special "feminine" trousered uniforms. This photograph from *American Machinist* (July 4, 1918) shows the uniform boilersuit and cap developed by a committee of women workers. "I should hate to go back to work in the old long skirts," said one munitions worker.

was devoted to the "problems of the average woman who makes and spends her own money," and who "disregards the tradition . . . that woman's work should be confined to the home." Wage earning women (whether working class or middle class) chose to wear the latest fashions. But some people complained that women's abbreviated skirts and transparent silk stockings were "cheap, tawdry, grotesque."

Asked for a remedy, one Englishman replied, "Uniforms. If you don't demand dignity of appearance in your rapidly growing wage-earning class, you will cheapen the standards of the new type of woman." He was greeted with laughter by both men and women: "Imagine American women in standard uniforms!" "They wore them in the war," he countered. "That was an adventure," explained the women. "Work is a daily grind. The wage-earner wants to wear the latest fashion as other women do. That is why most of them work. Clothes are their recreation. Put them in uniforms and you run the risk of destroying the female industrial class in this country."[38]

Women's work experience during the Second World War encompassed both "Rosie the Riveter" heavy industrial jobs (for which trousers were worn) and more traditional jobs in light industry (for which skirts were usually worn). But even when women wore trousers and performed "men's work," it was not uncommon for them to wear feminine hair styles, elaborate makeup, and fancy underwear. This 1942 photograph from the Bureau of Public Relations shows a team of women together with one man assembling an airplane.

But soon men and women were in uniform again. During World War II, Rosie the Riveter became an icon. Yet working women were perceived as merely pitching in temporarily to help their men overseas. Few people in government or industry expected that women would continue to hold jobs in heavy industry after the war was over. Articles written in the 1940s debated whether or not "girl operators" could lift heavy weights or handle heavy and complicated machinery.[39]

As the war progressed, however, women were actively encouraged to "shop for a war industry job."[40] They were reassured about bosses, machines, and uniforms. "Will I wear a uniform?" the hypothetical worker asked. It varied according to the plant, but "since skirts can so easily get caught in the machinery, they are mostly taboo. Where no uniforms are required, women are encouraged to follow the widespread custom of wearing slacks." But many companies did demand that women employees wear uniforms—even if the men employees were not required to do so. "Some companies even supply uniforms and keep them laundered at company expense." (This had been a problem during the First World War, when many women workers preferred to wear old clothes rather than buy overalls.) "Slacks, blouse, and visor-cap of matching material and color are now practically standard." They might "not enhance a girl's charms," but they were "good garments for fighting on the production front."

Many companies felt that "conventional working clothes" with "patch pockets, flaring trouser legs, belts, and wide sleeves" posed "grave accident hazards."[41] Moreover, "tight sweaters, snug slacks, and feminine articles of color and style were distracting influences involving equal hazard to the men." So, working together with the government and garment trade authorities, they developed special industrial attire, "to fit the wishes of the girls and the needs of their respective jobs." The "cap-blouse-slacks outfit" came in three colors—"white for laboratory workers, blue for mechanical, and khaki for operating departments. Piping on collars and cuffs add the feminine touch." If they wore trousers, however, women also frequently wore "glamour girl" hairstyles, heavy make-up, and ultra-feminine underwear. The "wife-dressing" of the 1950s and 1960s lay just around the corner.

IN THE OFFICE

As Hollywood fashion designer Edith Head pointed out in her book *How to Dress for Success* (1967), some women's definition of success might be "How to Get a Man—and Keep Him." She distinguished between "the girls in the stenographic pool," who wore sweaters and skirts (and might well be looking for husbands), and the female "executive in charge," who wore simple casual suits or tailored dresses.[42] The issue of sexual attractiveness was further complicated by the fact that more and more married women were working by the 1950s and 1960s. As Head pointed out in her other book, *The Dress Doctor* (1959),

> Working wives must cultivate two separate fashion philosophies: no man
> wants a brisk, executive-looking woman at the dinner table, and no man
> wants a too-alluring creature gliding around his office.[43]

The dress designer Anne Fogarty was a working woman, but in her book, *Wife Dressing* (1959), she emphasized that a woman's primary role was to be a wife: "The wife plays an increasingly important role in the advancement of her husband, especially in big industry and the professions."[44] She should, thus, dress in a way appropriate for the *husband's* job. Even when doing housework, she should look attractive: "Don't look like a steam-fitter or a garage mechanic when what you are is, purely and simply, a wife."

The business*man* faced few of these vexing problems. The rules about what to wear during business hours were rigid ("conform or get out!") but on the whole fairly straightforward: a gray, brown, or black hat, white linen, gray, blue, black, or mixed coat and trousers, etc.[45] Nevertheless there *were* significant changes in the dress of both businessmen and businesswomen, and the nature of those changes tells us a great deal about the vicissitudes of work "in the office."

Just breaking into the office was a struggle for women. When one woman applied for an office position in 1849, her potential co-workers protested on the grounds that, "Women were physically, mentally, and emotionally unsuited for the work."[46] Yet the male clerks and scriveners of the 1840s were gradually replaced by women, so that by 1900 seventy-five percent of office workers were female. Today, almost all office workers are female and the male secretary is a curiosity.

The feminization of clerical work got underway during the emergency conditions of the Civil War, but really gained ground as the structure of American business (and government) grew in size and complexity. The ante-bellum office was small with a simple chain of command. Clerks and employers came from essentially the same class, and clerks had considerable upward mobility. As one clerk wrote in 1842, "The majority of clerks are young men who have hopes and prospects of business before them."[47] Consequently, they dressed as much like their employers as they could afford.

After the Civil War, however, as the structure of capitalism changed and businesses became larger and more complex, there was an increasing division of labor and a growth of hierarchy, resulting in a simultaneous proletarianization and feminization of the clerical work force. Unlike the clerks and scriveners of earlier years, the new office workers could no longer hope to become business leaders.

Their clothing—as workers and as women—set them apart from the upper-middle-class male employers. The "dress for ladies of business" should be "serviceable" and "sober" in color. *The Ladies' Home Journal* advised "the clerk and typewriter" to wear clothing that was "simple in construction" and made of "a fast black material" that would resist "unpleasant rubbing or staining." *Good Housekeeping* added that "a necessary office apron" provided additional clothing protection.[48] Well-educated, middle-class men easily found better paying jobs with more upward mobility and personal responsibility. For middle-class women, though, the typewriter's position was at least *respectable,* and the office setting was relatively clean and safe.

There was as yet no distinction between female executives and female secretaries; almost all women office workers were in a respectable yet subordinate position. Their clothing reflected a sense of propriety. It was also supposed to be fairly asexual, and modeled on the masculine prototype. As we have seen, there was to be neither peek-a-boo blouses nor excessive "mannishness." When women began to wear tailored suits in the 1860s and 1870s, the material and cut (as well as the concept of a suit) were widely regarded as masculine, and there was some reluctance to accept the style. By the 1880s, however, its shocking associations had largely disappeared, leaving only the appearance of practicality.

In his book *Miss America* (1898) Alexander Black characterized both the working woman and her tailored suit in highly favorable terms. He described seeing a successful young saleswoman traveling alone in a western city (selling carpets wholesale): "In no way was she radically dressed. Her tailor-made suit was of a fine cloth, richly trimmed. Her clothes, like her manner, had not an unnecessary touch." Moreover, "she succeeded one of their New York men, and she beat his orders by forty thousand dollars the first year."[49]

As *The Woman's Home Companion* put it in 1908, "The correct business attire for the modern woman suggests the best tailoring worn by men and with just the touch of femininity which will save the woman from a certain hardness and harshness."[50] The author of *The Efficient Secretary* (1916) concurred, warning against both ultra-feminine and ultra-masculine dress:

> [Women] are apt to wear fluffy, frilly, chiffon-like garments and unnecessary furbelows, or they are apt to fly to the other extreme and dress in tweeds and cheviots, cut in masculine lines.
>
> That the first extreme mentioned is never in good taste and never permissible for business wear goes without saying. The latter is permissible, to be sure, but unbecoming, except when worn by a woman who is dainty, girlish, and very feminine.[51]

Notice, however, the beginning of a shift in emphasis: whereas many Victorians seemed threatened both by peek-a-boo blouses and by women who were "imitation men," the twentieth-century writer makes an exception for the "girlish and very feminine" woman, who looks attractive in masculine styles. *Attractiveness* in a working woman was beginning to become a more and more desirable attribute.

In the twentieth century secretaries were increasingly "valued for their decorative effect," almost like office mistresses or office wives:

> "An exceptionally attractive, intelligent young woman, not over twenty-five; must be educated and well-bred, with charming personality; a natural blonde, five feet eight inches tall, and slender; a smart wardrobe necessary." Laying down specifications very much as he would for a yacht, Charles Hewling Ballinger, vice president of Mastings and Co., automobile manufacturers, is ordering a secretary.[52]

Now, there is a figure!

Heléne
OF HOLLYWOOD

Heléne's exclusive shoulder-bra in fabrics to match Heléne brassieres, at all fine s...

By the twentieth century, the secretary was increasingly valued for her attractive appearance: "a smart wardrobe necessary," read one job advertisement. This advertisement for Heléne brassieres appeared in *Vogue* in 1945. It associates the secretary's clothes with her image as a working woman: subordinate and sexy. The businessman portrayed is older and physically rather unattractive, but is clearly in control. His suit functions as a badge of status and authority.

It was not so much that an employer actually expected to have sexual relations with "his" secretary, but it was nevertheless sexually gratifying to "have" such an attractive subordinate.

Many secretaries only expected to work for a few years before getting married. Movies and popular fiction often promoted the ideal of marrying the boss. After all, "A man chooses his secretary much as he chooses his wife, and for much the same reasons. She looks good to him."[53] In many ways a good secretary was supposed to be like a good wife, defined as an extension of her husband: attractive, loyal, self-effacing, with an even disposition and a good personality, performing her work efficiently. Ideally, she should be unmarried but display wifely tendencies, since in many ways her personality and social roles were consistent with those of the home. Like the wife or sweetheart, the secretary "thinks *with* her employer, thinks *for* her employer, thinks *of* her employer."[54] No wonder he didn't want to promote her and risk losing her.

Men's business dress also reflected changes in the masculine image. Beginning in the 1880s, the more formal and occasion-specific clothing of the "perfect gentleman" gradually gave way to the looser, more casual, and "manly" business suit. High, stiff collars and stiff bosom shirts gradually gave way to softer shirts and low collars, the top hat to more sporting styles.

Costume historian Jo Paoletti has demonstrated that ridicule played an important part in the transformation of men's business clothing from 1880 to 1910, a period when there were notable "threats to masculine self-confidence."[55] Many Americans worried that the "New Woman" was more active and competitive than her gentlemanly counterpart. Cartoons began to appear, portraying the well-dressed man as an effeminate fool—a dude in a stiff collar and a long frock coat, wearing a monocle, and carrying a cane. The new role model seemed more aggressively masculine in his casual, all-purpose business suit. One cartoon favoring the new man in his sack-type business suit showed a spinsterish aunt demanding, "What! Are you going to call on my niece in a business suit?" To which the young man replies, "Well, I mean business."

Actually, from the later eighteenth century onward, men's business clothing grew ever more casual, egalitarian, and self-consciously masculine. Initially, the emphasis was on dressing in a manner appropriate to one's station, but by the nineteenth century there was more stress on working one's way *up* the social ladder. Considerations of status always remained paramount: "There cannot be a more evident, palpable, gross manifestation of poor, degenerate, dung-hilly blood and breeding than a rude, unpolished and disorderly exterior." "To appear genteel" but "not ostentatious" was the ideal.[56] The businessman who wanted to "win the respect of [his] associates" needed clothing that contributed to a sense of ease and self-confidence. "But can a man be at ease in a coat out at elbows, a coat which hangs like a meal-bag upon his shoulders, a coat which reminds you of a specimen of fossil remains, or an heirloom from one of the company in the ark, a coat which is a badge of contempt, a sign of vulgarity, an expression of a dilapidated purse, a careless disposition or an uncultivated and barbarous taste? No."[57]

Today, despite the ubiquity of the business suit, the totally mannish look for women is still taboo. As this 1985 advertisement of Jos. A. Bank Clothiers shows, there are still significant differences between the way men and women dress for work: professional women usually wear a skirt, not trousers, and a softer suit together with more feminine accessories.

The essence of classic clothing.

In short, the psychological aspects of clothing were as important as the pecuniary aspects: "If he is slovenly and lax in his dress, it is reasonable to assume that the same characteristics will prevail in all other matters." "A seedy-looking . . . representative at once suggests a business house of similar limitations, while a bright, smart, well-dressed fellow suggests a good house and a successful one." On the other hand, all eccentricity or extravagance of dress—indulged in "under the impression that they stand for individuality and distinction"—were "foolishness." Conformity and conservatism in dress indicated reliability.[58]

More than a hundred years ago, men and women were dressing for success in business. Nevertheless, both their definitions of success and their mode of dress have changed, in part because women began entering the *executive* work force in ever increasing numbers. In the 1970s many women's magazines were describing so-called power dressing as "combat gear for the trip to the top."[59] It was all very well to say, "Just dress like your boss." But how possible was this for working women?

In the early 1970s, pants suits became temporarily popular for work, but many women found that colleagues and clients still regarded trousers as masculine or informal. As the unconventionality of the late 1960s gave way to a more conservative social climate, women began to return to skirts. The fashion historian Anne Hollander points out that a tailored suit with a skirt created an image that combined the supposedly practical, business-like uniformity of the man's suit with *a bland statement of female gender.* Such a costume said in effect: I am a business woman, not an imitation man; but while we are working, please treat me simply as a colleague.[60]

Only "underlings" wear provocative clothes, argued the guru of "dress for success," John Molloy, while repeatedly insisting that "suits are associated with . . . power."[61] Clothing that is "too sexy, light or low-cut" is inappropriate, echoed the *New York Times* as late as 1985. Low-cut or diaphanous blouses, tight, short (or long) skirts, indeed *anything* associated with feminine seductiveness was and remains taboo. Long loose hair or elaborate hairstyles, ruffles, cute clothing, extreme makeup, dangling jewelry, all were unacceptable. "There's something about really high heels in the office that makes a woman look dumb or like a floozy," reported *Mademoiselle.*[62]

But the mannish look for women was also still taboo; even a suit was supposed to be a softer suit than that worn by a man. Sensible shoes were defined as medium-heeled pumps, not man-styled Oxfords; too much makeup was only slightly worse than none at all; and so on.

In a very different spirit, the authors of the satirical volume *A Girl's Guide to Executive Success* (1984) also advised that women wear skirts with hems that were congruent with current standards of modesty:

> When in doubt, let a Catholic school dress code be your guide. . . . skirts should hit the floor when kneeling, although you should never kneel under any circumstances.[63]

All of this advice sounds familiar. In essence, it is simply an update of the advice existing since the 1880s: don't wear a peek-a-boo blouse, but also don't go severity-mad like an imitation man. There is one important difference, however. Women have become an accepted part of the work force; they have even made inroads on executive positions. Therefore, we see a more explicit distinction between feminine underlings and asexual executives.

By the mid-1980s a number of women had broken into male-dominated professions, and the standards for work dress began to evolve away from the very tailored and conservative look. Some observers suggested that (male) senior executives disliked women's boxy navy or gray suits. Professional women themselves may also have become bored with the uniform, since they have been less conditioned than men for extreme clothing conformity. Perhaps most important, it emerged that dressing like men "may not be the best way to reach the top."

In 1985 the *New York Times* carried a front page article entitled "Women Dressing to Succeed Think Twice About the Suit," which opened with contrasting opinions:

> The skirted suit should become the uniform for almost all business and political situations.
> John Molloy, *The Women's Dress for Success Book,* 1977

> We've brainwashed ourselves into thinking that executive wear is synonymous with a suit.
> Mary Fiedorek, *The Executive Style: Looking It, Living It,* 1983.[64]

Molloy continued to insist that "the suit is not dead," although he admitted that the woman executive could occasionally "wear something equally dark, conservative, and asexual." But he warned that if a woman abandoned power dressing entirely in favor of frivolous *Vogue* fashions, then "everyone will know she's fluffing out." "I mean something feminine," insisted businesswoman Mary Fiedorek, "—and not sexy at all. There cannot be any allusion to sex."[65]

Accessories for both men and women were also revealing. According to Egon von Furstenberg's *The Power Look* (1978), "Ideally, a man never wears the same pair of shoes twice in a week. Ideally, too, he wears the best shoes he can afford—shoes like the plain-toe Oxford and the Gucci loafer."[66] Meanwhile, women (who used to be criticized by men for wearing foolish and unhealthy high-heeled shoes) turned to wearing running shoes with their business suits while walking to the office. But an op-ed column in the *New York Times* declared that this was "A Sneaking Problem for Men." It does not look professional, complained Richard M. Goldstein, adding that women used to be able to wear high heels. An angry woman wrote in reply to complain about "High-Heeled Instruments of Torture."[67]

A headline in the *Wall Street Journal* announced: "Vive la Différence? In Business World, Quelle Différence? Women Are Told to Emulate Men and Shun Provocation Such as Open-Toed Shoes."[68] But can it really be (as image consultants maintain) that open-toed shoes "encourage men to think of women as a sexual partner rather than as a potential chairman of the board?" How potential a chairman is the average businesswoman? If men are so easily inclined to view women as sexual partners, this is more revealing than the shoes.

As Dress for Success became a cliché, and the executive woman's man-tailored business suit became a widespread fashion, it was increasingly satirized. According to *The Girl's Guide to Executive Success* (1984), from which this illustration is taken, "The skirted suit and briefcase were once the Woman Executive's unquestioned badge of authenticity. These days, she might find herself surrounded by imposters."

The skirted suit and briefcase were once the Woman Executive's unquestioned badge of authenticity. These days, she might find herself surrounded by imposters.

The necktie has also been regarded as an important nonverbal sign. "For the Power Look, choose [neckties] with the same consideration you would devote to selecting a business letterhead or a spot ad on TV." [69] And according to the magazine *Success,* only losers wear bowties. Does this mean that in the 1970s working women were unintentionally wearing loser's ties? A *feminized* version of the necktie became popular then, in the form of bowties and blouses with floppy bows. But by 1985, the president of a professional women's clothing store claimed that "secretaries wear bowties; women who are true professionals wouldn't be caught dead in them." [70]

Different professions, of course, have somewhat different dress codes: advertising agencies permit more leeway—a trendy, high fashion look is possible, even desirable for men and women; by contrast, law firms expect both men and women to dress more conservatively. But the 1985 article claiming that lawyers may deviate little from the standard gray or navy suit is already out of date. Law, in fact, is a particularly interesting field for exploring perceptions of dress for success.

In 1983 university researchers asked one hundred former jurors "what apparel gives a female lawyer the greatest credibility," and found that even the type of neckwear "affects perceptions of her authority."[71] A man's tie was not well received, nor was a "crisp" bow tie (of the sort that was then in fashion with some professional women). The researchers suggested that, perhaps, an unfavorably "masculine impression" was "created by this tie's crispness." An ascot was too "arty." The best tie was a long, narrow scarf tied in a flat knot and tucked inside the buttoned jacket—giving an "effect similar to that of a man's tie, but with a softness that identifies the scarf as belonging to a woman. . . . The second most positive response went to the traditional woman's bowed blouse—the floppy bow-tie. Although there is more than phallic symbolism at work here, it does seem suggestive that women's ties needed to be *soft* in order to be acceptably feminine.

Law was traditionally regarded as an aggressive, masculine profession, characterized by noisy courtroom scenes incompatible with gentle refined womanhood. Furthermore, lawyers consciously dress to meet the expectations of the judge and jury. According to the *Legal Times of Washington* (1982), "The male trial lawyer's suit conveys authority by it's propriety, quality, and completeness."[72] Said one D.C. resident, "I might hire someone in a cord suit to defend me on a traffic violation . . . but to defend my freedom or my life, I want someone who wears a dark suit, someone who can dominate a courtroom." The client, crime, locale, and socioeconomic status of the jury all affect the degree of conservatism the lawyer exhibits in his (or her) dress. Another Washington trial lawyer reported that he sometimes tailors clothing to the particular situation: "He wore boots once when he noticed the jury foreman did." But this tactic "must be used very carefully."

Woman lawyers needed to wear a suit "with a skirt—never pants. . . . While the right dresses might work in the office, the courtroom is not the place to break with convention," but by late 1987, suits seemed less important. One female lawyer added that "wearing understated jewelry and discreet makeup increases authority by adding polish." High heels were also advisable.

Did the need to look powerful and to dominate the courtroom conflict with the equal insistence on looking feminine? Judge, jury, and client might demand aggressive lawyers, while deploring aggressive women: "Even if your colleagues accept you, you still have to deal with clients without triggering their stereotypes about women," said one woman attorney in 1984.[73]

"Madame! Are you a lawyer?" demanded the court officer when a woman lawyer came to a court in the early-1970s wearing an "informal skirt and top." She compromised and adopted a more sedate look. Speaking in 1975, she believed that all the available role models for trial lawyers, from F. Lee Bailey to Perry Mason, were male—aggressive, loudly argumentative, with booming voices—and she reported that her students in Boston were concerned about how they could combine being a woman and a lawyer. Since law is something like acting, a man might have more leeway in dressing up for the jury, playing "just folks" or Perry Mason. Yet she reported, "The more experienced I get, the more irrelevant my costume becomes. . . . Either I'm known more, or it no longer matters."[74]

In job after job—police work, medicine, nursing, industry, business, law—we find varying degrees of sex segregation and stereotyping, which can be expressed in clothing symbolism. The feminine stereotype was helpful, kindly, and subordinate—her uniform was one of service, her dress, a badge of gentility, her dilemma, to avoid looking too masculine or too feminine. The masculine stereotype was strong, intelligent, authoritative. Whether a brain-worker, a muscle-worker, or a fighter, his clothing still owed something to that quintessential masculine dress—the military uniform—at least indirectly, as with the business "uniform." The very concept of uniformity applied first to men's clothes.

Nor has the situation changed as much as one might have assumed. Issues of class continue to intersect with gender concerns. By the mid-1980s, the woman's business suit became devalued as a symbol of professional success, in part perhaps because it had been copied by so many women who were patently not executives. "The skirted suit and briefcase were once the Woman Executive's unquestioned badge of authenticity. These days [1984], she might find herself surrounded by imposters."[75] Yet how many women are executives in a country where women earn, on the average, only a little more than half of what men do? And what does it mean when by 1987 the pendulum had swung decisively away from mannish, unisex, or androgynous work clothes back toward a revival of femininity?

Men have been even more constrained in what they wear. In 1984, a woman lawyer reported that "her male colleagues wonder if they dare to wear a striped shirt (or) . . . a sweater vest. . . . Partners *fantasize* about coming to work in a sports jacket." Perhaps, one writer suggested, "The fact that women are loosening their ties may end up giving permission to men to do the same."[76]

BARBARA A. SCHREIER

SPORTING WEAR

In seeking for exercise and recreation the athletic man has a large field from which to choose his favorite sport. He may play baseball, football, lacrosse, lawn tennis and many other games. How different it is with the athletic woman. She may ride and walk for exercise, it is true; she may row; she may, with perfect propriety, play at mask and foil; but when she tires of these and seeks for a game in which the elements of exercise and competition are combined, lawn tennis seems to be her only refuge. . . . we of the other sex . . . admire the woman who . . . bravely struggles against the awful handicap imposed upon her, viz., much dress and little strength.

Henry J. Slocum, Jr., *Outing* (1889)

Within the past 150 years, we have witnessed the emergence of a sport culture in America with the concurrent acceptance of athletic men and women as cultural ideals. Yet the leisure revolution diverged immediately into separate men's and women's paths.[1] Gender served a transcendent role in shaping our sporting experiences, and the development of sports clothing was an integral part of this process. To an extraordinary degree, definitions of the virile male and the athlete have been synonymous. Only war has rivaled sports as the proving ground for masculine behavior. The female athlete, however, has long been considered a contradiction in terms. The presumed frailty of the weaker sex raised serious questions about the advisability of letting women participate in sports; and even in today's sports culture, the aggressive, competitive sportswoman arouses uneasiness. Conditioned by a long tradition of sex-role stereotyping, we seek reassurance that womanly instincts supersede athletic aspirations as we scrutinize sportswomen's appearances for tangible signs of femininity.

What are the differences between masculine and feminine sports? In the nineteenth century, men were thought to be active, competitive, sexual, and strong, while women were described as delicate, emotional, spiritual, and aesthetic. These carefully constructed distinctions, based on an upper-class model, offered a philosophical justification for categorizing sports as either masculine or feminine. Before the Civil War, women generally limited their exercising to walking, riding (sidesaddle) and mild calisthenics, activities believed to promote improved health and beauty. These could easily be incorporated into existing social patterns without compromising the aesthetic ideal. In contrast, masculine sports, such as baseball, running, and rowing, emphasized endurance, self-control, and competition. Partici-

By the twentieth century, sports heroes embodied the strong physical ideal, much to the delight of female admirers. This football player from a 1932 song sheet is protected by the leather shoulder pads on his jersey and the cane inserts in his knickers.

pants could validate their masculinity as they strengthened both their bodies and moral character.

The clothing of these early athletes was based on the traditions of fashionable dress and reinforced male/female stratifications. Sportswomen in floor-length skirts and corsets and sportsmen in formal business suits but without jackets provided visual reassurance that the sexes still adhered to the nineteenth-century codes of propriety even when engaged in sporting events. But increased interest in leisure during the second half of the century was an important catalyst for clothing modifications. Not surprisingly, men were first to adopt special sportswear combinations. Gymnasium suits, football helmets, and baseball uniforms all were developed in response to the sportsman's need for clothes that offered increased freedom of movement, protection, and team identification.

Since functional sportswear often clashed with the nineteenth-century image of the fashionable woman, it took longer for feminine active wear to gain acceptance. Yet within the framework of traditional clothing norms, important changes did occur. Although many sportswomen clung tenaciously to feminine trappings, within the confines of women's colleges and athletic clubs women experimented with new sports attire. Conservative women favored a looser, shorter, and less decorative version of fashionable dresses; their daring sisters enjoyed the freedom of divided skirts and bloomers. From 1850 to 1870 these examples of dress reform appeared only within the institutions' secluded walls; subsequent generations went public. As a result, women's sport clothing—no less than men's—helped to mold as well as mirror gender expectations.

By the beginning of the twentieth century, women's increased participation had begun to challenge definitions of masculine and feminine sports. With the widespread success of bicycling and basketball, for instance, women openly declared their sporting rights, often linking them to broader women's issues. Yet opportunity should not be confused with equality. In the twentieth century, the masculine/feminine polarization merely shifted its emphasis. Instead of defining appropriate sports for men and women, such gender bias delimited and prescribed the acceptable limits of behavior and appearance within each shared sport.

The evolution of sports clothing reflects the development of our gradual then increasing participation in sports activities, an especially significant change for women. Its study reveals attitudes in society toward the functional, even if controversial, deviations from everyday dressing required by those activities for both men and women.

AFTER EXERCISE.

The sporting attire of the athletes depicted in this illustration for an 1886 soap advertisement is based on the traditions of fashionable dress. Women played tennis and rode horses, but because they wore long skirts, they performed these activities somewhat differently than their male companions in trousers. Only men rode the high wheel bicycles.

FOOTBALL

Of all the masculine sports, football heads the list as the ultimate expression of male prowess and aggression, and the football hero is one of our most powerful symbols of masculinity. The football field remains essentially a men-only club where strength, toughness, courage, and endurance are tested. Even for spectators, like the legions of Sunday quarterbacks, the game offers an important opportunity for masculine validation.

Football is often criticized for its excessive displays of violence, yet the modern game is tame compared to late nineteenth- and early twentieth-century spectacles. Before World War I, football seemed little less than ritualized warfare. An 1880s newspaper account described a Yale-Princeton match in vivid terms: "The spectators could see the elevens hurl themselves in kicking, writhing heaps. . . . Those inside the lines . . . were nearer and saw something more. They saw real fighting, savage blows that drew blood, and falls that seemed as if they must crack all the bones and drive the life from those who sustained them."[2] The combative nature of the sport proved to be a mixed blessing. Many observers countered that the essential manly virtues and strategies of winning that football fostered were transmitted to other tasks. In the words of Theodore Roosevelt: "In life as in a football game . . . hit the line hard."[3]

In addition to their analogies between warfare and football, turn-of-the-century authors noted the parallels between primitive behavior and gridiron action. In 1917 Raymond Gettell, a professor at Amherst College, relied on this imagery to strengthen his defense of football. "The love of physical combat, of the matching of man against man to determine bodily supremacy, is a masculine trait, especially strong in primitive and vigorous people, and in the young men of even the highest civilizations."[4] The football field was the place where man "could legitimately act out aggressions" in a structured way.[5] Rather than denying the existence of these primitive urges, it was the coaches' responsibility to shape, stimulate, and incorporate them into the sports ritual.

The violent nature of the game, however, was an obvious target for social reformers who described it in terms of mayhem, homicide, carnage, and savagery. By the 1890s, college presidents, sports writers, civic leaders, and physical education instructors were debating the question "Is football worth saving?" Even ardent supporters of the game like Theodore Roosevelt and Walter Camp criticized the win-at-any-price sentiment that dominated college contests. Concerned individuals concluded that, if the game was to continue, football had to be relieved of its more dangerous features. To this end, the "flying wedge" formation was outlawed, playing time was cut, and the game was divided into halves.[6]

In keeping with the spirit of reform, the football uniform fell under scrutiny. Like mid-century baseball players, early football teams had "laid aside their hats, and coats and vests, reduced their clothing to serviceable limits," and walked onto the field unprotected.[7] Caps were worn but solely for the purpose of identification. One of the players in the first intercollegiate football game, which took place in 1864, later reminisced: "We had no team uniforms. Our college [Rutgers] color then was scarlet as it is today. To distinguish the Rutgers players from the Princeton team, many of our men wore either scarlet colored turbans or flaming red jerseys."[8]

As the number of injuries and fatalities increased, more attention was placed on devising safer equipment. In their 1896 book *Football,* Walter Camp and Lorin Deland traced the nineteenth-century evolution of the uniform.

The football players in this 1900s print test their physical strength in an exclusively male arena. The excessive brutality of the early version of football led to changes in the game and in the uniforms. These players wear nose guards, leather jackets, and padded knickers for protection.

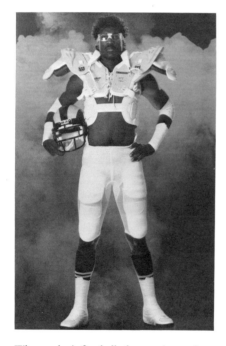

When today's football player suits up, he puts on an arsenal of protective armor to improve his chances of physical safety on the gridiron. In the process, he transforms himself into an athletic warrior, whose massive shoulders, well-defined muscles, and bulging thighs typify the modern super-masculine ideal. "Eric the Ready" (Eric Dickerson), photographed here in 1985 when he was with the Los Angeles Rams, exemplifies this ideal.

The original uniform consisted of tight-fitting jerseys, and tight, as well as rather thin, knickerbockers. There was no padding whatever, and nothing to break the force of falls. The first step in reform was the adoption of the canvas jacket worn over the jerseys. . . . The next reform in uniforms was the line of padding, and the trousers or knickerbockers we see to-day are practically loose bags heavily padded at the knees and thighs. Padding is also used more or less in the jackets and jerseys. . . . A leather uniform was brought out three years ago, and is undoubtedly a valuable help on a wet day. . . ."[9]

Nose guards, leather padded helmets, shin guards, and pants with cane reeds at the thighs offered the player additional protection.[10]

The development of protective sports gear had an uneven early history because the athlete's desire to prove himself on the playing field sometimes conflicted with the need to defend his physical well-being. Nineteenth-century sports fans mocked the effeminacy of protected players. Will Irwin described the response elicited by baseball players wearing gloves in the 1890s. "Hundreds of men are playing big league baseball now who aren't natural players. Take away those pillows and see how long they'd last."[11] Fans were less critical of football players' protective clothing, largely due to the contact sport's aggressive style of play. Who could accuse these fighting men of cowardice? The helmet and padding were the equivalent of the sport soldiers' armor, enabling them to perform even more heroic and superhuman feats. As a result of twentieth-century technological advancements, particularly the development of Fiberglas, the uniform-as-armor metaphor has become even more appropriate. Protective equipment exaggerates the male physique and hides the player's face behind a threatening mask, transforming players into larger-than-life athletic warriors.

GYMNASTICS

Even though the historical record proves it was not a realistic characterization of many women (especially working women), the mythical delicacy of

Women working at home needed no distinctive uniform, unlike the men who went out to work in offices or factories.

The man in this picture (1908) wears a navy business suit—an appropriate white-collar uniform. The woman, about 1908,

wears a black and white plaid cotton dress with a white cotton apron, clothing regarded as suitable for housework.

PLATE 20.

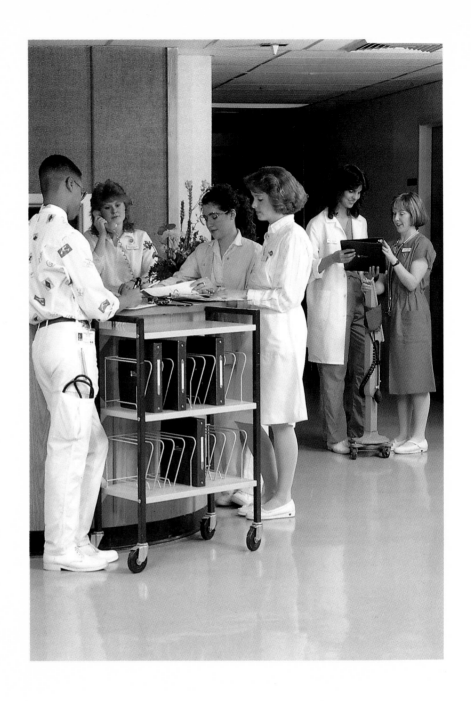

In the 1980s, most hospital physicians—male and female—continued to wear the doctor's traditional emblem of status: the white lab coat over street attire. With changing attitudes within the nursing profession, however, many nurses have abandoned their traditional caps and some have experimented with colorful uniforms. At George Washington University Hospital in 1988, the variety of nurses' uniforms represents the different units within the hospital.

PLATE 21.

The double-knit uniforms worn by Pete Rose and Mike Schmidt in this 1973 photograph feature flyless fronts, tapered calves, and a snug fit that leave little to the imagination. During the 1970s, sports figures joined the ranks of the Peacock Revolution, both on and off the field.

PLATE 22.

At the time of this illustration, 1909, more and more women were challenging the traditional rules of riding habits and riding styles. Seated astride her horse, this woman enjoys the functional benefits of a divided skirt as part of her cowboy-inspired outfit. To meet the needs of the twentieth-century horsewoman, tailors and ladies' magazines offered a variety of bifurcated styles as well as the more standard skirted habits.

PLATE 23.

The men and women in this 1930s chocolate advertisement wear the popular bathing suits of their day. The cut-out portions exposed a great deal of the body, but the one-piece styling technically met the standards of proper appearance that were enforced on public beaches. The bathing suits are almost identical in design and fit, which emphasizes, rather than eliminates, the physical differences between the sexes.

PLATE 24.

Jantzen used the ideal form of the late 1930s to show off these bathing suits to the best advantage. The muscular male body that appears to be chiseled in stone has come out of hiding from behind swimsuit tops. The woman's "Coquette" suit with its vestigial skirt clings seductively to her "perfectly" balanced body.

PLATE 25.

Left. Before Joan Crawford's 1932 movie *Letty Lynton* Sears did not sell the big-shouldered styles that were being featured by some Paris designers. After the movie was seen by thousands of enthusiastic customers, Sears responded to the demand in their Spring 1933 catalogue, including a dress named after the movie. *Right.* Men's waistcoats in the second quarter of the nineteenth century were made to produce the illusion of a fashionably small waist. In this 1832 garment that belonged to Dr. Jona F. Gay from New England, the cut as well as the upper-chest padding and the diagonal placement of the fabric pattern contributed to the desired effect. The longer-waisted vests of the 1840s were made with darts to make the waist even smaller than the chest.

PLATE 26.

BLOOMER COSTUMES OR WOMAN'S EMANCIPATION.

Satirical illustrations of the early 1850s Bloomer Costume emphasized its masculine connotations by further shortening the skirt to reveal more of the wearer's trousers. They also depicted the acceptable male (but not female) habits of smoking and carrying walking sticks.

PLATE 27.

the "gentler sex" exerted a powerful influence on the place of sport in nineteenth-century women's lives. For many years, the word *sport* rarely appeared in connection with women's activities: exercise, games, healthful recreations, and physical culture were the feminine components of the masculine sport theme.

The first serious efforts to promote organized physical education for women began as early as the 1830s.[12] As part of their campaign for increased educational opportunities for women, social reformers such as Catherine Beecher and Emma Willard began to espouse the benefits of exercise. While this trend paralleled the male gymnastics movement, the specially designed women's system of exercise employed a less vigorous approach and was labelled calisthenics. Stressing the inseparable nature of women's intellectual and physical development, they established a critical model, which would grow stronger with each succeeding decade. The goals of these physical education programs were restorative, corrective, and preventative. In addition to enhancing "mental vigor," exercise was said to make girls more cheerful, graceful, and feminine since "without health, both industry and enjoyment languish." In her *Letters to Young Ladies,* Mrs. Sigourney went on to attack the "physical imbecility" of women and stress the importance of multiplying "those modes of exercise, which are decidedly feminine."[13]

Enthusiasts also promoted exercise as the panacea for almost every infirmity. An 1827 treatise on calisthenic exercises for ladies declared that

> the particular diseases, in the cure of which Gymnastic Exercises have been found the most effectual, are: 1. The Gout; 2. The Rheumatism; 3. Consumption; 4. Nervous Disorders; 5. The Bilious Cholic; 6. The Dropsy; 7. The Palsy; 8. Diseases of the Mind;—besides many other disorders.[14]

Calisthenics was not the only form of exercise touted as a cure-all by early physical educators; many in the physical culture movement spoke out in favor of walking, dancing, drawing, or even "running about the fields and gathering fruits or flowers" as ideal forms of feminine exercise.[15] In 1836 Mrs. Farrar encouraged her readers to rethink the advantages of housework. "Next in healthfulness to exercise in the open air, is that which is taken in the various occupations of a notable housekeeper. Making a bed is such very good exercise of the whole body."[16]

Nineteenth-century views of women's piety dictated that their physical and intellectual efforts had to be channeled into the moral culture. Although male and female roles were both rooted in the mind-body-soul trinity, women's reproductive function intensified the "divinely ordered gulf" between the sexes. Women's child-bearing capabilities were a constant source of anxiety to popular writers and members of the medical community. They warned that unhealthy women produce sickly children. Therefore, physical fitness was every woman's obligation and her most important legacy to future generations.[17]

To physical culturists, fashion was the enemy. They lamented the dangers of long skirts and bemoaned styles that inhibited movement, but, most of all, they declared war on tightly laced corsets. "By far the most frequent difficulty with our women arises from uterine displacement and

". . . the utter disuse of the muscles . . . which are kept inactive by the corset."[18] Unable to stem the tide of this "crippling practice," physical educators directed their attention to two related areas. They promoted exercises that would relieve some of the health problems associated with tight corsets, and they encouraged a looser style of exercise clothing.

The earliest styles of exercise clothing emphasized freedom of upper body movement and loose-fitting waistlines. Hemlines generally fell to just above the ankles and women were advised to remove most of their petticoats. By mid-century the skirts were shortened to mid-calf with bloomers worn underneath. The adoption of this costume illustrates the dichotomized rules of the nineteenth-century private and public spheres. Although acceptable in the gymnasium setting, this is the same Bloomer Costume that provoked such outrage when it became part of the dress reformer's public attire. Gymnastic manuals of the 1900s and 1910s illustrate women in middy blouses and bloomers.

The evolution of the gymnastic costume reflects not only a loosening of dress codes but a change in the exercises as well. Before the 1850s, female calisthenic programs concentrated on upper torso movements. Indian clubs, dumbbells, wands, and bean bags were employed to improve coordination, encourage graceful movements, increase flexibility, and tone the muscles. Only men were depicted performing leg-spreading, knee-lifting, and lunging exercises. When women began to add these to their athletic repertoire, bloomers became the preferred styles. The popularity of bloomers also increased with the rise in the 1870s and 1880s of women's colleges like Vassar, Smith, Mount Holyoke, and Wellesley, whose founders believed that the success of their endeavors depended on the health of their students.[19] Training in rhythmic gymnastics and/or calisthenics became an integral part of the curriculum.

The man and woman illustrated in this 1866 gymnastics manual perform rhythmic exercises with Indian clubs. Calisthenics was one of the earliest forms of exercise designed to improve a woman's beauty, grace, and physical stamina. Men often followed a related, but more vigorous, gymnastics program. In the privacy of an all-female setting, women wore looser-fitting, shorter dresses over a pair of bloomers. Men performed their male-only workouts in loose trousers worn with or without a shirt.

FIGURE 19.   FIGURE 9.

In mid-nineteenth-century America, men often turned to gymnastics and calisthenics for moral, physical, and spiritual improvement. Public and private gymnasiums accommodated the growing number of men interested in becoming physically fit. In this 1878 advertisement, men practice a wide range of activities and many are stripped down to "fighting weight."

As college women developed their physical side, they also experimented with unconventional attire.[20] Protected from the public's censorious eyes in the privacy of the educational setting, these young women steadily advanced the evolution of gymnastic attire. In order to maximize the benefits of their exercise regimen, colleges required students to abandon their fashionable garb and don loose bloomers with a short dress while they were in the gym. Some colleges even allowed the gym suit to be worn to classes.[21] Although most college women wore the traditional long skirts when exercising in public, their early experiments with bloomer outfits paved the way for a widespread acceptance of special gymnasium costume. By the turn of the century, secondary schoolgirls were also changing into gym suits as a normal part of their daily routine. Voluminous bloomers and loose-fitting middy blouses were replaced by shorts and skirts, and eventually the two pieces were combined into a one-piece style with an elastic waistband.

Interestingly, although gymnastics fulfilled all the criteria of a feminine sport, the regulation school gym suit never incorporated the feminine touches that appear in most sports styles. For most of us, the mention of "gym suit" conjures up grim memories. They may have been practical but their aesthetic charms were carefully hidden. In an article for *Women Sports*, Carol Maccini vividly summarizes the horrors of the 1950s gym suit.

> First of all, it was u-g-l-y. I mean really ugly. . . . it was usually a green or orange heavy cotton denim garment whose wrinkles no iron could conquer. . . . As an added torture, we had to cross through the boy's half of the gym in order to get to the girl's half. . . . Most of us were worked up into an emotional sweat even before the roll was called.[22]

BASKETBALL

By the turn of the century, women's increased athletic participation posed a direct challenge to nineteenth-century distinctions between male and female sports. In addition to ladylike pastimes such as calisthenics, riding, croquet, and walking, women were swimming, playing tennis, and cycling. What is more, before any agreement could be reached as to the advisability of these sports for women, the New Woman began making ever-increasing demands for more strenuous games. This polemical behavior sharply collided with the predefined images of woman in sports. The sport that brought this argument to a head was basketball.

In contrast to other sports such as rowing, baseball, or football, whose status as male events went unchallenged for years, the crossover in basketball was almost immediate. Dr. James Naismith, a Y.M.C.A. leader, invented the game in 1891, and one year later Senda Berenson of Smith College introduced the sport as part of the college's physical education curriculum. For students who were bored with the repetitiveness of calisthenics, basketball held a special appeal.

The sport combined the benefits of individual gymnastic exercises with the fast-paced strategy of cooperative teamwork, and the students went onto the court "willingly and even eagerly."[23] Soon other colleges and secondary schools followed Smith's example. "We had never heard of 'penetrating' our opponents, of getting credit for 'rebounds,' or 'containing' a threatening basket shooter," wrote Lillian Randall about her early school days in Iowa. "We just played as hard as we could. And loved every minute of it."[24] At Wellesley College in 1898, basketball had "become such a popular sport that even the members of the faculty have taken it up. In the evening, after dinner, strange shadows may be seen flitting to and fro before the gymnasium windows."[25]

The loose-fitting bloomers and middy blouses that female basketball players wore surely contributed to their sense of freedom. Each leg of these voluminous bloomers was a skirt in itself, yet some schools, bowing to the

The girls in this illustration from a 1902 issue of the *Delineator* testify to the widespread popularity of women's basketball at the turn of the century. The bloomers shown here were standard *indoor* uniforms; however, a costume change was required when the game was played *outdoors*. Skirts were worn over, or instead of, the bloomers when the girls went public.

dictates of modest feminine behavior as well as to weather conditions, required players to appear in a shortened skirt and sweater or blouse when the game moved outdoors.[26] Schools sometimes issued regulation outfits, but if funds were lacking, the girls either purchased the suits themselves or made them.

Unlike other sports where controversy raged over women's dress codes, the major concern in basketball was over the style of play. As the first team sport to reach large numbers of women, basketball broke new ground. But what would happen to the gender dividing line if women played a men's game according to men's rules? Disputes centered on two themes: basketball's vigorous style, a putative threat to women's health, and its competitive nature—a threat to women's docile femininity. The latter concern was deemed the more ominous. If immoderate rivalry was allowed to infest basketball, traditionalists warned, no "feminine" sport would be free of its "choking grasp." It was far better for women to "profit by the experience of our brothers and therefore save ourselves from allowing . . . objectionable features to creep into our athletics."[27]

The game was too popular and the health benefits too obvious for detractors to curtail women's participation. Instead, college directors began revising Naismith's original game to accommodate the requirements of women's "condition." Codified in 1899 at a physical training conference in Springfield, Massachusetts, the revised rules divided the court into three equal parts with players assigned to each, prohibited any player from snatching the ball away from another, and forbade more than three dribbles of the ball by one player. These changes were sparked by the desire to equalize the importance of the players, reduce the amount of physical exertion, and encourage teamplay.[28] Men compete, women cooperate. The result was the transformation of a man's sport into a woman's game.

The rise of women's college basketball expanded the scope and direction of women's physical education programs. It also opened up a new sport for the enjoyment of non-collegiate women in the twentieth century. Following the general acceptance of the revised game, women's basketball became an important component of many industries' recreation programs.[29] And by the 1950s women physical educators, inspired by women's continuing interest in basketball, were working to eliminate distinctions between the male and female versions of the game.

Today men's and women's basketball are virtually the same, proving that masculine and feminine sports categories are not immutable. Significantly, the uniforms are also indistinguishable. The unisex shorts and tank tops proclaim that men and women play the same game by the same rules, and demand the same requirements of their uniforms.

BASEBALL

As individuals move from a private to a public sphere or leave an all-male or all-female gathering to mingle with members of the opposite sex, the rules governing social intercourse tend to change. In most cases, greater

The New York Knickerbockers in 1858 are wearing an early version of a baseball uniform. The game was still a gentleman's sport at this time and the players dressed accordingly. Their long blue pants and starched white shirts descended directly from the mid-nineteenth-century business suit.

pressure is exerted on an individual in a coed, public situation to conform to social stereotypes. The history of American sports follows this basic pattern. The way the game is played and the way the players look are affected by the presence or absence of spectators and the gender relationship between the spectators and the players.

The history of baseball, from its early origins in a predominantly gender-segregated arena to a sport spectacle enjoyed by both sexes, offers a unique look at the interaction between onlooker and performer and the concommitant influence on the presentation of the sport and sports figures. The Knickerbocker Baseball Club, founded in New York City in 1842, was the first formal American team, followed in rapid succession by other clubs. In the early years of its development, baseball was perceived as a healthy vehicle of social interaction for club members. Membership was often controlled by a system of blackballing that protected the code of exclusivity so highly prized by upper-class clubs.

The early baseball rules and regulations fostered the values of precision, teamwork, and self-control.[30] The excessive physicality that typified football play by the end of the century was eschewed during the early years of baseball's history. During the 1840s and 1850s Americans still were grappling with questions of sport etiquette. As a non-contact sport, baseball fulfilled the requirements of a pleasurable pastime without threatening mid-century codes of gentlemanly behavior. Players appeared in an abbreviated version of their business suits, removing their jackets and sometimes rolling up their sleeves and strapping on a pair of removable cleats to signify that they were ready to leave the sedentary world of work and enter into the spirit of play.[31] Even the umpires reinforced this air of gentility and commonly "officiated wearing a silk hat, sporting a Prince Albert coat and carrying a cane."[32]

By the 1850s, the Knickerbockers were appearing in a standardized outfit consisting of blue woolen pants (referred to as cricket pants) worn with white flannel shirts and straw hats. This early version of the baseball uniform, dubbed the "Knickerbocker Look," was adopted by other teams with variations in color and trimming to individualize the outfits. In his book *Baseball,* Harold Seymour bestows the mid-century sartorial banner to the Charter Oaks of Brooklyn who sported "white pants with pink stripes, pink shirts with white facings and stars, white caps with blue peaks and black belts on which the name Charter Oaks was inscribed."[33]

Although these uniforms declared the players' status as sports participants, early associations with the business suit left an indelible impression on later uniforms. Neckties or scarves were worn for many years, and it was some time before the clean, white collar, which was such an important clothing cue in the nineteenth-century business world, lost its distinction on the diamond. Wes Fisler who played for the Philadelphia Athletes in the 1860s earned the nickname "the icicle" for his ability to finish "nine innings without soiling or rumpling the new paper collar he had put on at the start of the game."[34]

These lingering vestiges of formality supported the notion of baseball's respectability, which promoters relied on to attract female spectators. In 1867 the *Ball Players Chronicle* reassured its readers that baseball was "a sport every lady in the land can grace with her presence without fear of offensive language or deed."[35] To protect women's "delicate sensibilities," players were cautioned to watch their language, curb displays of rowdiness, and, in some instances, to roll down their shirt sleeves if ladies were in the stands. Clubs courted the attendance of women, since their presence underscored baseball's image as a wholesome, untainted activity; special days were designated as Ladies' Days, when it was common practice to admit women free if accompanied by a gentleman.[36] It appears that women needed little encouragement. Their enthusiastic participation is well documented and their role as spectators played a vital part in baseball's meteoric rise in popularity. Women's presence also influenced the subsequent evolution of the baseball uniform.

The first dramatic change in the baseball uniform occurred in 1867 when the Cincinnati Red Stockings replaced the traditional full-length pants with loose-fitting knickers and bright red socks.[37] The implications of this change were threefold. First, the adoption of knickers reflects a change in the way baseball was played. By the late 1860s baseball was well on its way to becoming the national pastime. Unlike many sports that were frozen in time during the Civil War, baseball flourished during those years as the favored sport of Billy Yank and Johnny Reb.[38] As the appeal of the game became widespread, it lost its elitist association with upper-class recreation. As a result of this democratization process, the players assumed a more aggressive posture on the diamond, pulling at the reins of the formality that had characterized the earliest games. By offering greater freedom of movement than the tight-fitting trousers, knickers accommodated, and even encouraged, more vigorous participation.

Second, knickers were children's clothes. Usually, boys cast off knickers in favor of long pants around the age of nine or ten; it was a tangible sign to the rest of the world that the boy was ready to leave his childhood days behind and assume adult responsibilities. Thus, the appearance of knickers on baseball players was bound to create a stir, and fans taunted the Red Stockings' captain, Harry Wright: "Say Harry, you've got whiskers like a man and pants like a boy."[39] Players exclaimed about the freedom they felt when they ran out on the field and recaptured the pleasure of being boys again.

Finally, and most important for this discussion of spectators' influence on sport clothing, the knicker outfit fulfilled the prophecy of the social power of the uniform. It expressed group cohesiveness by identifying individuals as members of a team, it established visual boundaries between teams, and it strengthened the image of the sport figure as cultural hero. His public demonstrations of competition and aggression, which normally would threaten gentlemanly standards in other social spheres, were appropriate within the context of the game. The thousands of fans who witnessed sports events eagerly embraced these uniformed heroes, and the presence of cheering spectators undoubtedly heightened the players' impulse to display their male prowess.

> We are a band of baseball players
>   From Cincinnati City;
> We come to toss the ball around
>   And sing to you our ditty;
> . . . The ladies want to know
>   Who are those gallant men in
> Stockings red, they'd like to know.

Cincinnati Red Stockings Team Song, 1869

With the advent of professional teams in the 1870s and 1880s, baseball uniforms became more colorful, and, according to some accounts, more revealing. Reporting on the Red Stockings-Eagles match in 1869, the San Francisco Chronicle commented that "It is easy to see why they adopted the Red Stocking style of dress which shows their calves in all their magnitude and rotundity. Everyone of them has a large and well-turned leg and everyone of them knows how to use it."[40] In 1888, when the Chicago White Stockings appeared in their black uniforms with white neckties, *Weekly Sporting Life* complained "that the pants were so tight that they were positively indecent."[41] Although some critics lamented the passing amateurism and criticized the new brand of athlete who prostrated himself before "the shrine of baseball vanity," the crowds clearly disagreed. These flashy players were part of the entertainment, and fans were willing to accept a different set of norms regarding body exposure for the male athlete.

More recently baseball owners have also acknowledged the importance of the game as spectacle and have tried to capitalize on the drawing power of unusual uniforms. In the 1960s Charley Finley broke away from the gray and white tradition by putting his Kansas City Athletics in green, gold, and white uniforms. Despite the initial embarrassment of some players who complained about playing in women's "softball uniforms," bolder hues and mix-and-match color schemes caught on quickly.[42] And although Bill Veeck's experiment with shorts for his Chicago White Sox in 1976 was less successful, the current style of tight-fitting double-knit pants often reveal more than they conceal.

Though the male baseball uniform symbolized changing perceptions of the male athlete, the clothing of female players offered an important reminder of woman's perceived physical limitations and her decorative function. Throughout the last half of the nineteenth century and much of the twentieth century, critics challenged female dress codes on the diamond, while raising the more fundamental question of whether women should play this so-called masculine game at all. Once again, the presence or absence of spectators figured prominently in the debate.

There are instances of women playing amateur and professional baseball during the last quarter of the nineteenth century, but crowds did not take the spectacle seriously. At best they were entertained. More typically the response was one of horrified outrage at the women who played in bloomers or "indecently short" skirts (above the ankle). During the 1880s the Female Baseball Club sponsored by Mr. Freeman aroused the wrath of more than one fan. "The female has no place in baseball, except to the degradation of the game. For 2 seasons . . . people . . . have been nauseated with the spectacle of these tramps. . . ." [43]

A host of experts emphatically stated that the game was simply too strenuous for women. Dire physical consequences were predicted for the women who overtaxed themselves in this way. Albert G. Spalding believed that women's participation in baseball should be limited to the grandstand, where they could share in the full enjoyment of the game by voicing their approval and directing "smiles of derision" at the umpire. [44] Women's colleges offered a safer haven for the female player. A Vassar graduate reminiscing about playing baseball in the 1880s wrote, "the public, so far as it knew of our playing, was shocked, but in our retired grounds, and protected from observation even in these grounds by sheltering trees, we continued to play in spite of a censorious public." [45]

The rules and regulations surrounding the All American Girls Baseball League during the 1940s offers a striking illustration of the influence of spectators in defining appropriate feminine demeanor and sports clothing. Founded in 1943 by Philip Wrigley as entertainment for war industry workers and as a way to keep the ball parks open during World War II, the AAGBL, at its peak, had 160 women under contract. Although the aspiring player had to demonstrate her skill to make a team, Wrigley's standards of ladylike behavior proved to be the ultimate test of her success. Disturbed by the masculine image of women's softball, Wrigley and his successor, A. Meyerhoff, instituted rigid standards of appearance and behavior that established the player's femininity as the first priority. [46]

Between practice sessions, the women received advice on deportment and grooming from such beauty consultants as Helena Rubenstein. Ever-present chaperones protected the players' reputations and reminded them, when necessary, of their allegiance to the higher goals of womanhood. "I remember one of them saying to me, as I went to the plate in a tight situation—a game-winning situation—'Oh, my dear, you don't have on your lipstick.'" [47] The approved uniform skirt (never shorts) had to fall within six inches of the knee, offering tangible proof that the players were ladies who also happened to be athletes. Even off the field the image had to be upheld; slacks and shorts were forbidden.

Wrigley's femininity concept provided welcome reassurance during wartime when preconceived notions of gender-related behavior were being shattered. In addition to this glamorous image, however, spectators were also treated to some very fine displays of baseball. From all accounts, these women were highly skilled athletes who played the game with a forceful, competitive spirit and helped to bring greater visibility to women's base-ball.

RIDING

Many observers have bemoaned the restrictions woman's dress has placed upon her emotional and physical well-being. These fashion crimes seem even more heinous when compared to the freedom men have enjoyed in their dress. Although careful study of men's clothing reveals that theirs has been not a complete, but rather a relative freedom, the scales have been heavily tipped in men's favor. Certainly, the male athlete was accorded greater latitude to develop the physical skills required in the mastery of any given sport. Therefore, as more nineteenth-century women began to train their bodies as well as their minds, they looked to the male wardrobe for clothing cues. This cross-fertilization caused many changes, not all of them physically liberating. The switch from skirts to bloomers expanded the gymnast's potential range of motion just as the masculine-styled swimsuits of the early twentieth century encouraged safer and more active swim-ming. But the importance of other borrowed components lies in their symbolic value, such as the silk top hat worn by equestriennes or the neck-ties favored by turn-of-the-century female tennis players.

Women's riding has had a long history both as a means of transportation and as healthy and elegant recreation. Approved by the medical commu-nity and endorsed by the upper class, riding managed to escape some of the nineteenth-century gender barriers that posed a threat to women's par-ticipation in other sports. Women not only enjoyed the benefits of riding together, but they also could indulge in the pleasures of a mixed company outing. Sidesaddle riding seemed to offer the perfect opportunity to dem-onstrate the best of womanly virtues—grace, gentleness, beauty, and con-trol. In 1857 Mrs. Stirling Clarke posed the questions "whether a graceful woman managing a noble steed does not present a finer picture of power over-ruled by gentleness?" and are grace and beauty "never more finely displayed than in the practice and enjoyment of this invigorating exer-cise?"[48]

As the physical culture movement took hold, proponents of riding stressed even more emphatically the healthful and beautifying benefits of the sport. "Riding tends to bring the body to a normal healthy state; it is the secret of perpetual youth, for it keeps the body, the figure and the heart young."[49] It was also credited with "stimulating a torpid liver," "quicken-ing the vital powers," and giving "color to the cheek and a brightness to the eye that no cosmetics can rival." By mid-century, riding was described as an eminently fashionable form of exercise, and riding schools and man-uals offered detailed instructions in the finer points of equestrian deport-ment and dress.

Although the authors of these nineteenth-century manuals largely ig-nored the question of male riding clothing, they devoted entire chapters to detailed descriptions of the correct female habit. Outfits designed exclu-

The sidesaddle riding habit featured in this 1850s American print combined masculine details with feminine styling. From the waist up, the outfit imitated a man's formal suit, but, from the waist down, women covered their legs with full and often dangerously long skirts.

sively for riding had been an established custom since the seventeenth century. Tradition prescribed the dress for a formal hunt, but pleasure riding habits offered greater flexibility in the subtleties of cut, style, and decoration. Looking the part was essential to a lady's reputation as a skilled horsewoman; if she ignored the former, the latter would forever be beyond her grasp. "If she looks right, she probably rides well; but if she does not so appear, no accomplishment by field and no victories in the arena will ever allow her the reputation as an expert to which she may be entitled." [50]

The desired look was one of precision, perfect fit, and sober elegance—qualities that men's tailors had been perfecting for years. Indeed, the crafting of the female habit fell within the tailor's domain. As the jacket construction, choice of accessories, sleeve placement, and neckwear arrangement assumed a distinctly masculine look, the habit became more standardized. In 1871 Midy Morgan described a "close-setting bodice style" that had been "in fashion for the past 15 years." [51] It was impossible for the habit to be "too plain." *Peterson's Magazine* cautioned its readers in 1877 that "velvet-collars, military or other ornamental braiding . . . are never worn by ladies who understand how to dress for riding." [52]

By 1890 the female riding habit bore a striking resemblance to male styles. Worn with a waistcoat, the hip-length jacket featured an open collar and lapels that revealed a hunting shirt and stock tie underneath. Mrs. Allbutt advised her readers in 1893 to "look to men's clothing" for the proper arrangement of the collar and tie. [53] Even the colors mimicked the male palette—navy, gray, black, brown, and bottle green being favored hues. A bowler hat or a straight hat, "like a man's," with the addition of a veil completed the outfit.

Although the merging of male and female styles met with widespread approval, it only affected the rider's appearance from the waist up. The question of appropriate leg coverings was closely linked to the larger concepts of feminine modesty and demeanor. Much of the intensity of the heated debate over whether to ride aside or astride was related to questions of dress, since the astride, or cross-saddle, method demanded that the rider wear some form of bifurcated garment. Women were forced to make a choice between upholding traditional gender ideals and embracing a more masculine riding style and habit. It was an emotional issue that began in the 1880s and continued well into the 1920s.

During the first half of the nineteenth century, habit skirts grew in length to ensure that a woman's ankles and feet were completely covered when she was mounted. Many men and women became so enamoured of the vision of a graceful horsewoman in a long, flowing skirt atop a horse that styles grew dangerously long. In a charming 1851 book entitled *A Conversation Between A Lady and Her Horse,* the horse explains the consequences of this fashion to his rider:

> I often feel irritated when I have a rider who wears her dress so long that it almost drags the ground, as it is continually flowing back over my hips until it covers my left side. It also wears and fatigues me. It drags around my left hind leg so I cannot move with ease and comfort.[54]

Walking was impeded and fashion plates of the period feature women in habits with yards of excess fabric draped over their arms. Apparently not all women were able to manage this task with ease; some manuals of the 1850s offer advice on how to hold "the Habit whilst a lady is waiting for, or walking to, her gallant steed."[55]

When placed into position by her groom with legs securely situated around the pommels, the sidesaddle rider was almost locked into position. Although this vise-like grip made for safer riding, the woman was unable to extricate herself easily if the horse stumbled and fell.[56] The problem was compounded by the riding habit. Even if the rider managed to free herself, the trailing skirt was apt to catch on the saddle or become entangled in the horse's legs. Shortening the skirt was one way to improve the dilemma, but the question of modesty remained. The shortened hemline increased the chances that even the smallest gust of wind would raise the habit to reveal more of the foot and ankle than was desirable. One solution was trousers worn under the habit, a means of psychological as well as physical comfort; to avoid unnecessary attention, their color matched that of the habit.

The safety skirt was introduced in the mid-1870s, although it took some time before women discarded the older style. Living up to its name, the

The debate over whether a woman should ride aside or astride a horse began in the 1880s and lasted well into the twentieth century. Ignoring the strict conventions of Eastern sidesaddle riding, these Colorado women wore divided skirts to ride astride their horses at the turn of the century. Many women in the West and Midwest, who rode for transportation as well as for leisure, delighted in the freedom and control that a cross-saddle offered.

tailored skirt depended on a complex system of darting and seaming instead of extra yardage to accommodate the raised position of the right knee when placed over the pommel.[57] Although, often hooked to one side, this artificial pouch looked awkward when the rider dismounted, it was designed to fit the mounted rider like a glove. First-class ladies' tailors commonly used a wooden horse complete with sidesaddle for their customers' fittings.[58] This was often a tedious process requiring hours of patient sitting but women were advised to endure it if they wanted to "soar above mediocrity." Although this figure-perfect fit was the standard of excellence in riding habits, it would have been shocking in fashionable dress. The irony of this was not lost on Mrs. Allbutt who wrote in 1893,

> . . . society, with characteristic inconsistency, decrees that, although when walking a woman may, on no account, show the barest outline of her figure from the waist down, yet once she finds herself in the saddle nothing must be permitted to mar this very outline, which on terra firma we should blush to think of unconnected with ample drapery.[59]

Although the astride riding style, with its looser fitting bifurcated habit, countered this inconsistency, women were extremely reluctant to change. Proponents of the sidesaddle mount stressed that their method was easier to learn, provided a more secure seat, and presented a more graceful and modest feminine picture. They ridiculed the cross-saddle style of dress for its blatant masculine connotations while reciting women's physical limitations to strengthen their cause. Belle Beach summarized these arguments in a 1922 article entitled "Why I Ride Side-Saddle":

> The average woman is not so constructed that she can ride that way (astride). As a rule, her legs are too short from the knee up, her thighs are too thick and not flat nor long enough. Her hips are too big, her knees are too round and she is cushioned too high to be able to sit down on the saddle, or get the proper grip. . . .[60]

By the second decade of the twentieth century it became increasingly obvious that the aesthetic ideal of the feminine rider who looked to her groom to place her in the saddle and adjust her skirts had lost much of its potency. The new breed of young horsewomen raved over the natural position and the degree of control that the cross-saddle offered.[61] Rather than wanting to tame the horse with their gentleness, they chose to become more active participants. Although some women rode astride in long divided skirts, many women opted to bring the riding breeches out of hiding.

Sidesaddle riding has undergone a resurgence since the early 1970s, however. A growing number of enthusiasts have revived the sidesaddle habit and wear an apron skirt over their breeches. When asked to explain the renewed interest in this sport, one rider declared ". . . there is nothing 'Women's Lib' about we side-saddle riders. We depend on our men to put us up. If unavoidably this has to be done by a woman it never looks right. Only a man tucks us in, and straightens our wrinkles, to our liking and secretly we know he's proud of us."[62]

BICYCLING

The bicycle craze that swept America in the 1890s epitomizes the challenge that masculinized sports clothing posed to the nineteenth-century conservative mind. Although questions surrounding the garb of the female cyclist lasted less than ten years, they captured the attention of a wider audience than the aside/astride horseback riding debate because of the mass appeal of the mechanical silent steed. The appropriateness of bifurcated outer garments was a concern common to both sports. However, there were circumstances surrounding the late-nineteenth-century cycling mania that distinguish it from riding: during the 1890s, there were far more women cyclists than horsewomen; women's physical exertion was more obvious in cycling than in riding; active forms of recreation for women had gained greater acceptability by 1890; the New Woman, often personified as a cyclist, had made substantial gains toward achieving greater social and economic freedoms; and while changes in the riding habit meant a head-on confrontation with tradition, the cyclist benefitted from the technological novelty of the "wheel."

All of these mediating factors, however, do not mean that the question of a suitable wheeling costume was settled without controversy or that the answer was found in only one fashion solution. Though many historians have concluded that the Bloomer Costume among 1890s cyclists was universally accepted, bloomers were worn by only the adventurous and daring segment of the female population. When the bicycle craze waned at the end of the decade, the issue of women in pants was still unresolved.

Various forms of the bicycle had existed since the beginning of the century, but the early models were hazardous, extremely costly, and ridden by a small number of thrill seekers. It took the technological developments and improvements in mass production methods of the 1880s to transform cycling into an affordable sport enjoyed by millions. Americans of all ages and backgrounds developed an instantaneous love affair with the safety bicycle (featuring chain-driven wheels of equal size). Cyclists formed clubs, founded associations, and opened instruction schools to promote the new sport. Advertisers, novelists, and song writers fueled the flames of this infatuation with their constant cycling references. Isaac Potter of the League of American Wheelmen estimated in 1896 that there were "over 2,500,000 bicycle riders in the United States."[63] Women cyclists accounted for a large percentage of that number—a fact that escaped no one's attention. "Bicycle-riding has changed the habits of hundreds of thousands who formerly took little or no exercise in the open air. . . . Women have taken to the sport with no less enthusiasm than men."[64]

The sharp acceleration in women's *public* physical performance is one of the most striking features of the hegemony of the bicycle. No longer confined to the private boundaries of upper-class athletic clubs or the sheltered walls of educational institutions, the female cyclist was mobile, independent, and highly visible. This phenomenon was not without opposition. Conservative groups such as the Boston Women's Rescue League denounced cycling as unwomanly and inveighed against its demoralizing in-

This advertisement from the 1890s illustrates the wide variety of bicycling costumes available to women at the turn of the century. Unlike riding habits that were rigidly prescribed down to the last detail, cyclists had more freedom of choice. More adventurous women followed the Parisian trend and wore bloomers; others preferred a skirted style.

fluence. Yet proponents far outnumbered opponents. The wheel was credited with curing a seemingly endless list of mental and physical infirmities, many of which were gender-related. In an 1895 article for *The Cosmopolitan,* an ardent devotee of the sport glowingly described its benefits. Mrs. de Koven stated that cycling exercised every muscle, expanded the lungs, strengthened the uterus, cured indigestion and insomnia, reduced flesh, and "in its applicability to nervous and mental troubles, it may almost be regarded in the light of a specific cure." [65] This promise that the wheel would restore emotional equilibrium and curb women's "hysterical tendencies" was a recurring theme. Some authors cited testimonial evidence such as the "authenticated case of an inmate of a retreat in Brooklyn who was restored to sanity by the use of the machine." [66]

Despite a general consensus about the benefits of cycling for women, there was disagreement over proper bicycle attire. As the *Delineator* reported in 1894, "tastes differ widely," and clothing experimentation lasted for the duration of the bicycle craze. [67] Popular opinion agreed on the necessity for a safe, practical costume, but opinions varied as to how this could best be achieved. Shortened skirts worn over knickerbockers, divided skirts (often with pleats and gores to simulate a round skirt when standing), "Syrian trousers" that reached to the ankle, and bloomers all had their following. Most of the controversy centered around the latter two styles, not because they were worn by the majority of cyclists, but because they represented the most radical change.

Once again, the image of women in pants threatened one of the crucial functions of nineteenth-century clothing: identifying and separating the sexes. Some observers responded with humor, such as the spoof on Hamlet's soliloquy that appeared in an 1895 issue of *The Queen of Fashion:* "To bloom or not to bloom, that is the question. . . ." [68] Others attacked the costume with the same angry vehemence that characterized the aside/

astride debate, scolding women for their lack of taste and unfeminine demeanor. In an 1895 article entitled "The Evolution of Dress," women were warned that "the wearing of such garments will do more to unseat womankind and rob her of that innate modesty which is her greatest charm than aught else."[69] The association of bloomers with "scorchers" (the male and female speed demons who terrorized the roads) did little to alleviate the anxieties about the consequences of this fashion. One point in the bloomers' favor was that many leaders of Parisian society had adopted the full knickerbockers and short jacket as their fashionable cycle costume. Yet as one 1895 writer wryly noted, "even the Parisienne looks like a guy in such an outfit."[70]

The more moderate position encouraged women to let their style of riding and common good sense dictate their wheeling costume. Although the divided or shortened skirt with knickers and gaiters provided sufficient freedom of movement for most short trips and casual riding, many authors conceded that it might be more practical to discard the skirt on long excursion rides. Valentine Lelong chose to ignore this advice. In 1896 she bicycled alone from Chicago to San Francisco wearing a "suitable skirt" and carrying a borrowed pistol. Her greatest fear during the trip, which took a little more than two months, was of the tramps she encountered along the way. In an account of her travels, she credits the respect they accorded her to the fact that she wore "a mediumly short skirt, properly cut" rather than "unladylike bloomers."[71]

Unlike the horsewoman whose habit was rigidly prescribed down to the last detail, the cyclist was relatively free to adopt a style that suited her temperament. The collective clothing advice offered to female cyclists of the 1890s is remarkable in its diversity. This increased flexibility is a strong indication that changes in attitudes were occurring—toward sportswear, sportswomen, and clothing in general. Although similar battles remained to be won in other sports, bicycling helped to smooth the way for future clothing changes and dramatically advanced the position of women in sports.

TENNIS

To a great extent, tennis managed to escape the growing trend in the nineteenth century toward the democratization of sports. Unlike other games (like baseball) that were rapidly assimilated into middle-class recreational patterns, wealthy Americans maintained their proprietorial grasp on lawn tennis for some time. And despite the burgeoning interest in the sport during this century, culminating in the 1970s tennis boom, associations with the upper class still linger.

When Mary Outerbridge first introduced the game to her friends at the Staten Island Cricket and Baseball Club in 1874, she established an important link between tennis and the sporting rich. During the 1880s and 1890s, tennis was fixed in the social orbit of the country club. Sports historian David Mrozek notes that the isolation of these fashionable institutions became the symbol of a "pleasure-oriented ethic" that was very different from the sporting mentality of the middle class. "Special costumes, special facilities, special identity among the players, special limits among the spectators—all became a part of the landscape of sports as an independent branch of leisure."[72] Within this spatially isolated milieu formality reigned supreme and athletic accomplishments often were subordinate to good manners. The sporting rich exploited tennis as a social and fashionable pastime, and tennis clothing became an important symbol of heightened class consciousness for men and women alike.

The protective enclave of the country club also helped in bridging men's and women's public and private spheres, as it freed upper-class men and women to fraternize unobserved by their social inferiors. Initially, this took place before and after tennis matches, since court time was carefully segregated by sex. At the Staten Island Cricket and Baseball Club, for example, arrangements were made "for the use of the grounds so that there should be no clashing of interest." Women "were permitted to play on all courts during the morning . . . and . . . every Friday the whole grounds were theirs exclusively."[73] By the 1890s, men and women were playing sets of mixed doubles. These matches were far more social than athletic due to the "gentler nature" of a woman's game, and they were governed by the rules of polite society.

Within the carefully constructed leisure arena, modesty was a central concern. For both sexes, most of the controversy focused on exposure of the legs. For the first twenty years of tennis's history, women closely followed the fashionable silhouette when they appeared on the court. An 1890 fashion plate in *Peterson's Magazine* featured a full-length tennis suit com-

The players in this 1892 magazine illustration enjoy a leisurely game of tennis dressed in the fashionable clothing of the day. The woman's draped skirt and tight-fitting bodice harmonize with the genteel style of play favored in this mixed-double setting. Gentlemen added color to the court with striped blazers and trousers.

plete with bustle. The length and width of the skirts prevented onlookers from catching a glimpse of a lady's ankle, but they were a great impediment to her game. Although by the mid-1890s, skirt lengths rose above the ankles, some of the more determined players, frustrated with the cumbersome styles, took matters in their own hands. Tennis champion Ellen Hansell recalled that "we did, now and then, grip our overdraped voluminous skirt with our left hand to give a bit more 'limb' freedom when dashing to make a swift, snappy stroke. . . ."[74] In 1889, Henry Slocum, Jr., also commented on the hampering effect of women's tennis clothing. "It is obvious that the wearing of a long and flowing skirt not only seriously interferes with quick movements . . . but . . . it prevents a woman from using her racquet and making a stroke in a correct manner."[75] Slocum's solution, however, was to reform woman's technique, not dress. "The most obvious remedy is that she should take as few balls as possible on the bound or, in other words, she should learn to volley. . . . when she has mastered that art, she will be very seldom annoyed by her manner of dress."

By the early 1900s, the rate of change dramatically accelerated. Tennis was commonly played at women's colleges and on public courts. Women had refined their game by mastering forehand strokes and overhead serves. Additionally, female champions began vying with male players for national attention. As they gained the public's seal of approval through their athletic accomplishments, these champions also legitimized reforms in women's tennis clothing.

During the next four decades, women such as May Sutton, Helen Wills, Suzanne Lenglen, and Helen Hull Jacobs helped to liberate women from the nineteenth-century "garden party" attire. Through their words and actions, these champions encouraged women to raise their hemlines, shorten their sleeves, and discard their petticoats. By 1940, a woman could confidently walk onto the court in shirt and shorts, *sans* hat, corset, and stockings, without fear of reprisal.

A partial explanation for the success of these women's influence is rooted in the nature of the game. In tennis, individuals, rather than teams, compete. With their heightened visibility, players are public barometers of changing tastes and customs. Yet visibility alone is not enough. These players fulfilled two important criteria that lent credence to their reformist stance. They were champions whose success on the court was undisputed, and they displayed a deep respect for tennis traditions even though they advocated change in dress.

When chronicling their careers, these women rarely linked the question of dress or sports to broader feminist issues. Instead, they endorsed clothing reform solely as a means of advancing a woman's game. In 1912 tennis star Dorothea Chambers noted that, "there has been a great improvement during the last few years in the costumes worn by those who take part in tournaments held all over the country. First-class players know from experience how to dress to be comfortable and least hampered by their clothing."[76] She went on to encourage amateur players "to remember that you want, above everything else, free use of all your limbs; physical action

It is easy to pick out Bunny Austin in this 1933 photograph—the man in shorts. Before this time, twentieth-century male tennis players dressed in long white trousers for professional matches. When Austin broke this long-standing tradition, he made tennis and sportswear history.

must not be impeded in any way by your clothing." Twenty-one years later, Helen Hull Jacobs (the first woman to wear shorts at Wimbledon) expressed the same sentiments. "There is only one bit of advice necessary regarding tennis clothes. That is to wear the simplest possible attire, and be certain that it allows for necessary freedom of movement."[77]

The game's strong ties to formalism, however, kept the changes in dress within careful limits. Interestingly, most official tournament rules contained very few specific guidelines regulating dress. Even the all-white clothing maxim was never formally legislated by the United States Tennis Association. Yet unwritten codes of modest tennis attire were deeply embedded in the sport's collective value system. If a player strayed too far, a polite reminder from a tournament official or a vehement protest from the crowd enforced the bounds of propriety.

In one memorable instance, however, it was a personal sense of modesty that inhibited clothing reform, and surprisingly it involved a modest male rather than a demure female. When British tennis champion Bunny Austin began his career in the mid-1920s, he wore the standard outfit men had been wearing for thirty years—long white flannel pants (cuffs turned up during play), white shirt with sleeves rolled up, white socks, and crepe-soled shoes. Fashion conscious players sometimes opted for a knit, short-sleeve polo short introduced in France in 1928.[78] By 1930 some amateur players, finding the long pants hot and uncomfortable, had switched to shorts. But professional men still played in their "longs" until Bunny took the plunge at the 1932 Men's National Tennis Championship at Forest Hills. In his book *Lawn Tennis Made Easy,* Austin described his personal battle of athletics over aesthetics:

> I myself took two years to summon up enough courage to wear shorts, although for years I had known how much more healthy, comfortable and reasonable they were for tennis. I hovered in my bedroom . . . putting them on, taking them off, putting them on again, wrestling with the problem of Hamlet—"To be or not to be." At last I summoned up all my courage, put and kept them on, and wearing an overcoat to conceal them as much as possible,

went out of the hotel to play. My bare legs protruded beneath the coat and I slunk through the lounge self-consciously. As I passed through the door an agitated porter followed me. "Excuse me, Mr. Austin," he whispered diffidently, "but I think you've forgotten your trousers."[79]

From an historical perspective, Austin's uneasiness appears exaggerated. Not only were women players beginning to experiment with shorts by this time but a man's bare legs had long been a common sight in the gym, on the basketball court, and at the beach. Yet his instincts were correct. A dichotomous code of modesty did exist and his shorts did create a stir. Newspapers covered the story with such captions as "'Long on Shorts,' 'Sawed-off Pants,' 'Air-cooled Trousers,' and 'Ventilated Pants.'"[80] Austin longed for the day when "old ladies will cease to pass such remarks as: 'Oh, hasn't Austin got hairy legs?' running the risk of being asked: 'Well, madam, what did you expect—feathers?'"[81] But he opened the door and scores of men followed his lead. Within a few years of Bunny's "immodest" court appearance, shorts were universally worn by professional, as well as amateur, players.

Tennis stars of the 1980s continue to endorse tennis clothing, only now the clothing bears the players' names. The public is buying status and identification, not increased freedom of movement. Men's and women's tennis wear has never been more colorful, more decorative or more fashionable. Yet the blueprints of correct etiquette remain for court attire as well as court behavior. The 1982 U.S.T.A. Encyclopedia observed "It is always reassuring to know that in white, you are right wherever you go."[82]

SWIMMING

The history of swimwear is connected to our changing perceptions of modesty and immodesty. Throughout its history, the swimsuit has typically been the most revealing form of sportswear, and it has forced an un-

Although men commonly swam in the nude during the early part of the nineteenth century, enforced codes of modesty became essential when women joined them on the beach. The men in this 1878 mixed bathing scene appear in long trousers and flannel shirts. These costumes gradually were replaced by the more functional, streamlined jersey and knit swimming trunks.

easy alliance between modesty and sexual display. Even today, when the body has become a marketable package, making a public appearance in a bathing suit can be a disquieting experience.

While it is true that women's swimwear followed a general progression toward greater body exposure, the history of men's swimming attire illustrates that the rhythms of modesty are sometimes erratic. In the early nineteenth century, men believed that "bathing is best performed when quite naked." ("Bathing" and "swimming" were considered to be closely related.) The rules of modesty were suspended within the privacy of all-male watering places, where men were encouraged to swim unfettered by clothing. Yet this freedom was temporary. By the mid-nineteenth century, when seaside resorts became popular attractions for both sexes, bathing time was carefully divided so that men and women were segregated in the water. At some resorts red and white flags were used to signal separate bathing times for the ladies and the gentlemen.[83] This enforced a code of privacy, and men still had the option to swim naked. But when mixed bathing was practiced, the flags of decency were waved and shirts and trousers were prescribed for men.[84]

By the end of the nineteenth century, definitions of modest swimwear were challenged once again. As interest in vigorous swimming expanded, the dimensions of men's swimsuits began to shrink. The male physique received increased exposure as the early 1900 tank suit with short sleeves and knee-length pants was replaced in the 1920s by a "one-piece suit with short skirt and deep armholes."[85] The changes did not go unnoticed nor unchallenged. Public ordinances were passed and private club regulations were issued to establish the boundaries of propriety. The upper torso became the new focus of concern, and male swimmers who bared their chests in public not only forfeited respectability but faced the penalty of arrest as well. However, male swimmers exhibited the same rebellious spirit that pervaded other sports and their diminution of the swimsuit sorely tested the limits of the law.

Throughout the 1920s swimsuit manufacturers chiseled away at the swim shirt until it resembled a jigsaw puzzle with most of the pieces missing. In 1930 *Men's Wear* commented that "there is so little left of the present popular bathing shirt, that if anymore trimming away is done, it will no longer be a shirt."[86] Although these glorified suspenders technically adhered to the codes of decency, the "nude look" in swimsuits made a mockery of the laws. *Apparel Arts* in 1932 reported that "many of the bathers of this year followed the Lido libido and swam shirtless, wearing only a pair of trunks."[87] The death knell for swim shirts had clearly sounded and, from 1932 to 1934, men at private beach resorts began to follow the European lead of swimming *sans* shirt.

European beaches also inspired a new seaside activity—sun worshipping. During the 1920s tanned skins became an essential component of the sexy, sporty look. Sanctioned at first by such fashion leaders as Coco Chanel, tanning became an international cult by 1930. Basking in the sun to acquire the bronzed athletic patina was the new popular pastime, and the most popular swimsuits were those that offered maximum body exposure.

Shirtless styles eliminated part of the clothing barrier, but men were not content with this change alone. Trunks also had to be modified. The legs were cut higher and new knitted Lastex fabrics promised a garment that "fits skintight and is minute in size."[88] (It bears repeating that these figure-hugging suits appeared at the same time that male tennis players were trying to summon enough courage to wear shorts.)

To please their customers and appease the city fathers, swimsuit manufacturers offered a variety of styles that accommodated both private and public customs. In 1934 Jantzen introduced their exclusive Topper model, featuring a zipper fastening around the waist so that a man could transform a "complete suit to trunks in six seconds." That same year Merode advertised a "quick demountable model" in which the scanty shirt buttoned onto the trunks. "Thus, by a jiffy's adjustment, the swimmer can be either as nearly shirtless as public beaches allowed or completely so, as private beaches both permit and favor." As the irony of the double standard increased, the legislation of male modesty became anachronistic. By 1935 most public beaches conceded defeat and men were allowed to swim in their trunks.

For women, the preservation of modesty became a crucial concern during the last three decades of the nineteenth century, when they made the uneasy transition from bathing to swimming. Throughout most of the century, women's aquatic endeavors were limited to brief immersions in water for the purpose of health, rather than exercise. Female bath houses, protective bathing machines, and "sentry-houses" carefully separated the woman bather from male swimmers, and early bathing costumes were utilitarian garments with few fashionable features.[89]

But by mid-century men, women, and children were escaping to this seasonal world by the thousands as a retreat from the pressures of urbanization and industrialization, and out of this pleasure culture the "summer girl" was born. She took obvious delight in tantalizing male vacationers with her daring antics and costume and thought that bathing was "just too awfully nice for anything."[90] One bewildered nineteenth-century commentator confessed that she is a "type which baffles all attempts at classification and description."[91]

As the summer girl and her more conservative followers became a common sight on public and private beaches, bathing developed into a highly social form of co-ed recreation. Functional bathing clothing was no longer adequate, and women adopted styles that showed off their charms. "Motivated by the presence of men at the seashore and by the competition with other women for masculine attention, ladies were more concerned with the style of their bathing dresses and appropriate trimmings. Thus bathing costume joined the ranks of other fashions described in women's magazines."[92]

In spite of the fact that some daring young women flirted with bathing costumes that emphasized their "roBUST and HYPnotic figures,"[93] the vast majority of women adhered to the more stringent definitions of modesty. Unfortunately for them, the yards of fabric that disguised a woman's figure on the shore often clung to every curve after a dip in the ocean, and some opaque colors became transparent when wet. Writing about her visit to the French seaside in the 1890s, a woman offered a frank account of her costume's transformation. Feeling quite fashionable in her "'ravishing get-up' of pure white serge . . . with . . . white silk stockings and sandals," she dove into the water at Les Bains. Upon returning to shore, she discovered that the "beautiful white bathing-dress was quite transparent after such a wetting, and was evidently intended only for the 'Baineuses Parisiennes' who trip about on the soft sand and never let the water come above their knees. . . ." The lady quickly decided a black serge costume was in order and rushed to town to make her purchase.[94]

Contrary to popular etiquette codes, young men not only refused to avert their eyes but some of the more brazen "Kodak fiends" often gathered at the water's edge to watch these living pictures of "Venus rising from the Sea." As women abandoned the protection of the bathing machines to socialize with men before and after bathing, modesty was a constant concern. At Atlantic City, three girls discovered too late the "terrible shrinking powers of salt water." They ran to the bath house for cover "but on their way thither ran a gauntlet far more awful than any ever encountered by Fennimore Cooper's Indian Fighters."[95]

A more pressing problem was the distracting and often dangerous impediment the bathing costume posed to swimming. As more women made the transition from playful bathing to athletic swimming, costume requirements changed. The emerging sportswoman was still concerned with modesty and fashion, but she also challenged the anchor-like effect of her voluminous bathing outfit. Reform efforts were supported by numerous male swimmers who promoted swimming as a valuable exercise for women. One swimming instructor went so far as to duplicate the female experience by swimming in a close imitation of her bathing costume. Describing this adventure in 1902, Edwin Sandys wrote,

> Not until then did I rightly understand what a serious matter a few feet of superfluous cloth might become in water. The suit was amply large, yet

This photograph was taken in 1897, a time when millions of Americans were enjoying the summer pleasures offered "by the beautiful sea." The men wear two-piece woolen swimsuits that are similar in cut and styling. Their fashion-conscious female companions are dressed for bathing, *not* swimming. These costumes, with sailor collars, puffed sleeves, and full skirts could weigh as much as thirty pounds when wet.

119

Today's swimsuits are fashion statements designed for swimming, sunning, and attracting attention. These 1985 styles feature bikini bottoms that are almost identical in design and fit, which emphasizes rather than eliminates physical differences between the sexes.

pounds of apparently dead weight seemed to be pulling at me in every direction. In that gear a swim of 100 yards was as serious a task as a mile in my own suit. After that experience, I no longer wondered why so few women swim well, but rather that that are able to swim at all.[96]

The controversy over bathing versus swimming, and the related issue of body concealment versus body display, continued well into the 1920s. In their pursuit of greater freedom and maximum exposure, women abandoned the overskirt, modified the chemise, and eventually adopted a one-piece or two-piece suit based on the male prototype.[97] The sexes also shared a strong preference for swimsuits that showcased their tan, trim bodies. Although public resistance and legal prohibitions designed to enforce a code of modesty were even stronger for women than they had been for men, standards did change. The fun-in-the-sun mentality encouraged a heightened sense of body awareness, and women's swimsuits became increasingly more revealing. Once again, women's persistent advocacy for athleticism was an important catalyst for sportswear changes.

> With the women in their swimmin'
> Turning Records into wrecks
> With the ladies raising hades
> In a matter quite complex,
> With their biceps getting stronger
> Where their strides are getting longer
> In about four generations
> Who will be the weaker sex?[98]

TODAY'S FITNESS IDEAL

How are sports played out today? If, as sports historian Dale Somers concludes, the eighteenth-century gospel of work yielded to a gospel of play in the nineteenth century, the current sports and fitness craze is a combination of both.[99] We work at our play. Indeed, the legions of men and women who pursue the athletic ideal often resemble sport soldiers as they train their bodies through a daily regimen. In their passion for muscularity, they push their bodies far beyond pleasurable limits while silently repeating, No pain, no gain. As a result, product overshadows process. Sport once shaped moral character; it now shapes perfect bodies.

We take the phrase *shaping-up* quite literally. Sport and exercise enables us to restructure as well as condition our bodies. The fact that the sleek, taut, muscular body is the aesthetic ideal for *both* men and women represents a direct attack on long-held beliefs about fundamental physical differences between the sexes. In his 1956 study of the nude, Kenneth Clark described the female form as "an oval, surmounted by two spheres."[100] By comparison, males appeared stronger, harder, and more angular. Yet as women break away from Clark's model, replacing historical softness with well-defined muscle, it becomes harder to define the sexes in diametric terms. Female body builders address this head-on when they ask, "Why can't muscles be feminine?"

By today's standards, a well-conditioned body is a sexy body, and this is true for both sexes. The Charles Atlas promise—"you can improve your life by improving your body"—now appeals to women as well as men. A new kind of body consciousness is emerging and athletic men and women appear eager to display their hard physiques. Some sociologists have

Unlike nineteenth-century women who were concerned that too much exercise would eliminate their voluptuous curves, twentieth-century women avidly turned to exercise, dieting, and gadgetry to achieve the new slender ideal. The women in this 1929 photograph attempt to slim down by shaking off excess weight with reducing machines.

The man and woman in this 1983 illustration are part of today's fitness-conscious generation. Originally, men pumped iron to build muscles, while women used weight training to trim and tone their bodies. Now both sexes use exercise and weights to shape a new, muscular physical ideal.

Build Up, Slim Down, or Both

With The Lean Machine™ the options are all yours. Wrist-curl 20 pounds or leg-curl 250 — you can do any of 45 exercises in the privacy of your own home, at your own pace, at your own convenience — night or day, summer or winter, rain or shine.

The Lean Machine is sturdy, compact, and infinitely adjustable. It's the ultimate fitness system. We'd be proud to send you a free brochure that will answer all your questions.

Call Toll Free: **1-800-621-1203**
(In Illinois 1-800-821-7143)

THE LEAN MACHINE.™
Inertia Dynamics Corp., 3550 N. Central Ave., Phoenix, AZ 85012

pointed out, however, that fitness addicts have gone far beyond the point of getting in shape for purposes of sexual attraction. They caution that we are becoming a culture of physical narcissists who are more interested in interacting with machines than with each other.[101] The sexual pleasure may exist but it is autoerotic.

Another aspect of sports' appeal is status. Despite the trend toward a democratization of sports in the early twentieth century, it has become an ideal vehicle for flaunting wealth, time, and dedication. High-priced club memberships, home fitness centers, and a wide array of expensive apparel, apparatus, and accessories all serve to delineate the new sporting hierarchy. Because of the growing popularity of these items we are continually encouraged to seek new expressions of status. Personal fitness coaches recently have become popular in large urban centers catering to individuals who are willing to pay from $40 to $80 per workout for custom-tailored fitness.[102] And for the "take-out" generation, there are now mobile health clubs in California that offer at-home exercise service. Thanks to these customized vans, which are equipped with weight equipment, exercise bikes, and rowing machines, a private gym is only as far away as your driveway.[103]

Finally, sports are fashionable. Trendy health clubs have become our new social arenas. Looking good is more than fitness, it is a matter of style. The once sharp division between public and private sports clothing is blurred to the point that sports wear is now marketed as active wear. And although many Americans still rely on sports to conform to the fashionable ideal, physical changes that result from an active life style are now dictating new directions in everyday clothing. Manufacturers of men's suits are selling "athletic style" suits, which feature a bigger "drop," that is, a greater difference between the chest and waist measurements, to accommodate a built-up physique.

This, however, is one reality. Recent statistics reveal that the vast majority of Americans fail to qualify as members of the physical elite. Even for those individuals who diligently pursue good health and a healthy body, the ideal always demands more. It also is shortsighted to conclude that the sports arena is neutral territory free of gender stereotypes or that the symbols that act as social determinates of gender are absent from today's sports wardrobe. While it is important to acknowledge that the sporting experience has broadened our vision of men's and women's potential, we must also remember that the history of sports and sports clothing is wedded to fashionable ideals. The present fitness cult does not escape this pressure either in style or in spirit. And so we must ask if the athletic images that are so deliberately apportioned and promoted to merchandise everything from cosmetics to breakfast cereal are created as ideals or found as facts. Is the ideal of the sports-shaped body another time-bound variant of the same drive to meet an unattainable standard of attractiveness?

CLAUDIA BRUSH KIDWELL

GENDER SYMBOLS OR FASHIONABLE DETAILS?

. . . big-shouldered women appeared during the Second World War, when rather square-cut, military-style clothing was adopted even by civilians. It was an appropriate display for a wartime period when women were playing a bigger role in hostilities than ever before.

Desmond Morris, *Bodywatching* (1985)

We tend to associate broad shoulders and narrow hips with men, and sloping shoulders, small waists, and wide, rounded hips with women. As Morris reports, one of the most striking (nonreproductive) differences between male and female bodies is the difference in shoulder mass. "The male shoulders are much broader, thicker and heavier than those of the female, a difference exaggerated by the female's wider hips. The typical male body shape tapers inwards as it descends while the typical female shape broadens out." This description of men and women, as well as our tendency to interpret broad shoulders as masculine, is shaped more by forty years of an exaggerated athletic ideal for men than by an accurate knowledge of biological differences.

Fashion does not necessarily follow biology, and Desmond Morris, who is also the author of *The Naked Ape,* errs in suggesting that, "If men wished to appear more masculine, they had only to add some kind of artificial width to their shoulders."[1] Despite the biological association with masculinity, broad shoulders do not always signify power. Nor is he correct in concluding that "When women have wished to assert themselves, they have frequently adopted artificially broadened shoulders." The examples he cites (women's leg-of-mutton sleeves in the 1890s and the shoulder pads worn during World War II) actually have more complex origins and significance.

Consider the following column on men's fashions, which appeared in 1938 in *Fashion Digest:* "Broad shoulders and slender hips are new suit points of interest borrowed from more feminine counterparts."[2] From the perspective of professionals in the American women's clothing industry, men's fashions in 1938 copied the extra broad shoulders characteristic of the latest fashions in *women's* dress. Moreover, initially at any rate, these

In 1942, both student and teacher at Scripps College in California are wearing broad-shouldered suits, a style that evolved from a fashion trend dating from the late 1920s.

broad shoulders were not associated with military uniforms, but rather with the latest Parisian style.

New fashions evolve, gradually changing in one part of the costume and then in another. Sometimes clothing emphasizes biological differences, but not always. No style feature has the same meaning at all times in all places. In the one hundred years before World War II, an entirely different set of clothing shapes and symbols ruled fashion. Consider the following hypothetical scenario, based on fashion plates of the period:

In 1840 an individual strolled through the city park cutting a fashionable figure in bottle green cloth and yellow brocaded silk. The figure was shaped like an hourglass. The fashionable silhouette had sloping shoulders, a padded chest, and a narrow, cinched waist. The clothing was seamed to fit snugly over the waist and flared over the hips into a full skirt. This could have been a skirt of a woman's dress or the skirt of a man's coat.

Thus Alison Lurie was not quite correct in titling one section of her book *The Language of Clothes* "Rectangular Men and Rounded Women." In the 1830s and 1840s the fashionable silhouette was rounded for *both* men and women, while in the late 1930s and the 1940s, both men and women wore "rectangular" clothes.

The language of clothes is not static. The only constant seems to be that distinctions will always be made between men and women, though the significant gender symbols change. When the language of clothes from one time period is learned, this knowledge does not necessarily help one understand the vocabulary of another time or place. To translate the meaning of clothes with any degree of accuracy requires a thorough knowledge of the specific way in which it was used.

THE HOURGLASS SHAPE FOR MEN AND WOMEN

John F. Watson, the chronicler of life in New York and Philadelphia "in the Olden Time," admired the early-nineteenth-century "graceful and easy habits of both sexes." But he vehemently objected to the latest 1840s styles: "Men and women stiffly corseted; long unnatural-looking waists; shoulders and breasts stuffed and deformed . . . and artificial hips."[3] Watson confirms for us that he saw the similarity in the fashionable appearances of contemporary men and women, and he objected to the form of these new fashions for both. He did not worry about the feminization of small-waisted, full-hipped men or the masculinization of wide-shouldered women. He knew that although the fashionable silhouette for both sexes was similar, it did not mean the same thing for both sexes.

A study of 1840s garments confirms the similarity of men's and women's silhouettes, while also revealing that some different techniques were used to create these shapes. Women were more likely to use undergarments to construct their fashionable figures—corsets to rearrange their flesh, petticoats and "bums," or cresent-shaped bustle pads, to enhance the hips. Their dresses served primarily as an outer covering, cut and trimmed to emphasize the form they had built. Men's fashionable silhouettes, however,

The gentleman and the lady in this 1840 fashion plate both have an hourglass shape created by constricting the waist and padding the shoulders and the hips. This shape was a sign of a fashionable person of the period. In other respects, masculine and feminine fashions were strikingly different. Courtesy of Cooper-Hewitt Museum, The Smithsonian Institution's National Museum of Design.

were more often built into their clothes by their tailors. It was the skillfully cut and artfully padded coat, vest, and trousers that transformed the average masculine body into the desired hourglass shape. As a Philadelphia tailor reported in 1843, "coats for city wear are made long waisted with wide shoulders, the . . . skirt has three gores cut out, well wadded on the hips, so as to give them a full appearance. . . ."[4] Garments for both men and women were cut with extended sloping shoulders. This was true of a ball gown, a cotton wash dress of a middle-class woman, or a dark wool broadcloth suit coat worn by a merchant.

A self-improvement book published in 1845 advised its readers that "health and beauty in both sexes require that the chest should be thrown well forward, the shoulders carried back, the carriage erect, free and unconstrained."[5] The 1840s ideal of a broad, full chest "thrown well forward" exceeded what most men and some women could achieve unaided. Extensive padding was essential in men's suit coats and, to a lesser extent, in women's garments. When padding was used in a dress it was usually in the front of the bodice to produce the desired rounded curves. This was particularly necessary when the natural endowments of a woman did not produce the ideal mass even when rearranged by the usual corset. Most men, not just the slightly built ones, however, required "wadding," or padding, to approximate the fashionable ideal.

When an 1840s man dressed for business or for a formal occasion, he

This measuring diagram from an 1844 "treatise on the art of tailoring" illustrates how the skillfully cut coat, sewn with sculptured padding, contributed to the making of a fashionably shaped man.

began constructing his upper torso when he put on his vest, which was padded over the chest. But his suit coat was most important: the padding in this garment started at the shoulder and extended into the sleeve to maintain the desired broad, sloping shoulder line that smoothly curved into a full upper arm. The padding also flowed from the shoulder over the chest and down and around the body—particularly adding breadth under the arms—then thinning to nothing at the waist.

Both vests and coats were cut to fit the waistline closely and then flare out for broad hips. Frock coats—the standard business attire of the period—had skirts cut with full gores. The cutaway skirts of the more formal dress coats were padded and eased into the waistline to produce a full rounded hip shape. A man's waist, located between the padded shoulders and chest above and the fullness below, looked small by contrast.

Most women wore corsets to shape their bodies. These were usually not heavily boned garments, but rather were made of sturdy cotton fabric with one central busk board down the front. Corsets were not necessarily pulled very tightly, as moderate pressure on the lacing would have provided adequate shaping.

One man's corset from this period, worn by Samuel Wise, an Englishman, when he married in 1843, was a remarkably engineered garment, with encased rows of fine metal springs. It is stamped "Henry Adcock London" and "His Majesty's Royal Letter's Patent."[6] Unlike women's corsets, which relied on the unyielding pressure of sturdy cotton to shape the female figure, this masculine undergarment compressed the male waist through the elastic action of stretched springs.

When John Watson criticized 1840s fashions, he referred to both men and women as being "stiffly corseted." At no time did he suggest that men should not wear corsets because small waists were for women only or even that corsets were a feminine garment. He was as critical of the new vogue for the cultivation of "whiskers, mustachios and sidelocks" as he was of corsets for men. Characterizing these innovations as "passing caprices" he wished that at least "businessmen who have to live by their employments" would go "unbarbed and uncorseted."[7]

A man could also cinch his waist by means other than a corset. There are extant several men's drawers that are made with multiple sets of drawstrings at the waistline. These could be pulled and adjusted, drawing in the waist. The drawers are also cut with extra fullness eased into the lower edge of the wide waistband, which would have contributed to creating a broad-hipped look. Fashionable men's "pantaloons" (trousers that strapped under the foot) also helped shape the masculine body. Pantaloons at this time were made without waistbands and were cut to "fit closely at the hips."[8] When this garment was put on, the rounded, close-fitting shape of the hips and the tension created by strapping each leg beneath the shoe created a full, curving shape that gradually narrowed to fit closely at the ankle.

Thus, through the cut and padding of their clothes, men as well as women created a rounded silhouette. This figure-eight outline was enhanced in both sexes by the optical illusion of certain design details. For example, the apparent breadth of the shoulders and chest and the narrowness of the waist were exaggerated by the placement of the wide lapels of a man's suit coat and by the angle of the gathers, pleats, or other trimmings on a woman's bodice. Although the specific techniques used to change the body were different for men and women, the overall effect was the same.

If, as Desmond Morris and Alison Lurie suggest, certain features of appearance always have the same meaning, then the rounded 1840s masculine fashions might have meant that men at that time were trying to appear softer and less powerful. But middle-class men and women in the 1840s lived very different lives—men focusing on business in the public arena outside the home, and women operating primarily within the private sphere of domestic life. In spite of their similar silhouettes, male and female fashions differed strikingly in other respects. Men wore trousers, and strode purposefully forward. Women wore long skirts, which they cleared out of their way at every step by moving each leg in a circular motion. Even when the same type of clothing was worn, distinctions were made between the masculine and feminine versions by the use of the materials with different textures, patterns, colors, and motifs. Women's apparel was characterized by a greater variety of possible materials and a much wider range of design choices. Because of the limits of acceptable masculine choices, men were more restricted in the degree of individual expression that was deemed appropriate. Conformity to exact standards of correct fit became more important for men than women (which, for women, resulted in the development of very different sizing systems in the fledgling ready-to-wear clothing industries).

Even what was similar in men's and women's dress was perceived differently. When contemporary writers made reference to the shape of a fashionable man's body, they most often described wide shoulders, while the reporters of feminine fashions focused on narrow waists. Any reference to the apparent width of the shoulders in women's dresses was in terms of how this feature showed off in contrast a small waist. Thus the optical illusion created by the V angle of the lapels on a man's coat and the V angle of the gathers on a woman's bodice were interpreted differently.

A similar phenomenon occurred in the late 1930s when men and women were again shaped similarly by their clothes. This time they were broad-shouldered with narrow hips. But again, similar silhouettes were interpreted differently, at least at first. In the late 1930s, narrow hips on men were seen to emphasize broad shoulders, while broad shoulders on women were perceived as drawing attention to small waists and slender female hips. The wealth of information that is available from this period demonstrates how important it is to understand the history of a particular fashion before making conclusions about its meaning.

THE INFLUENCE OF MILITARY UNIFORMS ON FASHION

When civilians adopt square-cut styles, they are often said to be influenced by military uniforms. This notion assumes that military uniforms are by

Between 1926 and 1937, a series of revised specifications transformed the oval outline of the World War I army uniform on the right to the upside-down-triangle silhouette of the uniform on the left. The army uniform committee made the changes following civilian fashions.

definition square cut. In fact, the 1917 World War I Army field uniforms suggested an oval silhouette. During World War I, the high-waisted service coats with a flared skirt worn over ample breeches created the appearance of a substantial body, wide at the hips. This rounded shape was visually reinforced by trim details such as the four large, curved patch pockets. It took a series of revisions in specifications starting in 1926 with a change in the collar, to transform this oval outline to a roughly inverted-triangle silhouette by 1939.[9]

The latest specifications in 1939 called for a service coat cut with wider shoulders, more ease in the upper back and chest, and a lower waist. The coat, with its skirt cut to fit smoothly over the hip, was worn over straight trousers instead of easy-fitting breeches. Even the increased width and length of the lapels and the alterations in the type, size, and location of pockets enhanced the broad-shouldered, narrow-hipped, triangular appearance of the body.

It took roughly twenty years for the Army to complete this major change. These alterations, however, were not fashion innovations of the uniform committee. On the contrary, the established bureaucratic decision-making processes responded to changes that occurred first in civilian life. Factors such as the huge stockpiles of World War I uniforms at the end of the hostilities and the slow procedures for making changes in uniform specifications prevented the Army from altering their garb as much or as quickly as is the practice in civilian life. Not only did military uniform not influence civilian styles, they lagged behind, following not every variation but the major changes in civilian fashions.

And civilian styles changed significantly in the first half of the twentieth century, transforming the ideal body several times. Fashionable silhouettes for men (as well as women) were continually evolving. But the timing and the extent of change for men and women were often different. A survey of fashions from 1900 to the mid-1920s shows the variable rhythms of these changes.

| 1904 | 1911 | 1917 | 1927 | 1933 | 1938 | 1944 | 1952 |

Figures from Fall Sears catalogues, 1904 to 1952, illustrate the evolving fashion silhouette. The century began with very different masculine and feminine shapes—even different postures. By the 1920s a slender, youthful figure was the ideal for both. In 1933 the big-shoulder fashions were more popular for women than for men, but by 1938 this upside-down-triangular shape was the common contemporary look for both genders. By 1952 the menswear and womenswear industries were again promoting different shapes. The reasons for these changes can only be understood after closely studying the history of each style and related events.

131

In the first years of the twentieth century, well-dressed men and women presented a substantial appearance. They were shaped, however, very differently. The ideal masculine body was portrayed as a massive rectangle while the woman's figure was shown as fleshy above and below a small waist. He stood firmly on two legs with a straight spine; she slanted—as if in forward motion—with a curved spine and with her pelvis tilted back.

Over the next two decades, the trend for both was toward a slender youthful body, but the details differed. Men started the twentieth century wearing a sack suit for business with a short jacket. Cut with little hint of a waist, this garment seems suited for an amply proportioned, wealthy gentleman. But gradually suits were cut narrower. By 1910 jackets were made with raised waists and shaped slightly for the hips. By 1923 the industry paper, *Men's Wear,* shows that the waist in fashionable men's clothes was dropping just as it was in women's fashions. *Men's Wear* correspondents from various European fashion centers revealed that the leading tailors had introduced other changes along with the natural waist. In 1923 one writer reported that English jackets were cut with shoulders that were broad "with plenty of chest," and a well-defined waist with the skirts cut straight.[10] In the same year, French models were noted as being "very wide at the shoulders, shaped to fit the body from the waist downward."[11] The advertisements in these same issues, however, suggested that manufacturers felt that while the majority of their fashionable customers were interested in English models, they would be put off by extreme styles. They wanted the "correct English model—the slightly wider shoulders, a lower waistline, the slender hips. . . ."[12] The actual width of the shoulders and the amount of upper back and chest fullness were controversial features and would continue to be issues of concern for several decades.

Men's Wear criticized President Coolidge in 1926, for example, saying that he was creating the wrong shape. One article shows a photograph of the president in his usual suit. This is contrasted with an illustration showing Coolidge's face superimposed above a suit with a jacket made along "smarter lines than he now wears." They admonished, "Ah, yes, your tailor *is* an honorable man, but the clothes he produces for you unnecessarily distort your figure. Perhaps you could never be transformed into an Apollo, but your clothes could be made to more naturally dress the body that God gave you."[13] They recommended a jacket that "gracefully follows the masculine lines of the body" and was both comfortable and smart. By 1926 *Men's Wear* writers visualized an attractive, masculine body in terms of the upside down triangle.

It would take years of exposure to this new body ideal before the majority of American men would agree. But it is clear that this look was established in the minds of America's young men long before the Army changed its uniforms from an oval outline to a triangular silhouette. By the late 1920s, an elongated, triangular look was also the fashionable ideal shown for the majority of women. More women were offered this new look than men, and civilians were ahead of the military.

The first hint of greater shoulder width for women appeared in the 1920s. At the end of the decade women's fashions changed from styles cut to hang straight from the shoulders to an ideal silhouette that approximated an upside down, elongated triangle. Dresses and, most dramatically, coats were made fuller above the waist than below. And the size and shape of collars and the placement of trimmings exaggerated the illusion of this top-heavy outline.

As early as August 1931 *Women's Wear Daily* reported that French designers were exaggerating the width of shoulders with new sleeve cuts, revers, and capelets. One headline announced, "Silhouette With Breadth at Top Cited as Designed to Make Waistline Appear Smaller."[14] A week later this industry paper reported that, "Daytime dresses emphasized broad shouldered and slender waisted effects."[15] In reaction to the straight look of the twenties fashions, curves at the waist were seen as the new feminine look, and the broadening of the shoulders was heralded as a contribution to the new femininity. The most extreme examples were shown on evening dresses.

The interest in shoulders increased. In January and February 1932, mentions of "broad shoulders" and "wide shoulders" are scattered through *Women's Wear Daily* with padding in coats and tailored suits and with large ruffles, ruchings, and huge puffed sleeves on evening dresses. Major Parisian designers such as Lelong and Schiaparelli are frequently mentioned, and the new styles are shown worn by socialites and theater personalities.

The April 28, 1932, *Women's Wear Daily* showed Joan Crawford in a white dress with the caption "Ruffles in Organdie Express a Cinema Version of Wide Shoulders."[16] The report tells that she wears this Adrian designed model in her forthcoming picture *Letty Lynton*. Joan Crawford was built for the part. She was slender, young, active, and as Adrian is reputed to have commented about her shoulders when he first saw her, "My God, you're a Johnny Weismuller."[17] In June 1932, *Letty Lynton* opened in neighborhood theaters. The costumes were a sensation. The public stormed their local stores buying the biggest-sleeved, most highly ruffled dresses they could find. Eventually these wider-shouldered, narrow-hipped styles would have been accepted without the impact of the movies. But the promotional power of the larger-than-life vision of Joan Crawford as Letty Lynton accelerated Americans' conversion to this style.

Sears, which had been lagging behind the trend for wide shoulders, making conservative selections for its mail order catalogue, found it was no longer offering its customers what they wanted. In Spring 1933, however, Sears offered dresses with puffed and ruffled sleeves along with conservative versions. One is described as "the alluring kind of dress that flashes across the screen on your favorite movie star!"[18]

Harper's Bazaar had already shown some versions of the "important shoulder" styles in 1932 before *Letty Lynton,* quietly observing that wide

In April 1932 *Women's Wear Daily* showed the gown worn by Joan Crawford in a forthcoming movie, *Letty Lynton*. The dress was described as the latest "cinema version of the high fashion wide shouldered look." No one expected that the movie audiences' enthusiasm for this design would so quickly make big shoulders for women a widely accepted fashion.

revers and square shoulders in a suit "accent slim hips."[19] After the movie, the magazine actively promoted broad shoulders. A diagram was included in the 1933 April issue demonstrating the optical illusion at work in a new Schiaparelli dress. Two drawings of the same woman with the same hips showed that broad shoulders made the hips look smaller.[20]

Women's Wear Daily escalated its promotion of the big shoulders. Every issue in 1933 was filled with stories about shoulders—padded and unpadded, sometimes high, always wide. They reported a fantastic variety of ways fabric could be contorted to get these effects. Everything from knitwear to wedding dresses was fair game.

By 1938 a beautiful woman's body, dressed or undressed, was ideally firm yet curvy. Broad shoulders emphasized a narrow waist and compact slender hips. The attention was directed downward to shapely legs and ankles. Broad shoulders had become an integral feature in the ideal female body. This feature was not intended to be a symbol of masculinity; it evolved as a design device that emphasized a woman's femaleness.

Broad shoulders also became a dominant feature of the ideal male body. In the late 1920s and early 1930s, the newest style innovations described in *Men's Wear* featured variations of wider shoulders. The most extreme versions came from two very different sources—English and European tailors and the American "Broadway Styles."

The high-fashion tailors' designs were routinely reported with each new season, and feature articles showed the fashionable men who wore these suits. The Prince of Wales was a particular favorite, while stories on Hollywood stars began to appear more regularly. The majority of the American menswear industry was eventually influenced by the innovations of these English and European tailors.

The Broadway suits were a distinctive interpretation of the style the high-fashion tailors were showing. According to *Men's Wear*, these flamboyant suits were first worn by "young actors, song writers, and members of the metropolitan jazz orchestras."[21] The typical wearer was ". . . the sporty young boy who stays out nights and frequents the dance halls and cabarets. . . ." His suit ". . . emphatically expresses, so he thinks, what is the latest up-to-the-minute sportiest-appearing garb he can buy, and, best of all, it is priced low enough to be within his limited means." *Men's Wear* predicted that

> In a few years . . . this young man will not be a customer for this style of clothing. The chances are . . . as his education proceeds, he will have completely changed his ideas. He will then . . . get married and raise a family, work to support it, and he will then be a conservative clothes customer who views extreme clothes with contempt.[22]

In 1932, using ideas first proposed in England and Europe, a *Men's Wear* advertisement expounded on the advantages of the latest "new" shoulder style. "The drape model will change the silhouette," they proclaimed,

> And the changed silhouette is more flattering to the average man than the present cylinder. For the Drape broadens his shoulders, deepens his chest, shapes his waist, gives contour to his legs. The Drape does the significant job of combining new style with new comfort. Put the ordinary man into the Drape Suit and you have put new style ideas into his mind. . . . The men of the country will be worked up to the change by the time they are ready to buy a new suit next Fall. . . . the Drape Model will be a powerful influence in the direction of making the clothes that men are now wearing—obsolete, old-fashioned.[23]

The menswear industry professionals saw the profitable possibilities of these new styles, but the general public did not adopt them quickly.

In Spring 1933, when Sears offered huge puffed, ruffled, and leg-of-mutton sleeves on women's garments, the catalogue offered at least four different variations of the triangular silhouette for men. The most flamboyant, described as "Swagger" styles, corresponded to the Broadway suits described in *Men's Wear*. "University Styles" were high fashion, without the jazzy extremes of the Broadway suits. (Sears's version of high fashion, however, was several years behind the latest trends in England as reported in *Men's Wear*.) And then there were the moderately stylish and the conservative options.

Each of the four categories of suits has ascribed to it certain attributes that may be admired or met with disapproval depending upon what man is wearing it, at which occasion, and with what group of people. Within the Broadway suit category the changes over time were dramatic and similar to the changes in women's fashions. The lines of conservative suits, however, evolved more slowly and within a narrower range of possibilities.

Between 1933 and 1938 Sears changed its offerings each season just enough so that by the end of this period more men were wearing suits cut with broader shoulders. Because the triangular broad-shouldered silhouette was initially offered to a greater number of women than men, to an industry professional it would appear as though the men were finally catching up to the women's triangular silhouette.

By 1938 the broad-shouldered figure was no longer just for the young man. This athletic ideal, personified by movie stars such as Errol Flynn, Clark Gable, and Cary Grant, was accepted by even the conservative individual as the way a male should look—whether he was naturally built that way or not. The menswear industry recognized this change and used it to promote that year's "new" big-shouldered look for men. In August 1938 *Men's Wear* observed that, "the major features" of "the new spring jackets" are "at the shoulders."

> Extra fullness, two inches or more, produced deep folds near the sleeve-heads that have an accordian-like quality. The chest too is of ample breadth and shows folds. The waist is shapely, and the bottom of the jacket fits closely.[24]

Big shoulders in feminine clothes were the mode five years before this latest push for bigger shoulders in men's fashions. Women were wearing shoulder pads about five years before the army converted the enlisted man's World War I uniform with its oval outline to the upside down triangular silhouette of the 1939 field uniform. Indeed, by 1940, French couturiers were beginning to show designs using less padding and fuller skirts, rejecting the style of exaggerated shoulders. American magazines also started to show these Paris innovations. In June 1940 *Harper's Bazaar* featured several of Alix's designs, a suit with "rounded shoulders" and a dress with "gentle" shoulders.[25]

Although the war did not inspire the wide-shouldered look for women, it did have an effect. The war prevented the broad shoulders in America from going out of fashion as soon as they normally would have.

With the German occupation of Paris, the international fashion industry was paralyzed. In response, the American industry shifted gears. Instead of reporting on the Paris collections, the September 1941 *Vogue* headlined their issue "AMERICAN COLLECTION—for the first time 'on their own.'" The same month *Harper's Bazaar* announced,

> This is the first issue of *Harper's Bazaar* that has ever appeared without fashions from Paris. We publish this record of the New York Autumn openings

with pride in the achievements of our American Designers and with full ac-knowledgment of our debt to the French. We have learned from the greatest masters of fashion in the world; learned, and then added something of our own. Such clothes have never been made in America before.[26]

The average reader knew little about American designers. It had been only nine years since Dorothy Shaver, then vice president of Lord & Taylor, began recognizing American designers by name.[27] Prior to that time, a designer worked anonymously—a policy encouraged by manufacturers and, until Miss Shaver, retailers. In 1940 no group of American designers commanded the psychological and creative authority of the leading French designers.

Without the leadership of Paris, the American fashion press attempted to predict and promote what they anticipated as the next step toward a new fashion. In March 1941 *Harper's Bazaar* used a full-page illustration of torn-apart shoulder pads to make the point that "SHOULDER PADS Are in the Dustpan." They predicted,

> Those little triangular pincushions that were sewn inside our dresses to give us that coveted broad-shouldered look are going-going-going. The eye looks fondly on narrower shoulders, the eye is kinder to larger hips. A few months hence, if you insist on having those pads sewn in your dresses, we predict that you'll no longer be a contemporary figure. You'll just be an old stuffed shoulder.[28]

The fashions did not change in the direction predicted. Shoulders may have been "smooth," they may have even been slightly sloped, but they were not unpadded or rounded to the extent suggested by prewar Paris. Manufacturers did not know what to believe without the French there to tell them. And the manufacturers did not dare believe what was being hyped at home by the fashion predictors.

Then the government entered the picture. Facing a need to conserve textiles, clothing, and leather to maintain supplies both for the military and the civilian population during the war effort, the War Production Board set about to establish regulations. Stanley Marcus of Neiman-Marcus in Dallas was recruited to head the women's and children's sections. In addition to writing regulations that would conserve fabric and be self-enforcing, these rules had to "*virtually freeze fashion . . .* thus forestalling any radical change in fashion making existing clothes obsolete." The regulations for women's outerwear, officially titled General Limitation Order L-85, accomplished all three objectives. The strategy was to limit readily observable character-istics such as the length and sweep of skirts, characteristics that any cus-tomer or competitor would notice. Marcus wrote later that

> The restrictions we put into effect froze the fashion silhouette; it effectively prevented any change of skirt length downward and it blocked any extreme new sleeve or collar development, which might have encouraged women to discard their existing clothes. At that particular moment, I had greater fashion power than any monarch or couturier in the history of the world.

But this power was only relative. With his retail experience, Marcus real-ized that no matter how well written the regulations might be, he had to present this conservation order in a manner that would get maximum sup-

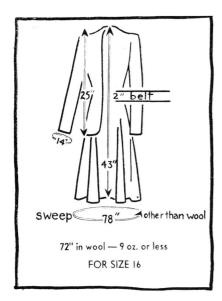

25"

2" belt

14"

43"

sweep 78" other than wool

72" in wool — 9 oz. or less

FOR SIZE 16

The War Production Board passed regulations in 1942 to conserve fabric during World War II. The diagrams illustrating the design restrictions show that the ten-year-old fashion for padded shoulders was part of the acceptable "basic body." The emergency conditions produced by the war temporarily prevented women's fashions from evolving toward a more rounded silhouette, a trend that was evident as early as 1940.

port from both the public and the trade. He went about selling the regulations. As he put it, he started by inviting editors from the "leading fashion magazines and newspaper, columnists, reporters for the various fashion newsletters, and anyone else" whom he "thought might give us a good send off" to a press conference in Washington, D.C. He also leaked the regulations to *Women's Wear Daily*'s Washington reporters in advance, against all War Production Board rules, so that they might be able to have sketches ready to accompany the publication of the order. As a result, the illustrations made the regulations crystal clear to members of the industry.[29] And because of his efforts at promoting the regulations, they were viewed as a patriotic opportunity to exercise creativity on behalf of the wartime effort instead of being seen as a wartime hardship.

The regulations did not eliminate shoulder pads. This feature had become so much a part of feminine dress that pads were included in the description of the "basic body," the government's way of defining the basic allowable dimensions and features in a woman's garment.

As a result of the war, communication with Paris was cut off, eliminating the usual flow of authoritative design information. And it was decreed both by government regulation and by popular opinion that it would be unpatriotic to use materials to experiment with changing the fashionable silhouette. Is it any wonder that manufacturers left the shoulder pads in?

Fashion was only revived with the first design reports from Paris after the city was liberated in August 1944. The French designs emphasized small waists exaggerated by full shoulders above and full hips and skirts below. Since L-85 was still in effect, Americans could not go too far with the trend for wider skirts. In 1945 *Vogue* reported that

New York fashion houses . . . have simultaneously staged a sort of bloodless silhouette revolution. And no L-85 rules broken. It is part pendulum swinging. Part Paris. Part reaction to the narrow tube silhouette, which is still a fashion form in high favour.[30]

Waist cinching and hip padding were described as essential for the new fashion, and it was said that "The smartest shoulders are the nearest-to-natural shoulders."[31] *Vogue* emphasized that

The new fashions are made not for tall little girls, but for women with indentations where Nature placed their waistlines.[32]

When, in the spring of 1947, Christian Dior introduced his first line, he so emphatically captured the essence of this new direction in his clothes that his designs were heralded as *the* New Look.[33] By the early 1950s even the Sears catalogue women were rounded while the men retained a wider, square silhouette, a result of the postwar fashion for ever broader shoulders known as the Bold Look.

FASHION CHANGES AND GENDER SYMBOLS

In thirty years, men made one radical alteration in their fashionable shape, while women made two. Although English and Continental tailors designed suits that were very wide at the shoulders in the early 1920s, the majority of American men were not influenced by this innovation for a number of years. By 1933 Sears was offering more broad-shouldered styles for women than for men, and the women's versions were more extreme. As late as 1938, a year before a final set of specification changes were made to produce the broad, square-shouldered military uniform, wide shoulders for women were a fashionable detail, an integral part of a total feminine look. But by the end of the war women were rejecting the square-shoulder silhouette as too masculine in favor of the more rounded (though sometimes still padded) shoulder thought to be more feminine. Who made the broad shoulders fashionable for women in the first place? And what happened between 1938 and 1948 to transform the interpretation of this silhouette? To understand how these changes transpired, we must first examine who controls fashion.

When the ideal silhouette for both women and men changed from an elongated triangle in the late 1920s to a heavily padded, sharply defined triangle in the late 1930s, was this the result of the inspiration of one creative person, such as the Hollywood film designer Adrian? Clearly not. Were consumers manipulated by the collaborative efforts of designers, manufacturers, advertisers, and sellers? Not exactly. Or are these changes simply a mirror of changing gender conventions and related gender symbols? Not really. These kinds of questions have always been raised in societies where styles regularly change in popularity. But they have been asked with increased intensity during the twentieth century with the growth of the ready-to-wear women's clothing industry and the decline of custom dressmakers and tailors.

An astute writer for the *New York Times,* Mrs. Eunice Fuller Barnard, observed in 1929, that

> The amazing democratization of fashion has made it at once more important and less easy to find its source. . . . with ever larger fortunes at stake, more and more strenuous efforts are being made to find . . . any clue to the course fashion is to take.

The manufacturers and retailers knew they could not direct fashion; yet they daily risked their business on guessing correctly. An entire industry within an industry sprang up in the 1920s including highly paid stylists in department stores and great fashion advisory organizations for both manufacturers and retailers. While in the 1920s "it is generally Paris through her couturiers who proposes, it is women, either in the individual or the mass, who disposes."[34] In this high-risk competitive business where artistic intuition and statistical analysis are both needed, it is the consumer who counts.

> What will . . . she . . . like, what will she accept? Or to ask the question more cynically, how much . . . can be "put over" on her? For after all, fashion is a business with quantity buying its aim. . . .

Barnard observed that

> These big organizations that make their bread and caviar from advising shops and factories on fashion proceed on two almost opposite theories. . . . One school of thought holds that what an exclusive group of women who live in Paris decide to wear, in the main sets the fashion for the rest of the world. . . .

The other theory, which pins its proof to statistics, is that the shoppers themselves ultimately do the deciding. Mass acceptance of any style both here and abroad makes it a fashion.[35]

The menswear industry was not as focused on Paris as the women's industry and fashions changed to different degrees and at different rates in some forms of men's apparel. But tensions similar to those Barnard describes in the women's fashion field were also a part of the manufacture and selling of men's apparel.

Similar relationships between manufacturer and customer existed even in the 1840s when middle-class men and women had their clothes custom made. That fashion system, however, was different in some significant ways. The fashion plates that the consumer studied for information were reports of existing garments worn by the most fashionable in France or England (wherever the plate was first drawn). These reports informed those at some distance (socially or geographically) from privileged society. In the 1920s, however, the illustrations in the editorial pages of a magazine represented the writing staff's educated selection. They presented what they thought was most interesting as well as most likely to be influential from the designer's and manufacturer's latest offerings. These were predictions rather than reports on what was fashionable.

Another difference was that the consumer had direct contact with a dressmaker or tailor. If an individual were wealthy, adventuresome, and a socially prominent person of style, he or she might actively participate in the creation of new fashions. This fashion leader's innovative attire might be copied by others in their circle who would in turn be copied by others. (This also occurs in the modern fashion system, but fewer people wear custom-designed clothing today.)

Tailors and dressmakers were always watching for the signs of new trends, and frequently influenced the choices of their less inventive customers. Even in the 1840s a middle-class person had to be assertive to have their particular ideas followed when they placed a new order, but it was possible.

Today the impact that most individual consumers can have on fashion is diffused as they are removed from the designers who suggest to the manufacturer what the consumer will want. Professional buyers for large stores have the most direct influence on manufacturers' decisions. As a result of the ready-to-wear industry, however, more people can afford to make choices between a variety of manufactured goods than in the 1840s, though the choices available are not as great as those open to upper-middle-class people in the 1840s. Unless consumers contact buyers directly to express their opinions, their likes and dislikes are recorded only in the buyer's statistics—the shifting patterns of what did and did not sell.

The awareness of these limits has encouraged some people to reach the erroneous conclusion that fashion is dictated and controlled by a small group of people in the industry. But today, as in the 1920s, a variety of intuitive and statistical techniques are used by professionals to anticipate the direction of the latest fashions. Sophisticated merchandising techniques are powerful persuaders, but no one controls the marketplace. Consumers

In the mid-nineteenth century, women studied the latest styles shown in steel engraved fashion plates in women's magazines, and they discussed with their dressmakers which new features they wanted in their next dresses. This 1850 illustration from *Godey's Lady's Book* shows the latest fashions worn in a domestic scene. One woman appears to be studying a fashion plate.

The modern system of mass producing and marketing apparel has made quality clothing available to more people today than in the nineteenth century. Individuals no longer communicate directly to the manufacturer of their garments. They make their preferences known indirectly through the purchases they make from open racks of apparel selected for them by store buyers. In 1987 Woodward & Lothrop, a department store in Washington, D.C., offered a range of attractively displayed merchandise representative of what their staff thought their customers would want.

today may feel pressured and they may feel limited, but they make or break whole industries by their decisions to buy or not to buy.

The process of changing fashions can be described as an interrelated series of choices. For example, in the modern clothing industry designers create by selecting from a range of design possibilities, manufacturers decide which creations to produce, and the fashion press picks which innovations they are going to spotlight. At the end of this process, store buyers choose the items they think their customers want, and the individual buys or does not buy what is offered to him or her.

The choices that are exercised are not made independently from an unlimited universe of possibilities. Each participant is restricted as to the kinds of choices they feel they can make and each is influenced by the constraints affecting the others. The most obvious type of constraints are those imposed by economic concerns. Most customers, for example, cannot afford to buy all they might want. Knowing this, the designer who is creating for a particular price market will avoid materials or complicated designs that would put a garment out of the price range of the intended customer.

The precedent set by the current fashions also influences the kinds of choices that are made. Rarely is a new season's popular fashion a dramatic departure from the past. The average consumer has seldom accepted new styles that were radically different from what they were already wearing. They prefer to get used to a new feature gradually. Designers, manufacturers, and merchandisers are aware of this tendency. Their choices are influenced by their perception of how adventuresome or how conservative their targeted customers might be. For example, in 1933 the Sears menswear buyers apparently defined their pool of customers very broadly to include very different groups. All four—the "snappy" dresser with jazzy styling, the "university," or fashion conscious, young man, the "business" man, and the "conservative"—were offered distinctive styles, each of which changed slightly each year, but not dramatically.

The adoption of big-shouldered styles by large groups of women in 1932 after the movie *Letty Lynton* is a remarkable exception to the rule of gradual evolution of fashionable details. More typical is the way hemlines changed between 1900 and 1926. In 1915 Sears showed skirts that ended several inches above the ankles. Predictably, the hemline did not drop to the floor the next year nor did it jump up to the knee. In fact, in 1916 Sears offered skirts that were two inches shorter. In 1970, some manufacturers and certain fashion publications misread the public and promoted a radical change in hemlines from miniskirts to maxiskirts. The public resisted and did not buy the new style. They were not willing to follow the fashion industry's dictates.

Although the clothing industry routinely proposes new fashions, it cannot make consumers buy every style they offer. Furthermore, ideas for new fashions do not always come from designers. A classic example is the streamlined knit swimming suit, which was worn by a number of women as early as 1915, although the editorial pages of *Harper's Bazaar* and *Vogue* featured only ore elaborate, skirty bathing suits as late as the early 1920s. This is a fashion that did not trickle down from the styles proposed by designers and worn first by the wealthy. On the contrary, this is a fashion that bubbled up as a result of popular demand. In 1920, before the high-fashion magazines had changed their prescription of what was fashionable, Sears was offering only the more abbreviated and functional style.[36]

A clothing designer can propose new styles, and an individual can adopt a feature very different from prevailing or proposed fashions. But whether an innovation is adopted by others and becomes a popular fashion depends in part upon its relationship to prevailing gender conventions and the related gender symbols. This critical point is specifically considered in the next chapter, which compares what happened in the 1850s when a small group of women began wearing bloomers with the results in the 1960s when young men began wearing long hair.

The fashionable shape of shoulders for women changed in relationship to parameters in consumers' minds about what was attractive for a woman. By the 1920s youthful bodies that were slender, compared to earlier ideals, were admired. With the widespread popularity of sports, active had become attractive. When designers experimented with lines and details that enhanced a slender image, the public bought them. The popularity of the new styles in turn reinforced the latest vision of the ideal body. The exaggerated shoulders of 1938 were viewed simply as a design detail that had been around for a number of years as part of what had become in the United States the healthy, athletic, all-American girl look. Three years later, when *Harper's Bazaar* was announcing that "Shoulder Pads Are in the Dustpan," they were denigrated as being old-fashioned, inappropriate for the new contemporary figure. The restrictions caused by the war had intervened and prevented the fashion system from operating normally. Six years later women were urged by the fashion press to abandon the padded shoulders, not just because they were old-fashioned, but because they were also too masculine.

In ten years the landscape had changed. Broad shoulders were seen everywhere on civilians and in the military. During the war the square-shouldered image of the military predominated. Square-shouldered women in military uniforms or in factory utility garb were filling in, doing jobs men would do during normal times. There were concerns about the consequences of women taking on too many masculine attributes. A 1944 advertisement for lipstick showed women in uniform and asserted that "We are still the weaker sex."[37] And movies explored the consequences for women who went too far and abdicated their feminine roles as wives and mothers to pursue careers. Square shoulders for women by 1948 were not only old-fashioned, they had become too masculine. They were rejected in order to affirm the normal nurturing role of women—not because broad shoulders were inherently masculine, but because by association they had become redefined as masculine.

A similar cycle of broad-shouldered styles for women started in the late 1970s. It is still widely seen ten years later as struggling manufacturers fumble, reaching for the next set of innovations that will stimulate sales. The broadest shoulders that were enjoyed for the way they visually diminished hips appear to be shrinking. More and more men are wearing broader shoulders, and padding the shoulders of feminine garments has become commonplace. Though this time there is not any drama comparable to the postwar reaction, fashions change, stimulated yet bound by many factors, including what the consumer believes to be appropriate gender symbols.

Because of the amount of popular media attention on fashions proposed by the industry, there is a tendency today to overlook the significance of the consumer in directing how fashion changes occur. As Barnard concluded in her 1929 discussion of the workings of the industry,

> . . . it is not primarily the couturier, the advertiser, the salesman, or the much maligned manufacturer, who cruelly forces the fashion, much as they may do to exploit it. As often as not they, too, are its victims. You who would know where fashion springs—cherchez la femme.[38]

To which one might add, "Look for the man, too."

SHELLY FOOTE

CHALLENGING GENDER SYMBOLS

Nature never intended that the sexes should be distinguished by apparel. The beard which they assigned solely to man, is the natural token of his sex. But man effeminates himself, contrary to the evident purpose of nature, by shaving off his beard; and then, lest his sex should be mistaken, he arrogates to himself a particular form of dress, the wearing of which by the female sex he declares to be a grave misdemeanor.

Amelia Bloomer, *The Lily* (May 1851)

In her proposal that women wear a trousered outfit (for comfort and health), Mrs. Bloomer contradicted the belief that natural law dictated how men and women should dress. Only men wore trousers in the mid-nineteenth century. The idea that women should wear such a garment sparked criticism across the country: blurring the visual lines between the sexes, Mrs. Bloomer's opponents felt, might lead to radical changes in the relationships between men and women. A century later, when young men let their hair grow long as part of their overall rebellion against the *status quo*, critics expressed the same concern. Many people saw long hair on men—a change in appearance—as a symbolic precursor to social change.

The intense reaction to some changes in men's and women's appearance proves there is far-reaching symbolic significance attached to certain elements of appearance. Our beliefs about how men and women should look are part of a powerful, complex, and pervading system of values about what is appropriate male and female behavior. When these values have been challenged, as they were with the Bloomer Costume and long hair, there have been strong reactions and pressure from society to conform. In the past, the acceptance or rejection of such changes depended on the existing social climate and exactly who proposed and who opposed the changes.

Among the most powerful of these gender symbols in America have been skirts, trousers, and hair. Men have traditionally worn trousers, women skirts. Women, since the early nineteenth century, have had longer hair than men. When members of one sex defied tradition by appropriating one of these symbols for themselves, the reaction was immediate. The Bloomer Costume in the 1850s and long hair in the 1960s are two of the most vivid examples of this phenomenon. Women bobbing their hair in

The social reformer Amelia Bloomer posed for this photograph in the early 1850s attired in the outfit named after her. Her short dress and Turkish trousers were made of fashionable dress fabric.

the 1920s, women wearing trousers to work in the 1970s, and men wearing skirts in the 1980s are others.

The Bloomer Costume and long hair have much in common though they had completely different origins and intent and disparate groups of people—for completely different motives—supported them. Both challenged the accepted appearance of men and women in fundamental ways. Many believed that the adoption of symbols from the opposite sex that would blur the lines between the sexes threatened the established relationship between men and women. Therefore, these changes have been seen as elements that could disrupt the equilibrium of society, and lead, possibly, to society's destruction. In reality, successful changes in appearance have been a part of larger changes in gender conventions. With the establishment of a new set of values and beliefs about male and female behavior, society has redefined what it is to be and look like a man or a woman. By studying these two cases, we can learn much about the profound identification of men's and women's appearances with their expected gender roles.

THE BLOOMER COSTUME

The Bloomer Costume, later nicknamed bloomers, consisted of a short dress and Turkish trousers. In 1851 the reform newspaper *The Lily,* owned and edited by Amelia Bloomer, presented the costume to the public as an alternative to fashionable women's attire. The Bloomer Costume, especially its masculine connotations, sparked an explosion of opinion and commentary, mainly negative, that was printed and reprinted across the country. As a result, women who wore the outfit were publicly ridiculed and sometimes privately ostracized.

The origins of the Bloomer Costume are not known. One writer claimed that Elizabeth Cady Stanton's niece, Elizabeth Miller, adopted a trousered outfit after visiting a health sanitarium in Switzerland; Mrs. Stanton then told her friend Mrs. Bloomer about it. According to another story, the editor of a local conservative newspaper recommended a trousered outfit to his readers. Mrs. Bloomer, although knowing the editor spoke in jest, declared that the idea had merit. Members of some utopian communities, such as the one at Oneida, New York, wore a similar type of apparel that some researchers suggest might have been the model for the Bloomer Costume. The circulation of these differing stories at the time indicates that at least a few people were experimenting with trousers for women. There had never been a tradition of exposed, bifurcated garments for women in this country.

We do know that by April 1851 Mrs. Bloomer herself had appeared in the short dress and pantaloons. From New England to California, the press ran stories on other women wearing the costume. By 1852, however, it was clear that most women were not going to adopt the outfit. After that date only a few dedicated reformers continued to wear it.[1] The outfit was called heathenish and immodest. But the heart of the issue was whether women had the right to wear what was then an exclusively male garment. Society's answer was no.

The reform of women's clothing was not a new idea; many had advanced the notion since the late eighteenth century. By the mid-nineteenth century the objections to women's fashionable attire had intensified. The new mid-century silhouette emphasized a small waist and a wide, flowing skirt, both thought by reformers to be detrimental to women's health because of the corset and the number of petticoats required to create the new appearance. Some people suggested women lace their corsets less tightly and shorten their skirts, because long skirts jeopardized a woman's health by sweeping up street debris, mud, and water. A more ambitious group of reformers, many of whom supported the women's rights and temperance movements, had a more radical change in mind. Their goal was to create a new society in which men and women would have the same legal rights, in which liquor played no part, and in which people would practice Christian principles of living. Although not a large group, they were vocal, visible, and mainly white, middle class, and married. For these reformers, a shorter skirt was not enough. They claimed that the bulk and weight of the petticoats put undo stress on a woman's internal organs. Moreover, the petticoats added to the bulk around the waist, forcing a woman to lace her corset even tighter to achieve the fashionable, small-waisted silhouette. This group supported, in addition to the Bloomer Costume, a number of other dress reforms, especially in underwear. Ultimately these latter reforms were more successful.

This small group of reformers believed in the contemporary rhetoric about the innate natures of men and women. And they used these beliefs in their writings and lectures to gain support for dress reform among a larger audience. They stressed the unhealthy and unsuitable aspects of fashionable attire for women to fulfill their role as mothers. They contended that the Bloomer Costume made women healthier and, thus, better mothers. They also ascribed part of the mortality and sickness of newborn children to the unhealthy attire of their mothers.[2]

The proponents of the Bloomer outfit also stressed its comfort and practicality. Mary C. Vaughn of Oswego, New York, described the ease of walking in the new outfit, and claimed she did not become out-of-breath or muddied as she had in long skirts. A writer for the *Boston Herald,* who reported seeing fifteen to twenty women in bloomers ice-skating on Back Bay, noted the women's gracefulness and the absence of mishaps.[3]

The editor of *The Lily* called the new outfit an American style, but some people objected to the connotations of *Turkish* trousers. Although oriental motifs and objects *à la Turque* were popular at the time, some people called the outfit heathenish because of its association with Muslim culture. At least one writer noticed the irony of women supporting women's rights wearing an outfit similar to Middle-Eastern women—who had fewer legal rights than American women.[4]

Critics declared the exposure of the ankles and legs to public view immodest. Mrs. Jane Swisshelm, a well-known writer for *The Pittsburgh Visitor,* wrote,

> There must be constant care and use of the hands to insure that the skirts do
> not lodge on the knees, but fall over. If they do not, one may exhibit her

trousers to the waist; and when a woman exhibits her form with no other covering than trousers, we do not want to be there.[5]

Mrs. Bloomer countered by stating that long skirts were no more modest, since a woman exposed ankles when she lifted her skirts to avoid debris and also exposed the insides of their underskirts when she stooped. The editor of a newspaper in Oregon that reprinted Mrs. Swisshelm's comments urged her, and his readers, to remember that "a leg is a leg whether on a man or on a woman."[6] He suggested that his readers should "contemplate a pair of legs in trousers with as much calmness [as] a pair of bare arms or shoulders."

But, the exposure of the ankle and the definition of the legs lent the outfit an erotic quality. The editor of *The Louisville Journal* stated,

> Oh, we are decidedly a short dress man. It is not in our power to pass much time with the ladies, and we wish, during our brief opportunity, to see as much of them as we can with propriety.[7]

In San Francisco, a group of men crowded around a store that sold bloomers and bribed passersby to enter the store so they could see the clerk in her outfit. Illustrations also emphasized the display of the ankles and feet. Some prostitutes and dance hall girls were also reported wearing the outfit, further blackening its reputation, and prompting critics to warn that "women of true modesty and stainless purity" should not don the outfit. The reformers rejoined that prostitutes also wore long skirts.[8]

It was ultimately the issue of the right of women to wear trousers that led to the costume's defeat. The outfit's opponents supported their argument with verses from the Bible, usually Deuteronomy 22:5, "A woman shall not wear anything that pertains to a man, nor shall a man put on a woman's garment; for whoever does these things is an abomination to the Lord your God." Proponents of the outfit declared that this did not name trousers as the distinctive garment of the sexes.[9]

Because trousers were so identified with men, women wearing them were accused of looking like men. For example, one writer suggested naming the outfit "The Tom Boy" rather than the Bloomer. When an engraving of Mrs. Bloomer appeared in *The Lily* in September 1851, she jokingly wrote that she hoped her female readers would not be shocked by her appearance or that her male readers mistake her for a man. When Elizabeth Cady Stanton attended a women's rights convention in 1852 wearing bloomers, one journalist accused Mrs. Stanton of being dressed like a man down to boots, pants, a dickey, and a vest.[10]

Women who wore trousers, said the detractors of the Bloomer, might start to behave like men as well as look like them. Since most women who advocated the Bloomer participated in the women's rights movement, the threat seemed all the more real. Many people saw the acceptance of the Bloomer as the acceptance of women's rights, also believing women's rights threatened to change existing gender relationships. As one letter sent to the *New York Tribune* claimed,

> This Bloomer movement is a spawn of the late Women's Rights Conventions, where the injuries of the sex, and their solemn determination to be women no longer were deliberately considered and voted upon.[11]

Mrs. Nicholls, one of the reformers, perceived the relationship between appearance and accepted gender roles when she said, "there are still some of that class remaining who will think that if women wear clothes that will allow them to walk, they will walk away from their duties."[12]

Women's duties as wives and mothers were part of a system of accepted gender conventions. This set of ideal attributes of male and female behavior had been firmly in place since the 1830s and was not to change again until near the end of the nineteenth century. They were believed to be ordained by God and confirmed by science. Men were aggressive, women submissive. Women were pure and a civilizing influence, men corruptible. Women were emotional, men rational. Women were domestic, men were ambitious in the marketplace. The list goes on and on.

The women dress reformers may have advocated equal legal rights for women, but they did not think this would change the inherent natures of men and women. Women would remain the pure and civilizing influence of society (hence their involvement in temperance and other social reform movements). But with legal rights they might be able to mitigate men's power by injecting some of women's values into national affairs. They also firmly believed in their roles as wives and mothers. Or, as Amelia Bloomer said,

> To make gentlemen . . . 'now a days' we must, in addition to the rattans, grey hounds and cigars, coax our whiskers and moustaches out a few inches, learn to chew tobacco and skirt the juice about over carpets and furniture, drink whiskey toddies, and swear genteely! Well, there is no telling what we may come to, but as God made us women, nothing less powerful than his Almighty arm can make us any thing else.[13]

The popular press, however, interpreted the adoption of trousers as a sign that women did want to act, as well as look, like men. For example, Arthur Nelson of *The Cottage Gazette* accused women of wearing shirt collars, and expressed his conviction that women would continue to masculinize their appearance by strapping down their pantaloons and wearing Wellingtons. Carrying canes and smoking cigars, he said, could not be far behind.[14] More than one illustrator echoed Nelson's fears by depicting women as he described them: wearing Wellingtons, carrying canes, and puffing on cigars.

The insinuations of gender role reversal usually appeared in satirical form. Several newspapers reprinted a fictional store advertisement that originally appeared in *The St. Alabama Messenger.* Women could purchase a Bloomer outfit, complete with the related goods of boots, pants, vests, dickeys, canes, cigars, and razors in the shop. The proprietress informed her customers that in her absence at women's rights conventions her husband was her authorized agent. He could be found in the shop or working in the adjoining kitchen. The store's address was Hen Peck Lane.[15]

Cartoonists capitalized on these insinuations. One cartoon printed in *Harper's New Monthly Magazine* depicted a woman proposing marriage to a man, who informed her that she must get permission from his mother. In another image from *Harper's,* two confident women in bloomers accost a meek young man in the street, offering to give him a ride home. He can only weakly plead that his mother is sending a coach for him. In both

Gender role reversal was a favorite theme in cartoons. In this 1852 example, the woman proposes marriage and the man replies, "You must really ask Mama." Note that the satire is not carried to the extreme of showing a man in a skirt.

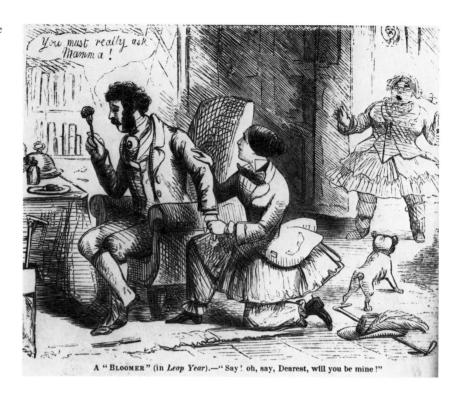

A "BLOOMER" (in *Leap Year*).—" Say! oh, say, Dearest, will you be mine?"

cases, the woman is exhibiting aggressive, male behavior, and the man passive behavior of women.

Women who wore the outfit were publicly taunted and ridiculed. Some dared not wear the outfit in public a second time. A parody of Hamlet's soliloquy in *Harper's Magazine* sums up the kinds of pressures brought to bear on a woman who publicly wore bloomers.

> To don the pants—
> The pants! perchance the boots! Ay, there's the rub
> For in those pants and boots what jeers may come.
> When we have shuffled off these untold skirts
> Must give us pause. There's the respect
> That makes calamity of so long a custom.
> For who could bear the scoffs and jeers of boys—
> The old maid's scandal—the young man's laughter—
> The sidelong leers, the derison's mock,
> The insolent press, and all the spurns . . .
> And makes us rather wear the dress we have,
> Than turn out Bloomers.[16]

One lady, who wished to remain anonymous, wrote *The Lily* confirming the power of this pressure. Men, she claimed, could withstand such pressure, but women must bow to the weight of public opinion. Social censure was all the more severe because it was other women, not men, who most stubbornly opposed the outfit.[17] In fact, pressure from friends and family forced Mrs. Stanton to abandon the costume not long after its introduction.[18]

An 1854 short story, "A Bloomer Among Us," published in *Godey's Lady's Book,* describes the forms of disapproval brought to bear on women. In the story, a young woman, Janet McLeod, visits her cousin in a small

New England town where she has been sent to learn Greek from a young professor. Her cousin and the professor are appalled when they meet Janet at the railroad station and find she is "A Bloomer." Neither wants to be seen publicly with her. At church Janet creates a sensation, so much so that the townspeople will not call on her or issue social invitations to her hosts. At the request of her father, whom Janet respects, she continues to wear the outfit. Eventually her health suffers. Learning the Bloomer is the cause of her ill health, her father relents. Once she resumes the long dress, the young professor proposes marriage, something he dared not do while she was still "A Bloomer." The moral of this story is twofold. First, Janet gets her reward—marriage—by conforming to public opinion. Second, Janet is a virtuous young woman who follows the wishes of her father until she falls in love, and then her allegiance shifts to the opinions of her fiancé. Only the most stout-minded could have withstood these pressures.

The Bloomer was quickly abandoned. Despite the publicity it received, few women actually wore the outfit. It was far too radical to gain widespread acceptance and it never truly threatened established styles. Today we have difficulty understanding the shock that greeted the first trousered women, but in the 1850s they appeared to most as ludicrous—similar to men in skirts in the 1980s. In the mid-nineteenth century, to appear in a garment exclusively worn by men—a powerful gender symbol—was to be masculine. If women were masculine, what were men? To accommodate women wearing trousers, the meaning of masculinity and feminity needed redefinition. Few were willing to question these conventions in the 1850s, leaving little chance that trousers for women would be accepted as normal daytime attire. Their acceptance was further hampered by their association with a group of reformers who advocated other controversial changes. While women did continue to wear trousers in the semiprivate arena of sports, they would have to wait until the next century to wear trousers freely, when new definitions of masculinity and femininity would allow them to do so without challenging the relationship between the sexes.

MEN'S HAIR LENGTH

Almost a century later, many young American men let their hair grow long. Although the older adults, especially men, who opposed the new look cited various reasons for their opposition, again the underlying fear was that more than appearance was being altered. They accused long-haired men of looking like women, and feared that long hair could encourage homosexuality.

As with the Bloomer Costume, we do not know the exact origins of the trend toward longer hair. No organized group adopted long hair as part of its program of social reform. During the 1960s a large number of youths both male and female participated in movements that advocated freedom of speech, supported civil rights, resisted the impersonality of a highly technical society, and opposed the Vietnam War. Rather than being a part of these movements, long hair became a rebellious symbol of identification

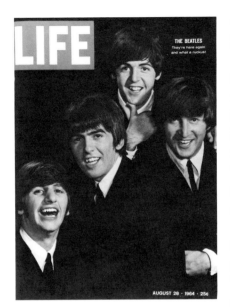

The Beatles drew national attention when they appeared on television in the "Ed Sullivan Show" in 1964. Although their hair seemed long to most Americans, they actually had shorter hair and were better groomed than many other British rock bands.

Young Edward Kores was suspended from his Connecticut high school when he appeared for classes in 1964. The school official stated that the boy's bangs were too much like those of the Beatles. By the late 1960s, this hairstyle would have been considered conservative.

with it. Even though criticism was intense, longer hair became acceptable by the end of the decade.

Although the complaints against the new look were different from those for the Bloomer Costume, the underlying fear was the same. Opponents charged that young men were defying authority by wearing their hair long, that the style was dangerous, and that long hair was dirty. But what bothered them most was the implied change in male/female relationships that could result from the blurring of the visual lines between the sexes. These fears were all the more real at the time because many aspects of society, including the definitions of masculinity and femininity, were being questioned.

Long hair, as a new look for men, probably originated in England. British rock-and-roll groups popularized the style in this country. The press usually singles out the Beatles for credit. When the band performed on the "Ed Sullivan Show" in February 1964, their tonsorial splendor caused as much controversy as their music. The press immediately labeled them "the mopheads." Ironically, even though Americans considered the Beatles' hair length radical, the Beatles were one of the best groomed of the British rock bands.[19] Guitarist Keith Richards of the Rolling Stones later said,

> When the Beatles were scruffy and dirty, we were just scruffier and dirtier. The long haired, dirty-rebel image was pushed on us here in the States. In London, we looked just exactly the same as the audience.[20]

A photo spread that appeared in *Look* on December 29, 1964, shows a variety of British male youths sporting longer and untidier hair than the Beatles.

When students reported to school in the fall of 1964, the reaction was immediate. The negative response was more intense in the eastern part of the country than on the West Coast. Edward T. Kores, Jr., of Westbrook, Connecticut, attended his first day of classes in the fall of 1964, only to have the school superintendent suspend him on the grounds that his bangs were too similar to those sported by the Beatles; the superintendent told Kores he could return to school if he brushed his bangs back.[21] A central issue was exactly who had the authority to decide what was masculine appearance. Was it the school, the family, the courts, or the boy? Fathers often disliked their sons' new hair length but found they had little or no authority to enforce their viewpoint. Sons did not politely follow their fathers' advice. Short of direct confrontation with scissors, there was little hope of changing their sons' appearance. Most schools had dress codes that were interpreted and enforced by the principals. For punishment, they suspended students or, sometimes, isolated long-haired students in separate classes. The headmaster in at least one private school cut students' hair as they passed through the front door if he thought it too long.[22] As a result of these actions and others, a few cases came to court as matters of personal freedom. However, the local judges who ruled on the cases often betrayed their own personal prejudices in their decisions. For example, an Indianapolis judge ruled that one boy should have his hair cut because it "would normally be described as feminine in style." He further stated that

STUDENTS OF NORWALK
BEAUTIFY AMERICA
get a haircut

Alan T Pearce

Many adults objected to long hair on the grounds that it looked dirty and unkempt. In 1968 billboards across the country urged young men to clean up themselves and, thus, America.

the trimming would not alter the young man's "opinions and beliefs, personality and individuality." Essentially the judge, like principals and superintendents, believed he had the right to define masculine appearance and the authority to enforce it.[23]

Others charged that long hair posed a safety threat to boys. For example, one high school physical education teacher maintained that long hair was dangerous to boys because it obscured their vision.[24] No one mentioned that girls, who often had long hair, might encounter the same problem. It is clear, as at least one author stated, that the distinction was being made, not on the grounds of safety, but on beliefs about appropriate masculine and feminine behavior.[25]

Some people worried lest vanity become part of the definition of masculinity. Well-groomed long hair implied giving time to caring for it. Some youths emphasized the fact that they had to wash their hair more frequently than when they had short hair.[26] Mick Jagger, lead singer of the British rock group the Rolling Stones, once stated in an interview "It [hair] is a sexual, personally vain thing. They've [men] always been taught that being masculine means looking clean, cropped and ugly."[27] The current definition of masculinity implied not being overly concerned with one's appearance. With the acceptance of long hair, vanity—formerly the preserve of women—crept into masculine behavior.

Others felt that long hair was dirty and unkempt because they associated the look with hippies. Hippies, first brought to national attention in 1967, "dropped out" of society by rejecting traditional values, living instead in groups or communes where they shared material goods, sexual promiscuity, and lack of concern with accepted norms of physical cleanliness.

Actually, there were very few true hippies. Many more American youths were trying to reform society, not reject it.[28] Some reformers railed against the impersonality of society, evidenced by technology and the corporate

"My daughter tells me you're a member of the opposite sex."

The older man in this 1967 cartoon is clearly confused by the mixed gender messages he receives from his daughter's boyfriend. Young people themselves had no difficulty in identifying each other's sex.

structure. Some supported the notion that all people had the right to equal opportunities and the right to live in peace. And many challenged the set of gender conventions that society had accepted after World War II. Some women in the 1960s refused to be defined as full-time wives and mothers, demanding education and jobs—including equal pay for the same work. Conversely, many young men, fighting their definition as breadwinners who conformed to the corporate structure, claimed that men could be nurturing. They felt they could assist in raising children and housework. The institution of marriage was challenged by young people of both sexes. They believed men and women could have sexual relationships without marriage and friendships between men and women could exist. All of these threats to the accepted gender roles caused great unease in society and hostility to their proponents. The lengthening of men's hair was visual evidence to many that these traditional roles of men and women were in transition.

Critics of long hair charged that men and women—even if only superficially—looked too much alike. In one cartoon, the father is disturbed by the ambivalence of the youth's sexual identity. Many found this blurring of the visual lines between the sexes frightening. As Bruce Jay Friedman, novelist and social commentator, explained, the behavior of people who opposed long hair

> implies that there is a *threat* in long hair and the choppers are worried about something much more subtle than sloppy thinking . . . but I guess that what frightens them is that if the boys wear their hair long, why then the boys are going to look like girls, and the lines between the sexes are going to get blurrier than ever. This can be frightening, and what better solution than to chop off a little hair so that the sex division can be all tidy again.[29]

One sociologist, Charles Winick, in a book entitled *The New People,* alleged that the unisex look, partly represented by hair, indicated that all mankind was undergoing a desexualization process; he predicted that the confusion over sexual identities would result in a decreased reproduction rate and the end of mankind.[30]

Many older adults worried that young men who looked like women might behave in a feminine manner. Young men themselves belittled this fear. In fact, they felt long hair made them more masculine and sexually attractive. In a *Good Housekeeping* feature, for example, a teacher who personally disliked long hair wrote an open letter to a father of a boy who refused to cut his hair. The father had told his son that only sissies wore long hair. The teacher pointed out that short hair did not create masculinity, and informed the father that boys with long, but clean, hair were the most popular with girls.[31] Other long-haired men, when interviewed, said they felt more masculine with long hair and their wives or girl friends liked the style.[32] In another story from the *New York Times,* two young long-haired men traveling across the United States reported their amusement when motorists, seeing them shirtless, were disappointed to learn that they were men.[33] One *Times* reader responded by expressing his surprise that young men could find it humorous to be mistaken for women and, by implication, to have their masculinity questioned.[34] These young men were only amused by the incident, however, knowing their peers accepted long hair as normal masculine appearance.

Organized sports and the armed forces vehemently opposed long hair because of its supposed feminization of men. Officials equated long hair with the passive behavior they associated with women. Sports in particular illustrate the resistance to the changing appearance of men. When the initial controversy over hair length erupted in the early 1960s, it was a moot issue for athletes. Few young men dared to confront a school coach for fear of being eliminated from the team. As *Newsweek* reported in 1965, forty-seven football players at Haverhill High School in Massachusetts promptly cut their hair when the coach told them, "Either get haircuts or don't play ball. I'm not coaching a girls' team."[35] But within a few years rebellion was in the ranks. By then school officials often sided with the youths. Some coaches quit rather than be associated with long-haired teams.[36] Some saw the acceptance of long hair as a loss of authority over the students, others saw it as a feminization of athletics. Tony Simpson, a football coach at North Short Junior High School near Houston, Texas, wrote on the subject for the *Texas High School Coaches Association Magazine* in 1973. He stated that American coaches should not allow themselves to be represented by male teams that looked like females.[37] He intimated that the appearance of his team reflected on his own masculinity. Newspapers, including the *New York Times* and the *Los Angeles Times,* reprinted his remarks; many readers responded. In Los Angeles, a man who had been both a player and a coach was upset by Simpson's attitude and what he termed a "gross lack of awareness." The reader pointed out that athletes played with their minds and their bodies, not with their hair, and that short hair did not make a player masculine.[38]

Some people viewed this "feminized" appearance as evidence of homosexuality. If men and women looked similar, they reasoned, and particularly if men looked like women, then men might as easily be attracted to their own sex as the opposite. The dean of one school suspended a long-haired youth "because he feared fighting in the school as a result of taunts to the boy, such as 'hello, fag.'" When asked by a reporter if there had already been encounters of this kind, the man admitted that there had been no incidents between long- and short-haired boys. His objections reflected his own uncertainties rather than the reality among the student population. The student was reinstated.[39]

There were occasionally violent responses to long-haired youths. One young man told how, only a few years previously, he had walked down Sunset Boulevard in Hollywood with onlookers staring, pointing, or yelling "Hi, Miss," but generally leaving him alone. By 1967 people were throwing things at him as he passed.[40] In the 1969 movie *Easy Rider,* two men, played by Peter Fonda and Dennis Hopper, travel by motorcycle across the country. Their appearance wins them acceptance at a commune but gets them arrested and harassed in a small Southern town. At a restaurant, a waitress ignores them at the same time a group of young women ogles them. The sheriff and a local man sitting at a booth have the following exchange:

The 1969 movie *Easy Rider* epitomized the long-haired rebellious appearance of male youth. The movie also suggested the conflicting implications of the look—that young men might look feminine on one hand but heterosexually attractive on the other.

Local: Check that yokel with the long hair.

Sheriff: I've checked him already. Like we might have to bring him up to the Hilton [jail] before it's all over with.

Local: Ha! I think she's cute.

Sheriff: Isn't she though?

Local: I'll guess we'll put him in a woman's cell, don't you reckon?

Sheriff: I think we ought to put him in a cage and charge admission to see him.[41]

Ironically, after these accusations of femininity, the young girls follow the men out of the restaurant and beg to be taken for a motorcycle ride. The men refuse, because the sheriff and customer are watching them through the windows.

On one hand, the sheriff and the local man accuse the men of looking like women. On the other, they fear the young men's sexuality, which they equate with hippie-like appearance. In the movie, Fonda and Hopper are beaten and eventually murdered. All the things long hair was thought to stand for—disrespect for authority, drugs, uncleanliness, sexuality, and, as the movie claims, freedom—caused visceral violent reaction. One journalist reported that the film imitated life, when, within a day or two of seeing the movie, he witnessed a long-haired youth being threatened by a cab driver and saw a waitress being rude to two long-haired students from California.[42]

In spite of opposition, however, longer hair came to be accepted for men of all ages. The hairstyles that Edward Kores and the Beatles wore in the early 1960s were conservative by 1969. The *Washington Post* noted the relatively longer hair lengths of some prominent Washingtonians in a 1971 article.

When both blurred the visual distinctions between the sexes, why was long hair for men eventually accepted but the Bloomer Costume unsuccessful? The answer may lie with the time in which the proposed changes occurred and exactly who opposed and who proposed the new look.

In the 1850s gender conventions were stable and firmly in place. Although the idea of universal reform was well known, it was supported by a relatively small group of people and few major changes were achieved. The identification of the proponents of the Bloomer Costume with the Women's Rights Movement further hindered its acceptance. Men and women of the same class were the main opponents of the outfit. Under these conditions the chance of success for such a radical change was minimal.

The situation was quite different in the 1960s, when all aspects of society, including gender relationships, were being challenged by a larger percentage of the population. In essence, the idea of any change fell on more fertile ground. Also, long-haired young men were supported by other youths, both male and female. It was older people who opposed the new length. With strong peer support it was easier to defy tradition.

The reaction to the Bloomer Costume for women and long hair for men prove that American society has in part defined masculinity and femininity in terms of appearance. As these two instances show, when one sex adopts a potent gender symbol from the opposite sex, the response is immediate. Many people fear that more than just outward appearance is being changed. These reactions demonstrate how intertwined are our views of male and female appearance and behavior. When a major change wins acceptance, it is an indication that society has redefined what it is to *be,* and thus, to *look* like a man or woman.

JO B. PAOLETTI and CLAUDIA BRUSH KIDWELL

CONCLUSION

We began with three basic questions. How does fashion express gender? What does it mean when gender conventions change or are challenged? And does the existence of gendered dress imply the existence of sexual inequality? Much of this book has addressed the first question, examining dress in a variety of settings: cross-culturally, in children's clothing, as an erotic stimulus, in the workplace, and in sports. The process of changing gender symbols has dominated the last two chapters. Within each chapter, an answer to the third question has been elusive. But looking over the finished work, we find that not only has truly androgynous dress never existed for adult men and women, but the closest we have ever come to androgyny is for women to dress like men.

How does fashion express gender? While dress can reinforce the physical differences between men and women, padded shoulders, for example, have been perceived as both feminine and masculine. Dress also reflects social differences between the sexes, such as women's more restricted public lives, the need for men to project authority, and the emphasis on physical attractiveness as the measure of a woman's value. As women entered occupations previously dominated by men, they have adopted more or less masculine styles. But despite these changes, men's and women's appearance is almost never identical. There is continuing pressure to retain some distinguishing features.

Certain symbols resist change stubbornly. Consider the time required for women to adopt trousers for everyday dress. In the process new feminine forms of trousers appeared, as if to mitigate the extent to which a potent male symbol was being usurped. Skirts are another rigid symbol. Their use for children in the nineteenth century was acceptable only insofar as infants and young children did not need to be identified publicly by gen-

This striking 1986 advertisement shows both the man and the woman wearing garments based on traditional masculine forms and materials. Significantly, men are much less likely to wear clothes drawn from feminine tradition, perhaps because male and female are valued differently.

der. Distinctions between male and female dress have been maintained both by keeping a few symbols tightly bound to masculinity or femininity and by transforming borrowed symbols.

The overwhelming direction in the borrowing of gender symbols is from the men's to women's dress. Nor is this a twentieth-century phenomenon, as women's adoption of hats during the sixteenth-century reveals. Examples of men imitating women's dress are rare. Even when apparently feminine symbols are borrowed, justification is offered by citing examples of *men's* earlier use of the style. Long-haired youths in the late 1960s countered criticism by pointing out that Jesus had long hair.

What does it mean when gender symbols change or are challenged? Fashion change is a complicated activity, involving individual choice and a vast manufacturing and distribution complex. The biggest gap in our understanding becomes evident when we attempt to find the motivation behind a fashion change. Consider the round-shouldered suit in the style of the New Look, for example. Did individuals see it as more feminine than previous styles, or as a welcome change from years of regulated sameness? There is a temptation to attach too great a significance to changes in gender symbols. When potent symbols of one gender are adopted by another (such as the introduction of trousers for women or long hair for men), the public reacts as if basic gender conventions are being threatened. But not all fashion changes have significant meaning. Clothing styles are influenced by more factors than gender, and they change more frequently than do accepted definitions of masculinity and femininity. To read gender significance into the nuances of fashion would be oversimplifying a complex form of communication. A brief vogue for three-inch heels does not foreshadow a repeal of the nineteenth amendment.

The period from approximately 1880 to 1920 was a time when gender conventions *and* gender images changed. Men, women, and children of the

1920s looked significantly different than their parents. But we must be accurate in interpreting the new look, since the connection between role and appearance is not usually simple and direct. Women's clothing of the twenties had become lighter in weight and much less restricting, allowing more physical freedom. The new body-skimming silhouette represented important changes: the acceptance of female athleticism and the introduction of a slimmer ideal of feminine beauty. In general, the options for women's and girls' clothing increased a great deal in the span of a generation, mostly by the appropriation of formerly masculine-style features. At the same time, women and girls did actually begin to enjoy more options in education, sports, and work, although these social changes were well underway in the late nineteenth century. In contrast, the changes that affected men's and boys' clothing did not reflect corresponding changes in conventional masculinity, but instead represented a new expression of the traditional masculine image.

Controversial fashion changes such as women adopting trousers can only take place after women's roles in society have altered. The mass acceptance of a style may accompany a change in public opinion, but does not precede it. Dress reformers were correct in seeing the connection between women's roles and their clothing, but erred in believing that by changing the costume, changes in gender conventions would automatically follow.

Do differences between men's and women's dress imply the existence of sexual inequality? Women's clothing prior to the twentieth century was usually more restricting than men's and there are still women's styles that hamper natural movement or distort the body. But men's clothing is hardly perfect: women's legs have been liberated since the nineteen-twenties, while men continue to suffer through the summer heat in long trousers, suit coats, tight collars, and neckties. Women enjoy a much larger range of choices than men, including personal styles drawing almost entirely from mens' clothing.

It would appear that truly androgynous dress, if it existed, could eliminate the disadvantages of feminine and masculine dress, while combining their advantages. Yet styles that combine male *and* female characteristics that are worn by men *and* women have never been widely accepted. Women have incorporated almost every conceivable masculine element into their dress, but for men to adopt potent feminine symbols raises questions about their masculinity. Why is it more acceptable for women to copy men's clothing than for men to adopt women's clothing? Could it be, in part, because masculine symbols are valued more highly? If this is true, then women's adoption of trousers represents an important readjustment of the definition of femininity, but not necessarily a change in the existing balance of power.

Will distinctive masculine and feminine apparel ever become obsolete? If there isn't distinctive clothing, what might be worn? In 1970 the avant-garde designer Rudi Gernreich predicted that by 1980 male and female dress would be interchangeable. From his vantage point amidst the upheavals of the 1960s, Gernreich envisioned men and women in unisex

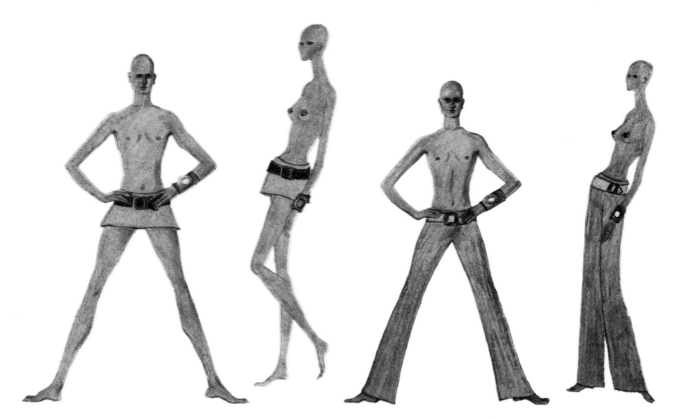

In 1970 the avant-garde designer Rudi Gernreich predicted that by 1980 young men and women would wear skirts and trousers interchangeably. Yet, his man and woman are posed in the familiar stances signifying male power and female submission.

styles with their appearance differentiated by anatomy alone. His clothing was functional, devoid of gender symbolism. Yet the differences in young masculine and feminine bodies were celebrated. Gernreich's view was radical even for his time. But Gernreich could not exorcise traditional patterns of gender imagery from his vision of an egalitarian future. His man and woman dressed identically but posed in the familiar stances of angular, erect male and curving, submissive female. Gernreich's designs are no less radical today than they were twenty years ago.

Men and women will never be the same, but their differences need not give them unequal status. It is possible that someday women and men will be valued equally, for all their differences. The clothes we wear today do not indicate that this will happen soon. If and when equality comes, both men and women will be free to express their unique individuality drawing from the broad vocabulary of masculinity and femininity.

NOTES

INTRODUCTION

1. Ann Oakley, *Sex, Gender and Society* (New York: Harper & Row, 1972), p. 16.
2. Roland Barthes, *The Fashion System*, trans. Matthew Ward and Richard Howard (New York: Hill and Wang, 1983).
3. Rudi Gernreich, *Life*, January 9, 1970.

APPEARANCE AND IDENTITY

1. Fred Davis, "Clothing and Fashion as Communication," in *The Psychology of Fashion*, ed. Michael Solomon (Lexington, Mass.: D.C. Heath & Company, 1985), pp. 15–26. See also Philippe Perrot, *Les Dessus et les dessous de la bourgeoisie. Une histoire du vêtement au XIXe siecle* (Paris: Librairie Artheme Fayard, 1981); and Domna Stanton, *The Aristocrat as Art: A Study of the Honnête Homme and the Dandy in Seventeenth- and Nineteenth-Century French Literature* (New York: Columbia University Press, 1980).
2. Eve Merriam, *Figleaf: The Business of Being in Fashion* (Philadelphia and New York: J. B. Lippincott Co., 1960), p. 9.
3. Jean Jacques Rousseau, *Emile* (1762), quoted in Susan Groag Bell, ed., *Women from the Greeks to the French Revolution* (Stanford: Stanford University Press, 1973), p. 263.
4. *La Toilette des dames, ou traité de la beauté* (1822), quoted in Grazietta Butazzi, *La Mode: art, histoire et société* (Paris: Hachette et Cie, 1983), p. 215.
5. Anne Hollander, "The New Androgeny," *The New Republic*, January 28, 1985, p. 28.
6. For a description of neoteny see chapter 10 of Stephen Jay Gould, *Ontogeny and Phylogeny* (Cambridge, Massachusetts, and London, England: The Belknap Press of Harvard University Press, 1977).
7. For recent anthropological studies on dress and adornment see Robert Brain, *The Decorated Body* (New York: Harper & Row, 1979), and Justine M. Cord-

well and Ronald Schwarz (eds.), *The Fabrics of Culture: The Anthropology of Clothing* (New York: Mouton Publishers, 1979).

8. Angela Fisher, *Africa Adorned* (New York: Abrams, 1984), p. 70.

9. *New York Times,* October 20, 1985, Business section.

10. For information on the history of trousers and skirts see Francois Boucher, *Histoire du costume en Occident de l'antiquité à nos jours* (Paris: Flammarion, 1967), and Shen Congwen, *Zhongguo gudai fushi yanjiu* [Researches on Ancient Chinese Costume] (Beijing and Hong Kong: The Commercial Press, 1981).

11. Valerie Steele, "The Social and Political Significance of Macaroni Fashion," *Costume: The Journal of the Costume Society* (London, 1985), pp. 94–109.

12. Robert Riegel, "Women's Clothes and Women's Rights," *American Quarterly,* vol. 15 (Fall 1963), pp. 390–401.

13. Valerie Steele, "Fashion in China," *Dress: The Journal of the American Costume Society* (1983).

THE CHILDREN'S DEPARTMENT

1. Lloyd de Mause, ed., "The Evolution of Childhood," *The History of Childhood* (New York: Harper and Row, 1974).

2. G. Stanley Hall, "Feminization in School and Home," *World's Work,* vol. 16 (May 1908), pp. 10237–44.

3. *The Twin Babies Cut-out Paper Doll Book* (New York: Merrimack Publishing Corporation, 1983), originally published in the late 1930s by an unknown company.

4. *Ladies Home Journal,* February 1905, p. 65.

5. Carol B. Seavy, Phyllis A. Katz, and Sue Rosenberg Zalk, "Baby X: The Effect of Gender Label on Adult Responses to Infants," *Sex Roles,* vol. 1, no. 2 (1975), pp. 103–109.

6. Harriet Spofford, *House and Hearth* (New York: Dodd, Mead, 1891), pp. 266–7.

7. May Byron, "The Little Boy," *The Living Age,* November 22, 1901, p. 489.

8. *Godey's Lady's Book and Magazine,* April 1870, p. 398.

9. Elisabeth Robinson Scovil, "The Art of Dressing the Boy," *Ladies Home Journal,* March 1895, p. 22.

10. "Children's Clothes," *New York Times,* May 7, 1892, p. 12.

11. Mrs. Burton Kingsland, "The Problem of the Small Boy," *Outlook,* August 25, 1894, pp. 307–308.

12. Robert Tomes, *The Bazaar Book of the Household* (New York: Harper and Brothers, 1875), p. 214.

13. Charlotte Perkins Gilman, "Children's Clothing," *Harper's Bazar,* January 1910, p. 24.

14. Kate Wiggin, *Children's Rights* (publisher not given, 1892), p. 12.

15. Gilman, p. 24.

16. Hunter Dickinson Farish, *Journal and Letters of Philip Vickers Fithian 1773–1774* (Charlottesville, Virginia: Dominion Books, 1968), p. 193.

17. Susanna Millar, *The Psychology of Play* (Baltimore: Penguin, 1968).

18. Alasdair Roberts, *Out to Play: The Middle Years of Childhood* (Aberdeen, Scotland: Aberdeen University Press, 1980).

19. Oscar Handlin and Mary F. Handlin, *Facing Life* (Boston: Little, Brown and Company, 1971).

20. Joseph Lee in Sarah Comstock, "Your Girl at Play," *Good Housekeeping,* February 1917, p. 24.

21. Jean Schick Grossman, *Do You Know Your Daughter?* (New York: D. Appleton-Century Co., 1944).

22. George Bush and Perry London, "On the Disappearance of Knickers: Hypothesis for the Functional Analysis of the Psychology of Clothing," *Journal of Social Psychology,* vol. 51 (May 1960), pp. 359–366.

CLOTHING AND SEXUALITY

1. James Laver, *The Concise History of Costume and Fashion* (New York: Abrams, 1969), pp. 268–9, 272–273, and James Laver, *Taste and Fashion* (London: George G. Harrap & Co. 1937), pp. 200–201.
2. Ruth Rubinstein, "Fashion and Passion—Designers are Shifting the Erogenous Zones Again," *Washington Post Magazine,* September 9, 1984, pp. 31, 43–45.
3. Elizabeth Wilson, *Adorned in Dreams: Fashion and Modernity* (London: Virago Press, 1985), p. 92.
4. Mark Cook and Robert McHenry, *Sexual Attraction* (New York: Pergamon Press, 1978), pp. 1, 6, (emphasis added).
5. S. Ginsberg, "Victoria's Secret is the subtle, sexy look," *Women's Wear Daily,* November 19, 1981, p. 12.
6. Alison Lurie, *The Language of Clothes* (New York: Random House, 1981), pp. 242–245.
7. R. W. Wildman, et al., "Note on males' and females' preferences for opposite sex body parts, bust sizes and bust revealing clothing," *Psychological Reports,* vol. 38, no. 2 (1976), pp. 485–486; E. A. McCullough, et al., "Sexually attractive clothing: Attitudes and usage," *Home Economics Research Journal,* Vol. 6, No. 2 (1977), pp. 164–170.
8. Studies by Terry and Doerge (1979) and Kanekar and Kolsawalla (1980) are cited in Susan B. Kaiser, *The Social Psychology of Clothing* (New York: Mac-Millan, 1985), pp. 48–49.
9. Brigitte Nioche, *The Sensual Dresser* (New York: Oxford University Press, 1981), p. 5.
10. Cook and McHenry, pp. 16–19.
11. *Home Journal,* February 13, 1858, in William Leach, *True Love and Perfect Union* (London: Routledge & Kegan Paul, 1981), p. 219.
12. *The Complete Beauty Book* (New York, 1906), pp. 258–262.
13. Peter Gay, *The Bourgeois Experience from Victoria to Freud,* Vols. 1 and 2 (New York: Oxford University Press, 1985, 1986); Valerie Steele, *Fashion and Eroticism: Ideals of Feminine Beauty from the Victorian Era to the Jazz Age* (New York: Oxford University Press, 1985).
14. See, for example, *The Ladies' Realm* (April 1903), p. 767; Mrs. Eric Pritchard, *The Cult of Chiffon* (London, 1902), pp. 15, 20.
15. E. Ward & Co., *The Dress Reform Problem* (London, 1886), pp. 52–53.
16. *The Englishwoman's Domestic Magazine,* January 1871, p. 62.
17. *Society,* January 28, 1899, p. 1176. See also Steele, Chapter 9, "The Corset Controversy."
18. *La Vie Parisienne,* May 17, 1884, p. 271.
19. Beatrice Faust, *Women, Sex and Pornography* (Harmondsworth: Penguin, 1981), p. 49.
20. "Calvin's New Gender Benders," *Time,* September 5, 1983, p. 56.
21. *Esquire Magazine,* September 1985, p. 65.
22. Jo Paoletti, "Ridicule and Role Models as Factors in American Men's Fashion Change, 1880–1910," in *Costume* (London: The Costume Society, 1985), p. 124.
23. *Wall Street Journal,* October 15, 1984, p. 35.
24. See the sections on "Beefcake" and "Men and Beauty" in Robin Tolmach Lakoff and Rachel L. Scherr, *Face Value: The Politics of Beauty* (London: Routledge & Kegan Paul, 1984).

25. Kaiser, p. 237.

26. *New York Times Magazine,* December 7, 1986, p. 113.

27. *New York Times,* February 5, 1985, and July 31, 1985.

28. Wilson, pp. 130–133.

DRESSING FOR WORK

1. "As Business Women Should and Should Not Dress," *Ladies Home Journal* (November 24, 1907), p. 25. See also Deborah Warner, *Perfect In Her Place: Women at Work in Industrial America* (Washington: Smithsonian Institution Press, 1981), n.p.

2. Personal communication.

3. Leonard Bickman, "Social Roles and Uniforms," *Psychology Today,* April 1974, p. 102. Thanks also are extended to Barbara Melosh and Dr. Pam Steele for their comments.

4. *Police Women* (New York: Dan Cooper Productions for the New York City Police Department, 1985), videotape.

5. A. E. Costello, *History of the New York City Police Department: Our Police Protectors* (New York: published by the author, 1885), pp. 127–8.

6. Clipping from *Gleason's Pictorial Journal,* 1856, month unknown, p. 16, in the collection of the Police Museum of New York City; Costello, p. 127.

7. Peter Horne, *Women in Law Enforcement* (Springfield, Illinois: Charles C. Thomas, 1975), pp. 26–28.

8. "Establishing Policewomen in Maryland in 1912," proceedings of the National Conference of Charities and Correction (1915), p. 420; Bertha Smith, "The Policewoman," *Good Housekeeping Magazine,* March 1911, p. 296. See also "Policewomen in Chicago," *The Literary Digest,* August 23, 1913, p. 271; "Policewomen and Their Work," *The American City,* January 1919, p. 59.

9. Patricia Peyser, *A Century of Women in Policing,* Police Department of New York City, 1985, n.p.

10. *Good Housekeeping Magazine,* December 1941, pp. 26–27.

11. Horne, p. 133.

12. Lee Michael Katz, "Top Cop," *The Washington Woman,* January 1985, p. 26.

13. Unidentified New York City newspaper article from 1957, on display at the 1985 policewomen exhibition at the New York City Police Museum.

14. *Wall Street Journal,* October 24, 1984.

15. *Wall Street Journal,* October 31, 1984.

16. "Police Uniforms: Navy is Good," *Psychology Today,* June 1985, p. 72.

17. Logan Clendening, *Behind the Doctor* (New York: Knopf, 1943), p. 386.

18. Dan W. Blumhagen, M.D., "The Doctor's White Coat: The Image of the Physician in Modern America," *Annals of Internal Medicine,* Vol. 9, No. 1 (July 1979), pp. 111–116, see especially p. 112.

19. Blumhagen, pp. 111, 113–115.

20. Florence Nightingale, *Notes on Nursing: What It is, and What It Is Not* (Boston: William Carter, 1860), preface, p. iii.

21. *Hospitals and Sisterhoods* (London: John Murray, 1854), in Victor Robinson, M.D., *White Caps: The Story of Nursing* (Philadelphia and New York: J. B. Lippincott, 1946), p. 392.

22. Robinson, p. 252.

23. M. Adelaide Nutting and Lavinia Dock, *A History of Nursing* (New York: Putnam, 1907) Vol. 2, pp. 400–401, in "The Student Nurse's Uniform," *American Journal of Nursing,* Vol. 40, No. 11 (November 1940), p. 1205, emphasis added.

24. "The Student Nurse's Uniform," *American Journal of Nursing,* Vol. 40, No. 11, pp. 1208–9.

25. "Why a Cap?" *American Journal of Nursing,* Vol. 40, No. 4, pp. 384–386.

26. *New York Times,* January 15, 1986, Sec. C, p. 10.

27. Quoted in Ruth Abram, ed., *Send Us A Lady Physician* (New York: W. W. Norton, 1985), p. 73; see also pp. 233, 126.

28. *Newport Daily News,* July 13, 1896, p. 2.

29. Quoted in Edward Shorter, *Bedside Manners: The Troubled History of Doctors and Patients* (New York: Simon & Schuster, 1986), pp. 104–5.

30. Claudia B. Kidwell, *Suiting Everyone: The Democratization of Clothing in America* (Washington, D.C.: Smithsonian Press, 1974), p. 20.

31. *The Bazaar Book of Decorum* (New York: Harper & Bros., 1872), pp. 160–161.

32. "Why Painters Wear Whites," *Painters and Allied Trades Journal,* December 1985, pp. 14–15.

33. Alice Kessler-Harris, *Out to Work: A History of Wage-Earning Women in the United States* (New York: Oxford University Press, 1982), p. 14.

34. *The Spectator,* November 30, 1912, p. 891.

35. "Skirts or Overalls for Women," *American Machinist,* September 12, 1918, p. 487.

36. "Safety Equipment for the Protection of Women Operatives," *Automotive Industries,* July 25, 1918, p. 150.

37. Emily Burbank, *Smartly Dressed Woman: How She Does It* (New York: Dodd, Mead and Co., 1925), p. 88.

38. Anne Rittenhouse, *The Well-Dressed Woman* (New York: Harper & Brothers, 1924), p. 71.

39. "Women and Heavy War Work," *Monthly Labor Review,* September 1940, p. 567.

40. "When Shopping for a War Industry Job," *Independent Woman,* October 1943, p. 308.

41. "Danger—Curves," *Business Week,* October 17, 1942, p. 48.

42. Edith Head, *How to Dress for Success* (New York: Random House, 1967), pp. 1–17.

43. Edith Head, *The Dress Doctor* (Boston: Little, Brown, 1959), p. 193.

44. Anne Fogarty, *Wife Dressing* (New York: Julian Messner, 1959), pp. 25, 145.

45. Ingersoll Lockwood, *The P.G. or Perfect Gentleman* (New York, 1881), p. 29; *The Haberdasher,* Vol. 16, No. 6 (December 1892), p. 51.

46. Quoted in Alice Kessler-Harris, *Out to Work: A History of Wage-Earning Women in the United States* (New York: Oxford University Press, 1982), p. 70.

47. Quoted in Margery W. Davies, *Woman's Place is at the Typewriter: Office Work and Office Workers* (Philadelphia: Temple University Press, 1982), p. 21.

48. Walter Houghton, *American Etiquette and Rules of Politeness* (Chicago: Rand McNally, 1882), p. 266; *Ladies Home Journal,* April 1894, p. 27; *Good Housekeeping,* April 1906, p. 435.

49. Alexander Black, *Miss America* (New York: Scribners, 1898), pp. 60, 73.

50. *Woman's Home Companion,* August 1980, p. 33.

51. Ellen Lane Spencer, *The Efficient Secretary* (New York: Frederick A. Stokes, 1916), p. 27.

52. Elizabeth Hilliard Ragan, "One Secretary as per Specifications," *Saturday Evening Post,* December 12, 1931, p. 10, quoted in Margery W. Davies, p. 152.

53. Ragan, p. 11.

54. Kessler-Harris, p. 234.

55. Jo Paoletti, "Ridicule and Role Models as Factors in American Men's Fashion Change, 1880–1910," in *Costume,* (London: The Costume Society, 1985), pp. 121–134.

56. "Dress Proclaims the Man," *The Journal of Fashion and Tailoring,* Vol. 26, No. 5 May, 1893, p. 90. See also "Clothes Make the Man," Philadelphia 1772, reprinted as "Philosophy of Clothes," *Forum,* March 1912, p. 525.

57. George P. Fox, *Fashion: The Power that Influences the World* (New York: Sheldon & Co., 3rd edition, 1872), p. 19.

58. *American Gentleman,* March 1906, p. 81; April 1911, p. 20; and August 1912, p. 31.

59. *Mademoiselle,* September 1977, p. 218; see also John Molloy, *Dress for Success* (New York: Peter A. Wyden, 1976) and *The Woman's Dress for Success Book* (Chicago: Follett, 1977); *New York Times,* October 13, 1985, Careers supplement, p. 42.

60. Anne Hollander, "Issue of Skirting," *New Republic,* December 17, 1977, p. 27.

61. Molloy quoted in *Mademoiselle,* September 1977, p. 218; Molloy quoted in Susan Craighead, "Some Women Graduate from Business Suits," *Wall Street Journal,* August 14, 1985.

62. *New York Times,* October 13, 1985, Careers supplement, p. 42.; *Mademoiselle,* September 1977, p. 221.

63. Sandra J. Shea and Mary Todd Lyon, *A Girl's Guide to Executive Success* (Berkeley: Ten Speed Press, 1984), p. 50.

64. Sandra Salmans, "Women Dressing to Succeed Think Twice About the Suit," *New York Times,* November 4, 1985, sec. A, p. 1, and sec. D, p. 4.

65. *New York Times,* October 13, 1985, Careers supplement, p. 42. See also *Wall Street Journal,* August 14, 1985.

66. Egon von Furstenberg, *The Power Look* (New York: Holt, Rinehart and Winston, 1978), p. 87.

67. "A Sneaking Problem For Men," *New York Times,* October 26, 1985, Op-Ed page and *New York Times,* November 5, 1985, Letters column.

68. *Wall Street Journal,* September 5, 1984.

69. von Furstenberg, p. 72.

70. *New York Times,* November 4, 1985, sec. D., p. 4.

71. "Dress for Success in Court," *Harper's Magazine,* May 1984, p. 26, originally published in the *American Bar Association Journal.* See also *New York Times,* October 13, 1985, Careers supplement, p. 42.

72. Wendy Adams, "Proper Clothing Transmits Powerful, Positive Image," *Legal Times of Washington,* November 1982, sec. A, pp. 2–8.

73. *Ms. Magazine,* April 1984, p. 36.

74. "Life Styles," *The Real Paper,* March 1975.

75. Shea and Lyon, p. 12.

76. *Ms. Magazine,* April 1984, p. 36.

SPORTING WEAR

1. Henry J. Slocum, Jr., "Lawn Tennis as a Game for Women," *Outing,* Vol. 14 (July 1889), p. 287.

2. David L. Cohn, *The Good Old Days* (New York: Arno Press, reprinted 1976), p. 45.

3. Joe L. Dubbert, *A Man's Place* (New Jersey: Prentice-Hall, Inc., 1979), p. 180.

4. Raymond G. Gettell, "The Value of Football," *American Physical Education Review,* vol. 22 (March 1917), p. 139.

5. Peter G. Filene, *Him/Her/Self: Sex Roles in Modern America* (New York: The New American Library, 1976), p. 143.

6. John H. Moore, "Football's Ugly Decades, 1892–1913," *Smithsonian Journal of History,* Vol. 2 (Fall 1969), pp. 49–55.

7. Betty Spears and Richard Swanson, *History of Sport and Physical Activity in the United States* (Dubuque, Iowa: Wm. C. Brown, 1978), p. 136.

8. Dean Hill, *Football Thru the Years* (New York: Gridiron Publishing Company, 1940), p. 11.

9. Walter Camp and Lorin F. Deland, *Football* (Boston: Houghton, Mifflin and Company, 1896), pp. 27–28.

10. Hill, pp. 73–74.

11. Will Irwin, "Baseball: Working Out the Game," *Collier's,* vol. 44 (May 15, 1909), p. 15.

12. Patricia Vertinsky, "Sexual Equality and the Legacy of Catharine Beecher," *Journal of Sport History,* vol. 6 (Spring 1979), p. 39.

13. Lydia H. Sigourney, *Letters to Young Ladies* (New York: Harper and Brothers, 1837), p. 94.

14. Signor G. Voarino, *A Treatise on Calisthenic Exercise, Arranged for the Private Tuition of Ladies* (London: Chiswick, 1827), pp. 19–20.

15. Seba Smith, "Cure of a Hypochondrias," *Godey's Lady's Book,* vol. 20 (February 1840), pp. 55–57.

16. Eliza Ware Farrar, *The Young Lady's Friend* (Boston: American Stationers' Company, 1836), p. 42.

17. Carol Smith-Rosenberg and Charles Rosenberg, "The Female Animal: Medical Biological Views of Women and Her Role in Nineteenth Century America," *The Journal of American History,* vol. LX (September 1973), p. 342.

18. Julia Ward Howe, *Sex and Education* (1874), p. 10, quoted by Patricia Vertinsky, "Rhythmics—A Sort of Physical Jubilee: A New Look at the Contribution of Dio Lews," *Canadian Journal of History of Sport and Physical Education,* vol. 9 (May 1978), p. 37.

19. Sheila M. Rothman, *Woman's Proper Place: A History of Changing Ideals and Practices, 1870 to the Present* (New York: Basic Books, Inc., 1978), pp. 26–29.

20. Helen L. Horowitz, *Alma Mater: Design and Experience in the Women's Colleges from Their Nineteenth Century Beginnings to the 1930s* (New York: Alfred A. Knopf, 1984), p. 162.

21. Spears and Swanson, p. 124.

22. Carol A. Maccini, "Present in the Fifties," *WomenSports,* vol. 2 (October 1975), p. 52.

23. J. Parmly Paret, "Basket-ball for Young Women," *Harper's Bazaar,* October 20, 1900, p. 1563.

24. Lillian P. Randal, "Basketball, 1912–1916," *The Sportswoman,* vol. 2 (July/August 1974), p. 31.

25. Jeannette Marks, *Outing,* vol. 2 (May 1898), p. 118, quoted in Margery A. Bulger, "American Sportswomen in the 19th Century," *Journal of Popular Culture,* vol. 16 (Fall 1982), p. 13.

26. Ellen B. Thompson, "Athletics for Women—Basketball," *Delineator,* May 1902, p. 841.

27. Senda Berenson, *Basket Ball for Women* (New York: American Sports Publishing Co., 1901), p. 20.

28. Paret, pp. 1564–1567.

29. John R. Betts, *America's Sporting Heritage: 1850–1950* (Reading, Massachusetts: Addison-Wesley Publishing Company, 1974), pp. 314–319.

30. David Lamoreaux, "Baseball in the Late Nineteenth Century: The Source of Its Appeal," *Journal of Popular Culture,* vol. 11 (Winter 1977), pp. 605–606.

31. Don Schlossberg, *The Baseball Catalog* (New York: Jonathan David Publishers, Inc., 1980), p. 69.

32. Betts, p. 94.

33. Harold Seymour, *Baseball: The Early Years* (New York: Oxford University Press, 1960), p. 20.

34. Robert Smith, *Illustrated History of Baseball* (New York: Grosset & Dunlap Publishers, 1973), p. 35.

35. Seymour, p. 328.

36. Steven M. Gelber, "Their Hands are All Out Playing: Business and Amateur Baseball, 1845–1917," *Journal of Sport History,* vol. 11 (Spring 1984), p. 15.

37. Wells Twomby, *200 Years of Sport in America* (New York: McGraw-Hill Book Company, 1976), p. 75.

38. David S. Crockett, "Sports and Recreational Practices of Union and Confederate Soldiers," *The Research Quarterly,* vol. 32 (October 1961), pp. 335–347.

39. John Durant, "Though Beaten, Not Disgraced," in *Yesterday in Sport* (New York: Time-Life Books, 1968), p. 11.

40. Robert K. Barney, "Of Rails and Red Stockings," *Journal of the West,* vol. 17 (July 1978), p. 63.

41. Schlossberg, p. 67.

42. Schlossberg, p. 68.

43. *Sporting Life,* December 24, 1884, quoted in David Q. Voight, *American Baseball: From Gentleman's Sport to the Commissioner System* (Norman, Oklahoma: University of Oklahoma Press, 1966), p. 211.

44. Donald J. Mrozek, *Sport and American Mentality 1880–1910* (Knoxville, Tennessee: The University of Tennessee Press, 1983), pp. 144–145.

45. Ellen W. Gerber, et al., *The American Woman in Sport* (Reading, Massachusetts: Addison-Wesley Publishing Company, 1974), p. 12.

46. W. G. Nicholson, "Women's Pro Baseball Packed the Stands . . . Then Johnny Came Marching Home," *WomenSports,* vol. 3 (April 1976), pp. 23–24.

47. David Young "Seasons in the Sun," *WomenSports,* vol. 4 (October 1977), p. 51.

48. Mrs. J. Stirling Clarke, *The Habit and the Horse* (London: Smith, Elder & Co., 1857), p. 1.

49. Belle Beach, "Athletics for Women, No. 9—Equestrianism," *Delineator,* October 1902, p. 574.

50. F. M. Ware, "Learning to Ride, Part I," *Outing,* vol. 49 (December 1906), p. 415.

51. Midy Morgan, "How to Learn to Ride on Horseback," *Hearth & Home,* May 20, 1871, p. 371.

52. "Editorial Chit-Chat," *Peterson's Magazine,* September 1877, p. 22.

53. Mrs. Harry Allbutt (Annie Blood-Smyth), *Hints to Horsewomen* (London: Horace Cox, 1893), p. 96.

54. Thomas Craige, *A Conversation Between a Lady and her Horse* (Philadelphia: Thomas Craige, 1851), p. 96.

55. Clarke, p. 30.

56. Nancy Evans, "The Development of the Riding Habit, Part VIII: 1880–1900," *Side-saddle News,* vol. 12 (March/April 1985), p. 21.

57. Evans.

58. W. A. Kerr, *Riding for Ladies* (London: George Bell & Sons, 1891), p. 68.

59. Allbutt, p. 32.

60. Belle Beach, "Why I Ride Side-Saddle," *Country Life,* vol. XLII (July 1922), p. 72.

61. Ivy Maddison, *Riding Astride for Girls* (New York: Henry Holt, 1923), pp. 3–13.

62. Janet Macdonald and Valerie Francis, *Riding Side-saddle* (London: Pelham Books, 1978), p. 103.

63. Gary A. Tobin, "The Bicycle Boom of the 1890's: The Development of Private Transportation and the Birth of the Modern Tourist," *Journal of Popular Culture,* vol. 7 (Spring 1974), p. 839.

64. "Woman and the Bicycle," *The Forum,* vol. 20 (January 1896), p. 578.

65. Mrs. Reginald de Koven, "Bicycling For Women," *Cosmopolitan* August 1895, p. 394.

66. de Koven, p. 395.

67. "Bicycling and Bicycling Outfits," *Delineator,* vol. XLIII (April 1894), p. 419.

68. "Mrs. Hamlet's Soliloquy," *The Queen of Fashion,* vol. 22 (August 1895), p. 186.

69. "The Evolution of Dress," *The Queen of Fashion,* vol. 23 (October 1895), p. 18.

70. *The Queen of Fashion,* vol. 22 (June 1895), p. 149.

71. Irving A. Leonard, *When Bikehood Was In Flower* (Tucson, Arizona: Seven Palms Press, 1983), p. 120.

72. Mrozek, p. 126.

73. Charles E. Clay, "The Staten Island Cricket and Baseball Club," *Outing,* vol. XI (November 1887), p. 108.

74. Ellen Hansell Allderdice, "The First Women's Championship," in *Fifty Years of Lawn Tennis in the United States* (New York: United States Lawn Tennis Association, 1931), p. 41.

75. Slocum, pp. 296–298.

76. Mrs. Lambert Chambers, *Lawn Tennis for Ladies* (London: Methuen & Co., second edition, 1912), p. 64.

77. Helen Hull Jacobs, *Modern Tennis* (New York: Books, Inc., 1933), p. 181.

78. O. E. Schoeffler and William Gale, *Esquire's Encyclopedia of 20th Century Men's Fashions* (New York: McGraw-Hill, Inc., 1973), p. 415.

79. Bunny Austin, *Lawn Tennis Made Easy* (London: Methuen & Co., Ltd., 1935), pp. 105–106.

80. Schoeffler and Gale, p. 416.

81. Austin, p. 107.

82. Kate Broughton, "Survival of the Fittest," *Longwood,* July 7, 1982, p. 17.

83. Claudia Kidwell, "Women's Bathing and Swimming Costume in the United States," *United States National Museum Bulletin,* vol. 250, paper 64 (1968), p. 9.

84. *The Science of Swimming as Taught and Practised in Civilized and Savage Nations* (New York: Fowler and Wells, 1849), pp. 16–17.

85. Schoeffler and Gale, pp. 420–422.

86. Schoeffler and Gale, p. 424.

87. Loudon Murdock, "A Revolution in Beach Clothes on the Riviera," *Men's Wear,* September 23, 1931, p. 52.

88. "Bathing Apparel," *Apparel Arts* (Summer 1932), p. 139.

89. Kidwell, pp. 7–9, 14–15.

90. Charles E. Funnell, *By the Beautiful Sea* (New York: Alfred A. Knopf, 1975), p. 41.

91. J. Howe Adams, "Bathing At the American Sea-Shore Resorts," *Cosmopolitan,* July 1895, p. 319.

92. Kidwell, p. 25.

93. Cohn, p. 392.

94. Mrs. Samudan, "Swimming," *The Gentlewoman's Book of Sports,* ed. Lady Grebelie (London: Henry & Co., n.d.), pp. 118–119.

95. Funnell, p. 43.

96. Edwin Sandys, "Athletics for Women—Swimming," *Delineator,* vol. LIX (June 1902), p. 1004.

97. Kidwell, pp. 24–29.

98. Grantland Rice, "Look Out for the Ladies," *Collier's,* February 21, 1925, p. 19.

99. Dale A. Somers, "The Leisure Revolution: Recreation in the American City, 1820–1920," *Journal of Popular Culture,* vol. V (Summer 1971), p. 127.

100. Kenneth Clark, *The Nude: A Study in Ideal Form* (New York: Doubleday Anchor Books, 1956), p. 42.

101. Gay Talese, "Men and Women Are Working Out, but Are They Working it Out," *Esquire,* November 1984, p. 91.

102. Camille Duhe, "Custom Body Work," *Gentleman's Quarterly,* September 1984, p. 156.

103. William E. Blundell, "Workouts on Wheels Now Bring Exercise to Where the Flab Is," *Wall Street Journal,* July 16, 1985.

1. Desmond Morris, *Bodywatching* (New York: Crown Publishers Inc., 1985), pp. 129–130.

2. *Fashion Digest,* Fall 1938, p. 66.

3. John F. Watson, *Annals and Occurrences of New York City and State, in the Olden Time* (Philadelphia: Henry F. Anners, 1846), p. 247. Small waists appeared as the latest fashion for men in nineteenth-century England in the second decade, prompting numerous cartoons ridiculing this innovation as extreme dress of dandies. By the 1840s the silhouette had evolved, lowering the small waist and expanding the chest.

4. *Mahan's Protractor and Proof Systems of Garment Cutting,* Fall/Winter 1843/1844, p. 7.

5. *Art of Good Behaviour* (New York City: Hvestis & Cozous, 1850), p. 12.

6. C. Willett Cunnington and Phillis Cunnington, *The History of Underclothes* (London & Boston: Faber and Faber, 1981), p. 80.

7. John F. Watson, *Annals of Philadelphia and Pennsylvania, in the Olden Time* (Philadelphia: published by the author, 1850), p. 194.

8. *Mahan's Protractor and Proof Systems of Garment Cutting,* Spring/Summer 1843, p. 8.

9. Erna Risch and Thomas M. Pitkin, "Clothing of the Soldier of World War II," *Quarter Master Corps Historical Studies No. 16* (Washington, D.C.: U.S. Government Printing Office, 1946), pp. 30–41.

10. *Men's Wear,* March 21, 1923, p. 72.

11. *Men's Wear,* November 21, 1923, p. 72.

12. *Men's Wear,* January 23, 1924, p. 19.

13. *Men's Wear,* June 9, 1926, p. 83.

14. *Women's Wear Daily,* August 4, 1931, sec. 1, p. 1.

15. *Women's Wear Daily,* August 11, 1931, sec. 1, p. 1.

16. *Women's Wear Daily,* April 28, 1932, p. 3.

17. Joseph Simms, "ADRIAN—American Artist and Designer," *Costume, The Journal of the Costume Society,* (1974), no. 8, p. 15.

18. *Sears, Roebuck and Co. Catalogue,* Spring and Summer, 1933, p. 6.

19. *Harper's Bazaar,* February 1932, p. 41.

20. *Harper's Bazaar,* April 1933, p. 60.

21. *Men's Wear,* July 25, 1928, p. 94.

22. *Men's Wear,* September 21, 1921, p. 14.

23. *Men's Wear,* June 22, 1932, p. 19.

24. *Men's Wear,* August 10, 1938, p. 29.

25. *Harper's Bazaar,* July 1940, pp. 56–57.

26. *Harper's Bazaar,* September 1, 1941, p. 41.

27. *Women's Wear Daily,* May 4, 1932, sec. 2, p. 1.

28. *Harper's Bazaar,* March 1, 1941, p. 41.

29. Stanley Marcus, *Minding the Store* (Boston: Little Brown & Co., Inc., 1975), p. 78–84.

30. *Vogue,* September 1, 1945, p. 122.

31. *Vogue,* March 1947, p. 178.

32. *Vogue,* February 1947, pp. 151–152.

33. Christian Dior, *Christian Dior and I* (France: Amiot-Dumont, 1957), pp. 40–46.

34. Gaetan J. Lapick, *Scientific Designing of Women's Clothes* (New York: The Hobson Book Press, 1946), pp. 203–213.

35. Lapick, pp. 205–206.

36. Claudia B. Kidwell, "Women's Bathing and Swimming Costume in the United States," *United States National Museum Bulletin 250, Paper 64* (Washington, D.C.: U.S. Government Printing Office, 1968), pp. 27–28.

37. *Screenland,* October 1944, p. 2.
38. Lapick, p. 213.

CHALLENGING GENDER SYMBOLS

1. See Shelly Foote, "Bloomers," *Dress,* 1980, pp. 3–5, and Jeanette C. and Robert H. Lauer, *Fashion Power* (Englewood Cliffs, New Jersey: Prentice-Hall, 1981), pp. 246–259, for a discussion of the various stories given for the origins of the outfit. A contemporary reference to the garb worn by the Oneida community is in *Frank Leslie's Illustrated Newspaper,* April 9, 1870.
2. *New York Times,* June 28, 1851; *The Lily,* February 1851; *The Lily,* January 1852; *The Lily,* August 1852.
3. *The Lily,* June 1851; *The Boston-Herald,* reprinted in *The Lily,* January 1852.
4. *New York Tribune,* June 12, 1851; *New York Tribune,* June 17, 1851.
5. *The Pittsburgh Visitor,* reprinted in *The Oregon Spectator,* November 11, 1851.
6. *The Oregon Spectator,* September 9, 1851, and November 11, 1851; *The Lily,* November 11, 1851.
7. *The Louisville Journal,* reprinted in *The Oregon Spectator,* September 2, 1851.
8. *Alta California,* July 8, 1851; *The Lily,* July 1851; *The Oregon Spectator,* September 2, 1851, reprinted a report from *The Columbus Statesman* that a lady of a leading citizen was seen in the costume and *The Scioto Metropolis* reported that a judge's wife had appeared in public in the outfit.
9. *The Lily,* May 1851.
10. Fashionable women's dress fabrics were used to make the outfit. The basic construction of the bodice and the use of trimming corresponded to the fashionable long dress. *The Cincinnati Gazette,* reprinted in *The Oregon Spectator,* September 2, 1851; *The Lily,* June 1852.
11. *Portland Argus,* reprinted with comments, in the *New York Tribune,* June 17, 1851.
12. *New York Tribune,* June 28, 1851.
13. *The Lily,* June 1851.
14. *The Lily,* June 1851.
15. *The Oregon Spectator,* December 23, 1851.
16. *Harper's Magazine,* February 1852, p. 432.
17. *New York Tribune,* June 13, 1851; *The Lily,* January 1853; *The Lily,* July 1851; *The Lily,* September 1852.
18. Dexter C. Bloomer, *The Life and Writings of Amelia Bloomer* (Boston, 1895), p. 69.
19. "What the Beatles Have Done to Hair," *Look,* December 29, 1964, p. 58; *Newsweek,* November 29, 1965, p. 92; *Esquire,* July, 1965, p. 37; *New York Times Magazine,* September 6, 1964, p. 18.
20. "Pop's Bad Boys," *Newsweek,* November 29, 1965, p. 92.
21. *New York Times,* December 16, 1964, p. 45; December 17, 1964, p. 44; December 22, 1964, p. 31.
22. *New York Times,* September 10, 1966, p. 31; October 12, 1966, p. 1; October 14, 1966, p. 45; October 15, 1966, p. 31.
23. *New York Times,* September 18, 1969, p. 50.
24. *New York Times,* October 15, 1966, p. 31.
25. *New York Times,* September 13, 1965, p. 37.
26. "Beauty and the Beatles," *McCall's Magazine,* July, 1965, p. 78; *New York Times,* January 30, 1968, p. 43.
27. *New York Times,* July 23, 1964, p. 29.
28. For a theoretical discussion of the elements of a social movement, and, particularly, the origins of the Women's Liberation Movement, see Jo Freeman,

The Politics of Women's Liberation (New York: David McKay Company, Inc., 1975), pp. 44–62.

29. Bruce Jay Friedman, "Keeping Out of My Kids' Hair," *Saturday Evening Post,* January 15, 1966, p. 6.
30. "Uniworld of His and Hers," *Life,* June 21, 1968, p. 90.
31. Mary Groves, "Open Letter to the Father of a Boy Who Won't Get His Hair Cut," *Good Housekeeping,* November 1967, p. 64.
32. "A Groovy Beatle-Type Man is An Arthur," *Mademoiselle,* November 1965, p. 180.
33. *New York Times,* October 4, 1970, sec. 10, pp. 1, 24.
34. *New York Times,* October 25, 1970, p. 6.
35. "Long and the Short of It," *Newsweek,* September 27, 1965, p. 66.
36. *New York Times,* July 15, 1971, p. 25; April 16, 1970, p. 58; June 5, 1968, p. 54.
37. *New York Times,* May 22, 1973, p. 35.
38. *Los Angeles Times,* May 26, 1973, sec. 3, p. 3.
39. *New York Times,* November 3, 1966, p. 41; November 4, 1966, p. 23.
40. John Poppy, "The Generation Gap" *Look,* February 21, 1967, p. 28.
41. *Easy Rider,* 1969, Columbia Pictures.
42. *New York Times,* November 2, 1969, pp. 13, 27.

CLAUDIA BRUSH KIDWELL

ACKNOWLEDGMENTS

*M*en and Women: Dressing the Part is much more than this book. It is a long-term interdisciplinary project initiated in about 1979. This inquiry into the relationship between appearance and cultural definitions of masculine and feminine behavior involved many different groups of people as the scope, focus, and immediate objectives changed. But throughout the years, the core team has been the staff of the Division of Costume at the National Museum of American History: Barbara Dickstein, Shelly Foote, Karyn Harris, Carol Kregloh, and, since 1985, Eleanor Boyne. Joan Young was also part of the team for several years. I am deeply grateful to them for both their considerable talents and their willingness to take on new challenges. Their contributions are so extensive and varied that they can only be suggested here, as each step in the project has built on the work preceding it.

Roger Kennedy, Director of the National Museum of American History, was the catalyst for this work. Since his arrival at the museum in 1979, his energy, style, and new ways of thinking have stimulated numerous programs that continue to alter the museum. Mr. Kennedy's early interest in my research on changing postures and body types as well as his emphasis on social history encouraged me in 1981 to formally propose that an exhibition, then called "Ideal Images," be produced after conducting an extensive research program involving scholars from many different fields. With his support of the general objectives for the project, we expanded the circle of people who were regularly involved in our planning/research discussions. Michael Carrigan, Assistant Director for Exhibitions; William Pretzer, Historian; Jonathan Prude, 1983 First Ladies Fellow; Valerie Steele, 1984 First Ladies Fellow; and Fath Ruffins, Historian, made particularly extensive contributions to our discussions. They and others helped to expand the range of questions we might address. When it became necessary to narrow the focus, we were able to make choices being more conscious of what we were and were not addressing.

During these discussions, the division continued to collect data, frequently through the assistance of student interns. The following individuals contributed to research in the Division of Costume: Carrie Alyea, Karen Andrade, Kate Blow, Tina Brugioni, Penny Daulton, Heather Dodson, D'Anne Evans, Marvene Ewell, Elizabeth Gessner, Virginia Jenkins, Sally Jensen, Catherine Kidman, Michele Majer, Sarah McBride, Ann Mehrten, Christine Nicholls, Elizabeth O'Rourke, Audrine Piasecki, Anne Sachs, Candice Shireman, Rebecca Skidmore, Alden Tullis, Susan Wallace.

Donald L. Robinson, Government Department, American Studies Program, at Smith College became interested in our project when one of his students worked with us. He proposed the idea of a Smith-Smithsonian Conference. Gary Kulik, then Chairman of NMAH's Department of Social and Cultural History, encouraged this effort, expressing his belief in the significance of the questions we were addressing. Jill Conway, then President of Smith College, readily gave her intellectual and administrative support for this conference. In February 1984, the Smith-Smithsonian Conference on the Conventions of Gender was held at Smith College. The program was developed by Carol Kregloh and then refined and brilliantly produced at Smith College under the direction of Susan Bourque, Project on Women in Social Change. The interest and support of these two remarkable women, Jill Conway and Suzie Bourque, was crucial at this point. This conference was the first time that scholars investigating both male gender or female gender issues had been brought together on the same program. It was an affirmation of our project's objective to examine men and women together, not as isolated groups. This was an outstanding conference thanks to the contributions of those who presented their papers. The following scholars presented papers: Leigh Bienen, Johnnella Butler, William Chafe, Cynthia Enloe, Elizabeth Fee, Peter Filene, Elizabeth Fox-Genovese, Diana Hall, James O. Horton, William Leach, Barbara Melosh, Ellen Rothman, E. Anthony Rotundo, and Lois Scharf.

Before the conference I had thought that the book we might do could be produced by combining a selection of the papers presented at Smith with several commissioned articles focusing more particularly on appearance and gender. But the kinds of questions that were raised in the course of the conference demonstrated that more work was needed focusing on how changing forms of appearance functioned as symbols communicating and confirming current gender conventions or promoting or retarding change. Valerie Steele, co-editor of this book, is responsible for finally convincing me that not only should we be focusing the book on these issues, for which we could make a particular contribution, but that we could do so. Her energy, enthusiasm, and facile writing ability helped to carry the book through the first proposal stages. The project expanded to include not only the ongoing research effort, the development of the book, and the refinement of the exhibition concept, but now included fund raising to support all of the above. At this juncture, the project benefited greatly from Ron Becker, Assistant Director for Administration, who became our project manager. His leadership has been critical for the continuance and development of the project. Through the early interest of Ann Leven, Treasurer of the Smithsonian Institution, we were able to obtain a bridge loan that supported us during this intensive developmental stage. The exhibition became a certainty when the Special Exhibition Fund committee headed by Tom Freudenheim, Assistant Secretary of the Smithsonian Institution, awarded the project a basic production grant. Later, the National Cosmetology Association generously made a contribution that has allowed us to enrich the presentation of the exhibition as well as produce the related exhibition booklet and traveling exhibition. I want to acknowledge Eleanor Boyne and Marilyn Rue for their efforts on behalf of the project. And we all join together on behalf of the Smithsonian Institution to thank George Bright and the Board of Directors of the National Cosmetology Association for their farsightedness in becoming a partner with us for the benefit of the millions who will be visiting the museum.

As work progressed on this book, Barbara Schreier, at the University of Massachusetts in Amherst, joined our team. She also participated as contributing curator in one phase of developing the exhibition outline. Jo Paoletti, at the University of Maryland, also became an important part of our project team for the book.

Shelly Foote and I, along with Eleanor Boyne, paid particular attention to obtaining illustrations that would demonstrate in the book our discoveries concerning appearance. We are grateful to the individuals, corporations, and institutions who gave us permission to use the images listed in the back of the book under credits and sources.

The exceptional photographs of our museum objects were produced through the efforts of a small army of people. The dressed figures were researched, designed, and produced by the Division of Costume staff and Jim Sims, exhibit designer, working with the following staff at the Smithsonian Institution model shop in the Office of Exhibits Central under the leadership of Walter Sorrell, Chief of Production. They are Susan Wallace, Carol Walls, Reed Martin, Susan Arshack, Ben Snouffer, Tim Smith, Paul Rhymer, Mike Fuillo, Lora Moran, Cynthia Southerland, Craig Lochlear, Matt Stone.

Each figure required the sculpting of a form representing a posture, an arrangement of flesh, and a ratio of muscle to body fat different from what is common for modern human beings. This work was influenced by a study we had completed a year earlier with Gretchen Schneider, cultural historian in expressive behavior and performance, to produce two dressed figures in a costume study gallery in the exhibiton "After the Revolution: Everyday Life in America 1780–1800." Karyn Harris was project manager for the study. The mannequins we produced for this book were dressed with the additional assistance of Elizabeth O'Connell, Christine Magee, and Elizabeth O'Rourke.

The photographs themselves are the result of the long-range planning and support of James Wallace, Director of the Office of Printing and Photographic Services, and Richard Hofmeister, Chief of Special Assignments in the Photography Branch. The composition of the images are largely the result of the inspired eye of Dane Penland working with book designer Janice Wheeler. Her involvement in this early phase was very gratifying. The creators of the photographs are cited in the photograph credits and sources section, but they are gratefully acknowledged here for their exceptional individual talents and their impressive team work.

Many others supported the Men and Women project by assisting with research and/or by reading conceptual scripts for the exhibiton, or chapters for the book. My co-editor, Valerie Steele, wishes to acknowledge and thank Detective Thomas Krant, Curator/Historian of the Police Museum, New York City, and Ms. Janet Athanasidy, Assistant Curator and Administrative Associate, Police Department, City of New York, for their cooperation in providing information for the chapter "Dressing for Work." Grateful acknowledgments are made to the following staff of the National Museum of American History—*Archives:* Spencer Crew, John Fleckner, Lorene Mayo; *Division of Armed Forces History:* Donald Kloster; *Division of Community Life:* Carl Scheele, Ellen Roney Hughes; *Division of Domestic Life:* Anne Golovin, Rodris Roth, Anne Serio, Barbara Clark Smith, Bill Yeingst; *Division of Graphic Arts:* Elizabeth Harris, Helena Wright; *Division of Medical Sciences:* Michael Harris, Ramunas Kondratas, Barbara Melosh; *Division of Photographic History:* Peter Liebhold, Eugene Ostroff; *Division of Physical Sciences:* Deborah Warner; *Division of Political History:* Edith Mayo, Harry Rubenstein; *Department of Public Programs:* Lonn Taylor, Elizabeth Sharpe, Nancy McCoy, Robert Selim; *Division of Textiles:* Rita Adrosko, Doris Bowman, Katherine Dirks. And the contributions of the following people are greatly appreciated: John Gosen, Terry Hartnett at the George Washington University Hospital, Rachel Kidwell, Kathy Peiss from the University of Massachusetts in Amherst, Bernard Robinson, and Louise Wherle.

As this publication leaves for the printer, the production of the exhibition is underway for the opening in a year. Tom Crouch is the new Chairman of the Department of Social and Cultural History. With his experience and interest in producing exhibitions, he has already provided significant leadership. Barbara Clark Smith is writing the script for the exhibition. Drawing upon her resources as a social historian and a feminist, she is expanding on the work that has been done to this point, adding her particular point of view. She has long been an enthusiastic supporter of this project, and it is a pleasure for us to work with her in this new way.

Jim Sims is designing the exhibition with design assistant Annette Ames supported by museum interns Rachel Bernhart, Patrick Rogan, and Brian Sieling. Jim Sims brings to the project a unique range of experiences in education, theatrical design, and museum programs as well as a particular interest both in costume and cultural history. With this combination, he is designing an exceptional exhibition.

During the next year numerous individuals and institutions will be providing illustrations and objects for the exhibition. Dozens of people within the museum will be involved in tracking, conserving, and mounting objects and in producing the exhibition and audio-visual programs. Unfortunately, it is not possible to anticipate and acknowledge them here.

Looking beyond the exhibition, we can anticipate other results of the Men and Women project. A grant from the Smithsonian's Education Outreach Fund will support a pilot cooperative program between the National Museum of American History and Washington, D.C., area high school students. In this project, directed by Lonn Taylor and Elizabeth Sharpe, students will learn about the exhibition and as a follow up will research masculine and feminine fashions among their peers. The results of their investigations will, in turn, contribute to the documentation resources in the museum. During the exhibition's term at the museum a variety of additional public programs will be provided through the efforts of Dwight Bowers, Shirley Cherkasky, Robert Selim, Helen Snyder, and the museum's docents.

CONTRIBUTORS

SHELLY FOOTE is a Museum Specialist in the Division of Costume, National Museum of American History, Smithsonian Institution. She is the author of "Bloomers," published in *Dress,* the Journal of the Costume Society of America as well as one on "Fashions of the Federal Period." A specialist on sources for documenting and exhibiting costume, and on American jewelry, she has lectured extensively on these subjects. Her M.A. in American Studies was awarded by George Washington University.

CLAUDIA BRUSH KIDWELL is Curator in the Division of Costume, National Museum of American History, Smithsonian Institution. She was coordinating curator for the museum's first major bicentennial exhibition, "Suiting Everyone: The Democratization of Clothing in America," and was senior author of the accompanying book. Ms. Kidwell's writings include "Woman's Bathing and Swimming Costume," "Apparel for Ballooning," and "Cutting a Fashionable Fit: Dressmakers' Drafting Systems in the United States." Her graduate work for the M.A. was done at Pennsylvania State University.

CAROL L. KREGLOH has been a Museum Specialist in the Division of Costume, National Museum of American History, Smithsonian Institution. She has delivered papers on eighteenth- and nineteenth-century dress and also organized a show of miniature furniture for the Smithsonian Institution Traveling Exhibition Service. Her M.A. in American Studies is from George Washington University.

JO B. PAOLETTI is currently Associate Professor in the Department of Textiles and Consumer Economics at the University of Maryland, where she also received her Ph.D. She has published and lectured extensively on the subject of children's and men's dress in addition to serving as a consultant and reviewer of costume text books. Her work in progress is a book on children's clothing slated for publication shortly.

BARBARA A. SCHREIER is Associate Professor at the University of Massachusetts in Amherst. She is the author of *Mystique and Identity: Woman's Fashions of the*

1950s and currently has in press an article entitled "The Resort of Pure Fashion: Newport, Rhode Island, 1880–1914." She has written extensively on the history of leisure and sportswear and is currently working on a study of the clothing and Americanization of immigrant women. Her doctorate in Costume and Textile History was awarded by Florida State University, and she has held Fellowships from the National Endowment for the Humanities and Radcliffe College.

VALERIE STEELE is the author of *Paris Fashion: A Cultural History* (1988) and *Fashion and Eroticism: Ideals of Feminine Beauty from the Victorian Era to the Jazz Age* (1985). She received her Ph.D. in History from Yale University in 1983, and now teaches in the graduate division of the Fashion Institute of Technology (SUNY). Dr. Steele was the 1984 First Ladies Fellow at the Smithsonian Institution.

PHOTOGRAPHIC CREDITS AND SOURCES

Page 24. Courtesy of Lever Brothers Company.

Page 26 (Above). Historic Costume and Textile Collection, University of Maryland, College Park.

Page 26 (Below). National Cloak and Suit Catalogue, Fall and Winter 1917–18. Division of Costume, National Museum of American History, Smithsonian Institution.

Page 28. Ladies' Home Journal, February 1905.

Page 31. Collections of The Virginia Historical Society.

Page 32 (Above). The Metropolitan Museum of Art, Gift of Edgar William and Bernice Chrysler Garbisch, 1964.

Page 32 (Below). Division of Costume, National Museum of American History, Smithsonian Institution.

Plate 12 (Above). Museé de Versailles.

Plate 12 (Below). Manchester [England] City Art Galleries.

Plate 13. Smithsonian Institution, photo by Dane A. Penland.

Plate 14 (Above). Collections of The Virginia Historical Society.

Plate 14 (Below). The Metropolitan Museum of Art, Gift of Edgar William and Bernice Chrysler Garbisch, 1964.

Plate 15 (Left). Carol Kregloh.

Plate 15 (Right). Carol Kregloh.

Plate 16. National Museums and Galleries on Merseyside (Walker Art Gallery, Liverpool).

Plate 17. Courtesy of The Arrow Company.

Plate 18 (Left). Division of Costume, National Museum of American History, Smithsonian Institution.

Plate 18 (Right). Division of Costume, National Museum of American History, Smithsonian Institution.

Plate 19. Smithsonian Institution, photo by Dane A. Penland.

Page 33. Division of Costume, National Museum of American History, Smithsonian Institution.

Page 36. 1979 Christmas Catalogue. © J.C. Penney Company, Inc., 1979; reproduced by permission.

Page 40. Sandra D. Alyea, Bloomington, Indiana.

Page 43. Reprinted with the permission of Joanna T. Steichen.

Page 46. Andrea Blanch. Courtesy *Vogue* © 1987 by The Conde Nast Publications Inc.

Page 47. Hamburger Kunsthalle, Hamburg.

Page 48. Helmut Newton.

Page 49. Jockey International, Inc.

Page 50 (Left). Division of Costume, National Museum of American History, Smithsonian Institution.

Page 50 (Right). From the collection of Valerie Steele.

Page 53. From the collection of Valerie Steele.

Page 54. Horst P. Horst.

Page 56. Stan Shaffer.

Page 57 (Left). Calvin Klein Underwear and Sleepwear.

Page 57 (Right). Calvin Klein Men's Underwear.

Page 58. Agence France Presse, Pierre Guillaud.

Page 60 (Left). Library of Congress.

Page 60 (Right). Life, December 1889. Library of Congress.

Page 61. Corbin, Ltd.

Page 62. M. Julian.

Page 65. Scribner's Magazine, July 1913. Library of Congress.

Page 68. Division of Costume, National Museum of American History, Smithsonian Institution.

Page 69. New York *Daily News.*

Page 70. New York Police Collection, photograph by P.O. Virginia Conde, N.Y.C.P.D.

Page 72. Reprinted from *Psychology Today* magazine, copyright © 1974 The American Psychological Association.

Page 73. U.S. Office of War Information Collection, Prints and Photographs Division, Library of Congress.

Page 74. University of Pennsylvania School of Medicine.

Page 76. Library of Congress.

Page 79 (Above). Prints and Photographs Division, Library of Congress.

Page 79 (Below). Underwood and Underwood Collection, Prints and Photographs Division, Library of Congress.

Page 80. Division of Costume, National Museum of American History, Smithsonian Institution.

Page 81. National Air and Space Museum, Smithsonian Institution.

Page 86. Courtesy of Jos. A. Bank Clothiers, 123 Market Place, Baltimore, Maryland 21202, and Eisner & Associates, Inc., Advertising and Public Relations, Baltimore, MD.

Page 89. Illustration by Mary Todd Lyon. From *A Girl's Guide to Executive Success* by Sandra J. Shea and Mary Todd Lyon. Copyright © 1984. Used with permission of Ten Speed Press, Box 7123, Berkeley, CA 94707.

Page 93. Division of Costume, National Museum of American History, Smithsonian Institution.

Page 94. Division of Costume, National Museum of American History, Smithsonian Institution.

Page 96 (Above). The Collection of Advertising History, Archives Center, National Museum of American History, Smithsonian Institution.

Page 96 (Below). Peter Read Miller.

Plate 20. Smithsonian Institution, photo by Laurie Minor and Richard Strauss.

Plate 21. Smithsonian Institution, photo by Dane A. Penland.

Plate 22. Photography by Steve Reyes.

Plate 23. Division of Costume, National Museum of American History, Smithsonian Institution.

Plate 24. Division of Costume, National Museum of American History, Smithsonian Institution.

Plate 25. Division of Costume, National Museum of American History, Smithsonian Institution.

Plate 26 (Left). Sears Roebuck and Co.

Plate 26 (Right). Smithsonian Institution, photo by Dane A. Penland.

Plate 27. The Harry T. Peters "America on Stone" Lithography Collection, Division of Domestic Life, National Museum of American History, Smithsonian Institution.

Page 98 (Left). Simon D. Kehoe, *The Indian Club Exercise* (New York: Peck & Snyder, 1866). Division of Community Life, National Museum of American History, Smithsonian Institution.

Page 98 (Right). Simon D. Kehoe, *The Indian Club Exercise* (New York: Peck & Snyder, 1866). Division of Community Life, National Museum of American History, Smithsonian Institution.

Page 99. The Collection of Advertising History, Archives Center, National Museum of American History, Smithsonian Institution.

Page 100. Division of Costume, National Museum of American History, Smithsonian Institution.

Page 102. Picture Collection, The Branch Libraries, The New York Public Library.

Page 107. The Harry T. Peters "America on Stone" Lithography Collection, Division of Domestic Life, National Museum of American History, Smithsonian Institution.

Page 108. Peter E. Palmquist Collection.

Page 111. The Collection of Advertising History, Archives Center, National Museum of American History, Smithsonian Institution.

Page 113. Library of Congress.

Page 115. American Lawn Tennis Magazine, permission granted by *World Tennis.*

Page 116. Ehrlich's Fashion Quarterly, Summer 1878, in the Collection of Advertising History, Archives Center, National Museum of American History, Smithsonian Institution.

Page 119. The Metropolitan (1897), Library of Congress.

Page 120. Adam York, Leavitt Advertising Agency.

Page 121. Division of Photographic History, National Museum of American History, Smithsonian Institution.

Page 122. Inertia Dynamics Corporation, Chandler, Arizona.

Page 125. Ella Strong Denison Library of The Claremont [CA] Colleges.

Page 127. Cooper-Hewitt Museum of Decorative Arts & Design, Smithsonian Institution.

Page 128. D. Hull, *A Plain and Concise Treatise on the Art of Tailoring* (New York: 1844).

Page 130. National Archives. Photograph by U.S. Army Signal Corps.

Page 131. Sears, Roebuck and Co.

Page 134. (Letty Lynton)

Page 138. Woman's Wear Daily, April 8, 1942.

Page 140. Division of Costume, National Museum of American History, Smithsonian Institution.

Page 141. Smithsonian Institution, photo by Dane A. Penland.

Page 145. Seneca Falls [NY] Historical Society.

Page 150. Harper's New Monthly Magazine, January 1852.

Page 152 (Above). John Dominis, *Life* magazine © 1964 Time Inc.

Page 152 (Below). New York Times Pictures.

Page 153. The Bettmann Archive.

Page 156. Copyright © 1970 Columbia Pictures Industries, Inc. Courtesy of The Academy of Motion Picture Arts and Sciences.

Page 159. Calvin Klein Industries, Inc.

Page 161. The Rudi Gernreich Estate.

INDEX

identity of, 24–25, 28–29. *See also* Children; Toddlers

Jacobs, Helen Hull, 114, 115
Jagger, Mick, 153
Jantzen swimwear, 118
Jazz Age, 15
Jewelry, 15
Jobs, 79; sex-linked, 64–66. *See also* Work clothing; *various jobs; professions*
Jodphurs, 15

Kansas City Athletics, 104
Kilts, 9
Knee breeches, 14
Knickerbocker Baseball Club, 102
Knickerbockers, 33, 103–104, 111, 112

Laboratories: white clothing in, 73–75
Lace, 51
Lastex fabric, 118
Laver, James, 42, 44, 63
Law: authoritative dress in, 89–90
League of American Wheelmen, 110
Leather: eroticism of, 62–63
Leisure clothing, 9. *See also* Sportswear; Swimwear
Lelong, Valentine, 112, 133
Lenglen, Suzanne, 114
Letty Lynton, 133, 134(fig.), pl.26
The Lily (Bloomer), 144, 147, 150
Lingerie: sexuality of, 45–46, 56; in Victorian era, 50–52
Little Lord Fauntleroy suits, 34
Los Angeles: police uniforms in, 69
Lounge wear, 15, 58

Manet, Edouard: *Nana*, 47(fig.), 49
Manufacturing. *See* Garment industry
Marcus, Stanley, 137–38
Masculinity, 1, 2, 8, 24, 86, 139, 143, 144, pl.1, pl.2; adolescent dress and, 38–39, 40; broad-shoulder styles and, 124, 136; cultural definitions of, 14, pl.2; in fashion, 13, 15, 16, pl.7, pl.8; of football, 94–95; hair length and, 152–53, 154–56; hourglass shape and, 129; nineteenth century views of, 33–34; of sports, 92, 94; of ties, 89–90; trousers and, 148–49; of undergarments, 56–57. *See also* Men
Mass media, 4
Maternalism, 59
Medieval era, 14, 15; body type in, 17–19
Men, 2, 5, 6, 11, 15, 16, pl.1, pl.5, pl.6, pl.12; body exposure of, 104; as sex objects, 60–61; uniforms for, 67, 104. *See also* Masculinity
Men's Wear, 132, 135, 136
Merchandising, 140–41
Merode swimwear, 118

Middle class, 16, 78
Middle East, 6
Middy blouses, 99, 101
Midwives, 77
Military, 7, 155. *See also* Military uniforms
Military uniforms, pl.8; influence on fashion of, 129–30, 143
Miller, Elizabeth, 146
Miss America (Black), 84
Motherhood, 26

Naismith, James, 100
Nana (Manet), 47(fig.), 49
Neckwear: for baseball, 103; for business, 89–90
Nelson, Arthur, 149
Neptune and Amphitrite (Gossaert), 18(fig.)
New Guinea, 11
New Look, 138, 159
The New People (Winick), 154
Newton, Helmut, 48(fig.), 49
New York City: police uniforms in, 68–70
Nightingale, Florence, 75
Nineteenth century, 50, 66, 108, 144, pl.12; adolescence in, 37, 38; body types in, 19–20; business in, 83–84; child-rearing in, 25–26, 30, 31–32, 33–34, pl.14; fashion in, 126–29, pl.26; gymnastics in, 98–99; sports in, 92, 94, 95; swimming in, 118–19; swimwear in, 117, 119. *See also* Victorian era
Nurses: uniforms for, 73(fig.), 75–76, pl.21. *See also* Nursing
Nursing: as women's work, 75, 77

Office work. *See* Business
Ornamentation, 11, pl.12; on infants' clothing, 25, 27; on lingerie, 51
Outerbridge, Mary, 112

Padding: in broad-shoulder styles, 133–38; in hourglass shape, 126, 127–29
Paint: as clothing, 10, 11
Painters, 79
Pajamas, 58
Pantaloons, 128
Pants. *See* Trousers
Pant suits, 87
Paris, 112; fashion design in, 136, 138
Parties, 50
Peacock Revolution, 12, pl.22
Peer pressure, 29
Peignoirs, 57
Persia, 14
Petticoats, 147, pl.19
Physical activity: and dress, 30–31. *See also* Exercise; Sportswear; Swimwear
Physical culture movement, 97–98

Physical fitness, 123; sexual attraction and, 121–22. *See also* Exercise; Sports
Picts: body paint of, 10–11
Pink, 78; gender definition of, 6, 15, 22, 27, 35
Pink collar workers, 78; expansion of, 79–80; uniforms for, 80–82
Play, 34; dress-up as, 35–36; grooming as, 36–37
Police: uniforms for, 67–72; women as, 68–71
Power, 11; sexual appeal of, 62
Power Look, 88, 89
The Power Look (von Furstenberg), 88
Powers, Hiram: *The Greek Slave*, 17
Prince of Wales: as fashion plate, 135
Proms: as rites of passage, 39–40
Prostitutes, 45
Puberty, 34, 38, 39
Punk, 38

Ready-to-wear industry, 140, 141(fig.)
Recreation, 97, 118. *See also* Bathing; Sports
Renaissance: body types in, 18(fig.), 19; male décolletage in, 59–60
Revolutionary era, 78, 79
Ribbons, 51
Riding: women's dress for, 106–109, pl.23
Rites of passage, 23(fig.), 34; during adolescence, 37–41
Rittenhouse, Anne: *The Well-Dressed Woman*, 80–81
Robes: gender symbolism of, 13, 14
Rock-and-roll groups: hair length and, 152, 153
Rome, 13
Rompers, 26, 27, 34
Roosevelt, Theodore, 95
Rosie the Riveter, 82
Rousseau, Jean Jacques: on education of children, 30–31

Saxons, 14
Sears Roebuck catalogs, 27, 34, 135–36, 138, 139, pl.26
Secretaries: dress for, 83–85
Security guards, 72
Seduction, 42, 44. *See also* Eroticism; Sexual display
Seventeenth century, 19; child-rearing during, 24, 25
Sex: and gender, 1–2
Sexual display: concealment of, 55–56; exposure and, 59–60; factors in, 44–47; men's dress and, 60–61; office attire and, 82; physical fitness and, 121–22; swimwear, 116–17, 118–19. *See also* Eroticism; Sexuality
Sexual dualism, 8